SCIENCE
FICTION
AND THE
MASS
CULTURAL
GENRE
SYSTEM

SCIENCE FICTION AND THE MASS CULTURAL GENRE SYSTEM

JOHN RIEDER

WESLEYAN UNIVERSITY PRESS • MIDDLETOWN, CONNECTICUT

Wesleyan University Press
Middletown CT 06459
www.wesleyan.edu/wespress
© 2017 John Rieder
All rights reserved

Manufactured in the United States of America
Designed by April Leidig
Typeset in Garamond by Copperline Book Services

An earlier version of chapter 1 in this book appeared as an essay by John Rieder, "On Defining Science Fiction, or Not: Genre Theory, SF, and History," *Science Fiction Studies* 37, no. 2 (July 2010).

Library of Congress Cataloging-in-Publication Data available upon request

5 4 3 2 1

CONTENTS

Acknowledgments
vii

INTRODUCTION
Science Fiction and the
Mass Cultural Genre System
1

1

On Defining Science Fiction, or Not:
Genre Theory, SF, and History
13

2

The Mass Cultural Genre System
33

3

Genealogies of SF
65

4

Philip K. Dick's
Mass Cultural Epistemology
93

5

Communities of Interpretation (1):
Two Hollywood Films and
the Tiptree Award Anthologies

113

6

Communities of Interpretation (2):
Afrofuturism and Indigenous Futurism

139

CONCLUSION
Periodizing SF
161

Notes

171

Works Cited

183

Index

197

ACKNOWLEDGMENTS

I want to thank those generous colleagues who read drafts of sections of this book and made helpful suggestions to me about revision: Cristina Bacchilega, Carl Freedman, Rob Latham, Roger Luckhurst, and Sherryl Vint. Earlier versions of various sections of what ended up being the introduction and the second, fifth, and sixth chapters were presented at the annual Orlando meetings of the International Conference on the Fantastic in the Arts in 2013, 2014, 2015, and 2016; at the annual conferences of the Science Fiction Research Association in Lublin, Poland, in 2011 and Madison, Wisconsin, in 2014; at Weird Council: An International Conference on the Writing of China Miéville at the University of London in 2012; and at the Historical Materialism Conference at University of London in 2012. Without risking the inevitable omissions that would come with an attempt to list everyone by name, I want to thank all those who participated in and responded to these sessions. Special thanks to Grace Dillon for introducing me to Helen Haig-Brown's *The Cave* and for her helpful response to my reading of it. And thanks to Art Evans for last-minute long-distance help on bibliography.

The students in my graduate seminars on Science Fiction and Genre Theory at the University of Hawaiʻi at Mānoa in spring 2011 and fall 2015 sessions helped me think through my positions on genre theory and widened my knowledge of the range and variety of contemporary SF practices. I want to thank especially my dissertation advisee Ida Yoshinaga for many stimulating conversations about contemporary genre production and reception.

The research on early periodical fiction that I have incorporated into chapter 3 was carried out at the Maison d'Ailleurs in Yverdon-les-Bains, Switzerland, and at the British Library. It is a pleasure to express my gratitude to all those at the Maison d'Ailleurs for their generosity and helpfulness, and to acknowledge my debt to that magnificent and accessible resource, the British Library.

Thanks to *Science Fiction Studies* for permission to reuse, with slight revisions, my essay "On Defining Science Fiction, or Not: Genre Theory, SF, and History" (vol. 37, no. 2, July 2010) as chapter 1. Thank you also to the Dille Family Trust for generously allowing me to use the copyrighted image of the *Buck Rogers* comic strip reproduced in chapter 3. Finally a major thank you to Elizabeth LaPensée for permission to use her beautiful image, *Growth*, on the book cover.

This book is lovingly dedicated to my lifelong partner, Cristina Bacchilega.

SCIENCE FICTION AND THE MASS CULTURAL GENRE SYSTEM

INTRODUCTION

Science Fiction and the Mass Cultural Genre System

The basic premise of this study is that science fiction and the other genres usually associated with so-called genre fiction, such as the detective story, the modern romance, the western, horror, and fantasy, collectively compose a system of genres distinct from the preexisting classical and academic genre system that includes the epic, tragedy, comedy, satire, romance, the lyric, and so on; and that this more recently formed genre system is an important historical phenomenon worthy of, and in need of, further study. Because this newer genre system can be firmly associated with large-scale commercial production and distribution of narrative fiction in print, film, and broadcast media, I call it the mass cultural genre system.

For the most influential members of the first generation of scholars of SF,[1] legitimizing the study of the genre entailed separating the best, most literary examples of SF from the more familiar, popular, and supposedly inferior versions of it that predominated in mass culture. *Science Fiction and the Mass Cultural Genre System* is written on the premise that not only has this strategy of academic legitimization long ago run its course, but that the mass cultural genre system and the contemporary academic-classical genre system are best understood in relation to one another, so that twenty-first-century literary history needs to recognize and study both. The overriding thesis is that the field of literary production and the project of literary studies cannot be adequately conceptualized without taking into account the tensions between these two genre systems (or we should say, at least these two) that arise from the different modes of publicity—that is, the interwoven and codependent practices of production, distribution, and reception that are the "ground" or environments for those different systems.

This book is an exercise in literary history based on the implications of taking a historical, rather than formalist, position on genre theory. Although the careful reading of individual texts forms an important part of its methodology, the fundamental challenge presented to the literary historian is here conceived as understanding systemic change rather than locating and appreciating individual innovation. Perhaps the best approximation in contemporary scholarship to narrating a transformational episode in the history of genre systems within such a framework are the various accounts of the rise of the European novel in conjunction with revolutions in the technology of print and the emergence of the middle class. Early theories of the novel that sought to understand it as modernity's version of the epic contrast sharply with those more recent ones that instead track its emergence out of a dense eighteenth-century milieu of genres including travel writing, biography, memoir, the conduct manual, and others. It is this confusion and repurposing of genres that characterize the transformation of the genre system itself so as to allow the new form, the novel, to emerge into recognizability. A similar situation attends the emergence of science fiction, as it is gradually constructed out of different permutations of the marvelous voyage, the utopia, lost-race adventures, stories of time travel, and the future war.

As Michael McKeon remarks in the introduction to *The Origins of the English Novel*, the novel as a generic designation is an abstraction that came to be formulated only when the process of its emergence was complete: "'The novel' must be understood as what Marx calls a 'simple abstraction,' a deceptively monolithic category that encloses a complex historical process" (20). Its "deceptively monolithic" character indicates something of its force as an intervention in the reception of those fictional works that came to be identified with it as definitive examples. Furthermore, the tendency, already evident in Henry Fielding's *Tom Jones*, to make the novel into the descendant or heir of the epic traded upon the prestige classical literature enjoyed because of its central place in the educational curriculum. In the twentieth century, as the modern national literatures took the place of classical literature in the schools, construction of the "great tradition" of realist fiction—that is, of the realist novel—no longer needed to refer to the novel's affinity with the epic.² But even before this the novel's cultural prestige was being redefined by its difference from the commercially ascendant periodical and serial publications that ushered in mass distribution and mass culture.

The emergence of SF, like the rise of the novel that precedes it and is one of its preconditions, also needs to be understood in the context of a large-scale transformation of the system of genres. Too often the history of genres, and SF is no exception, has been overly fascinated with the appearance of master texts that encapsulate moments of influential innovation. A history of genre systems attentive to the power that generic attribution exercises upon distribution and reception is one just as emphatically punctuated by watersheds in the technology of publication, the distribution of reading material, and the social production and distribution of literacy itself. Thus the influence of the great innovators like Shelley, Verne, and Wells takes place within the context of "cultural and historical fluctuations in the composition of generic systems," and close attention to the reception of any of the three (as I demonstrate in chapter 3 with respect to Shelley's *Frankenstein*) will show that "the same texts may be subject to different generic classifications in different social and historical contexts" (Bennett 101).

This variability is not simply a matter of applying different sets of terminology to the same story, but rather of using entirely different sets of criteria to identify genres. There is certainly a good argument to be made, for instance, for reading Sophocles's *Oedipus the King* as a detective story, as some eminent critics have done (e.g., Bloch). The main character is a famous solver of puzzles. He learns of a horrible crime and is tasked with solving it. He collects evidence and interrogates witnesses. Gradually he unravels the truth, and he exposes and punishes the criminal. But here is the catch: none of this has any bearing on whether or not the play is a tragedy. One could just as easily imagine a play featuring a famous solver of puzzles, the unraveling of a crime, and the punishment of the wrongdoer that would be a comedy, or a satire. *Oedipus the King* is, of course, Aristotle's prime example of the genre of tragedy in the *Poetics*. But the features that distinguish it as a tragedy, rather than a comedy or a satire, have nothing to do with the features that distinguish it as a detective story, rather than, for instance, a piece of science fiction or a western (and it very clearly does not resemble either of those genres).

These semiotic variations in what counts as significant to genre identification point to more profound differences in the social uses of narrative. More than merely sets of interrelated genre designations, the systems are composed of the values, not always explicit or simple, that direct competent users to recognize genres, perform them, and enforce or resist their boundaries. If genre categories do not come to us in isolation but always in some sort of relational matrix, then we need to ask, what sort of relations form these matrices? What are the social underpinnings of the mass cultural genre system, and what are those that keep the classical-academic system in place? For the classical-academic and mass cultural genre systems each have a history that has entered into the production, distribution, and reception of texts, and that often forms substantial connections between the systems themselves and the history and significance of a given text. Thus, while it is certainly possible to read the *Oedipus* as detective fiction, its historical relationship to the genre of tragedy, and to the system of genres and literary values elaborated in relation to classical tragedy, is a good deal more consequential. By the same token, texts that are usually considered SF could be read simply as examples of satire, romance, comedy, tragedy, and so on—and the assimilation of SF to satire, in particular, has been a practice employed by some of those who have wanted to argue for taking such texts seriously in an academic context—but this strategy of canonization by assimilation to the classical genre system strips them of an important aspect of their historicity. What I hope to do here is to respect the literary values and historical substance embedded in both systems, not by giving them equal time, but by trying to understand how the tensions between the two have become part of the structure of the contemporary field of cultural production.

Those tensions are all too evidently the basis for the major flaws in Darko Suvin's influential theorization of SF as "the literature of cognitive estrangement" (see *Metamorphoses of Science Fiction*, chapter 1, and "On the Poetics of the Science Fiction Genre"). The enduring strength and usefulness of Suvin's conceptualization of the SF "novum" and the critical power of its estrangement of cultural norms have been convincingly argued recently by Rhys Williams, who urges that "the radically ethical and utopian demands that shape the true core of the Suvinian paradigm should not be diluted but instead renewed, retooled, and readied to once again join battle" (618). I entirely agree, and I applaud the way those "ethical and utopian demands" continue to be energetically forwarded in a work like Philip E. Wegner's *Shockwaves of Possibility* (2014). However, the limitations of Suvin's paradigm have to do with some basic issues of genre theory that this study hopes to address.

The first is simply a matter of basic assumptions. For Suvin a genre is defined by formal strategies, not by common usage. In its common usage, "science fiction" is for Suvin an incoherent bundle of conflicting generic tendencies trundled together for commercial purposes. "The literature of cognitive estrangement" is, in contrast, a precise formal definition. Chapter 1 of this book will address the question of generic definition at much greater length, but let me preface that discussion by saying that "the literature of cognitive estrangement" is what Tzvetan Todorov would call a theoretical genre rather than a historical one (*Fantastic*, 13–15). Unfortunately for the Suvinian paradigm, what we might call really existing SF is not a theoretical entity but rather a historically situated, and therefore ever-changing, set of practices, so that the historical ground of the really existing genre continues to shift under the theory's feet. This is what yields the situation described by Williams:

> Sf strictly defined is no longer capable of estranging us from the hegemonic discourse for which it operates as ideological cheerleader [because] ... the authority of specifically capitalist science and rationality and its promises of progress are falling into doubt.... It is for precisely this reason that the creative and utopian energy in genres of the fantastic is currently manifesting itself in erosion and destruction of the false, self-crowned purity of that discourse.... "reality" and "fantasy" ... have changed value over the years, and with them have necessarily changed the meaning and character of "scientific progress," "rationality," and even "utopia." The problem with the Suvinian paradigm lay in his creation of a universal abstraction of exactly the type he sought to dismantle. (626)

Williams's historical analysis is on the mark, but the theoretical issue here has to do with basic assumptions. One cannot have it both ways: either the genre is indeed a "universal abstraction," an enduring possibility in some eternal grammar of narrative forms, or it is the work of historical agents, subject to the contingencies of history, and therefore always liable to shift its ideological and formal moorings in response to those contingencies.[3]

Attending to the contingencies of history brings us to the second problem, the question of what exactly is at stake in genre theory. However robust Suvin's analysis of the formal strategies that impart critical power to the best examples of SF, his analysis nonetheless manages to simultaneously trivialize and exaggerate what is at stake. The trivializing consists in the tendency to nitpicking distinctions between what is and is not SF, best (or rather worst) exemplified in the "Annotated Checklist of Books Not to Be Regarded as SF, with an Introductory Essay on the Reasonable Reasons Thereof," in *Victorian Science Fiction in the UK* (86). The exaggeration comes when Suvin presents the ability to make these distinctions as immediately and drastically consequential in ways that certainly do not correspond to any sort of common sense—for example, the mere confusion of the genres of SF and supernatural fantasy is called a "pathological" phenomenon "stimulated by irrational capitalist conditions of life" (91). The key to this overvaluation of generic difference is the loaded term "cognitive logic," which SF has and other proximate genres such as supernatural fantasy do not, making a failure to tell the difference between the genres (or to care about it) tantamount to a general failure to exercise one's critical capacities.

There are two ways to respond. The first, which has been forcefully argued by China Miéville in his essay "Cognition as Ideology," and which Williams builds upon, takes the strategy of accepting Suvin's description of SF as the literature of cognitive estrangement and then working through the consequences to demonstrate that Suvin's privileging of cognition over ideology is itself ideological. The crux of the argument is that where Suvin asserts the operation of form and reason, Miéville sees rhetorical acts of persuasion that aim for power and authority. Thus, according to Miéville, Suvin's insistence on correct taxonomy depends on his identifying himself with the charismatic authority of the authors who deploy the "cognition effect": "This is a translation into meta-literary and aggrandizing terms of the very layer of technocrats often envisaged in SF and its cultures as society's best hope" (239).[4]

A second approach to Suvin's deployment of "cognitive logic" is to see it from outside Suvin's paradigm. This is a matter of asserting first of all that every theoretical genre is also historical in the sense that it is a construction put in place at a specific time and place under specific circumstances, and therefore always constitutes taking a position within a field of possibilities or, as Pierre Bourdieu puts it, the field of cultural production. The distinction between Todorov's historical and theoretical genres is not between genres that are formed in a historical process and others that are not, but rather between genres constructed in the academy by an identifiable theorist (and, for Todorov, along certain rigorously formalist lines) and genres constructed more or less anonymously in a collective process. What is at stake in the definition of SF as a species of "literature" with an ancient lineage is the difference between the cultural prestige associated with the academic-classical genre system, with its deployment in higher education, and the mass cultural genre system and its commercial milieu. The fairly obvious point is that Suvin's definition is a way of assimilating SF into the classical-academic genre system and gaining for it a share of the cultural capital invested in that system—this in spite of Suvin's aggressive assertion of SF's political resistance to the status quo. I think that this understanding of Suvin's pugnacious defense of SF's genre boundary against its noncognitive neighbors might put him in a more forgiving light than that afforded by Miéville's ideology critique. He was in a fight of sorts, though it was not really with those who pathologically intermingle SF and fantasy, but rather with those—and they were the majority of literary scholars when Suvin did this work—who simply would dismiss SF as unworthy of academic study. Suvin's animosity toward the fantasists could actually be read as a kind of peace offering to the powers that controlled the gates of academic legitimacy.

To insist on holding the academic-classical genre system and the mass cultural genre system separate from one another rather than trying to conflate them or to turn one into a subset of the other draws upon a rich vein of genre theory devoted to connecting specific media, venues, and purposes with sets of genres tailored to them. John Frow is the theorist of literary and narrative genres who draws most ably upon this rhetorical tradition that stretches back to Mikhail Bakhtin's work on speech genres. Citing Carolyn Miller's argument that genres are "typified rhetorical actions based in recurrent situations" (Miller 31), Frow stresses that "genres have to do with the strategic work accomplished by texts in particular circumstances" (*Genre*, 115). In chapter 2 I will draw on Clay Spinuzzi's ideas about the way entire ensembles of genres are integrated with one another into what he calls sets, repertoires, systems, and ecologies. The notion of a narrative genre system, however, derives more directly from the work of Rick Altman and Jason Mittel on film and television genres, respectively. As Frow puts it, "We should perhaps not speak of a single system. Rather, we could posit that there are sets of genres organized by domain, those of film or television or literature or architecture.... Indeed, it may be the case that there is not, or no longer, a single system of film genres or literary genres; there may be only relatively disconnected sub-systems representing relatively disconnected organizations of value" (*Genre*, 124–25). Indeed, I think it is clearly the case, if one thinks for a moment of the world and not of a single nation or a single language, that there has never been a single system of narrative genres, a thesis that could be abundantly supported by examples from the history of translation of indigenous narratives in colonial settings (see for example Bacchilega, Naithani, and Owen). The issue that needs to be explored as regards academic and mass cultural genre systems, however, and which this book makes some attempt to open up, is how disconnected those "relatively disconnected sub-systems" of value are from one another, and what kinds of pressures they continue to exert on one another.

John Cawelti's work on what he calls formula fiction represents an important approximation toward the distinction between the academic and mass cultural genre systems. According to Cawelti, "popular story types such as the western, the detective story, or the spy adventure... are embodiments of archetypal story forms in terms of specific cultural materials. ... Formulas are ways in which specific cultural themes and stereotypes become embodied in more universal story archetypes" (6). Cawelti's distinction between formula and archetype turns out to correspond to the difference between modern, popular genre categories and ancient, classical ones. "Many film scholars and critics use the term 'popular genre' to denote literary types like the western or the detective story that are clearly the same as what I call formulas.... Another usage of genre involves concepts like tragedy, comedy, romance, and satire.... Since such conceptions clearly imply universal or transcultural conceptions of literary structure, they are examples of what I have called archetypes" (6–7). A different way to put this is that the classical genre system is very much older and more prestigious than the mass cultural one, and it has been relatively stable for long periods of time. There is no question that many a television sitcom employs devices that one can find in Roman comedy. This does not justify turning comedy or tragedy into a universal category, as Cawelti does. But interestingly, Cawelti's distinction between formula and archetype depends entirely on context: "If one thinks of a western in comparison to other westerns one is using a 'formula-genre' ... [but if you] relate this same western to some more universal generic conceptions such as tragedy or romance ... [you] would be employing an archetype-genre" (8). In other words, one system of classification works for commercial production, another for the academy; the hierarchical relation between them is entirely obvious in the terms "formula" and "archetype." That hierarchy of values deserves to be reexamined in the light of the forty years' worth of cultural studies work that Cawelti helped make possible.

Although the subsystems of value set at play in the relation of the two genre systems to one another are central to the arguments of this book, the topic is a single genre, science fiction. My primary thesis regarding SF is that it is an organic genre of the mass cultural genre system. I draw the term "organic" here from Antonio Gramsci's distinction between traditional intellectuals, whose roles in the social system are residual effects of past cultural formations, and organic intellectuals who rise spontaneously to perform the work of organizing production and politics within the contemporary formation (5–17). I suggest that the same distinction one would apply to the intellectuals working within the entertainment industry and the academy can usefully be applied to the genre systems that in significant ways help to organize their labors. The relation between the genre system organic to mass culture and the traditional genre system, lodged primarily in the schools, produces effects of stratification that pervade the entire field of modern literary production. I contend that instead of merely being manipulated by those effects, literary and cultural studies scholars in general, and science fiction studies scholars in particular, ought to be making them part of the object of their inquiries into the workings of contemporary culture and the powers exercised by various forms of narrative within it.

The thesis that science fiction is an organic genre of mass culture does not imply that mass cultural practices necessarily or inevitably included the development of this specific kind of fiction. I am not arguing that SF expresses the essence of mass culture or that the political economy of mass culture is expressed by or reflected in SF. The argument advanced here is simply that since SF takes shape within the milieu of mass culture, its generic form is "determined" by mass culture insofar as generic form is itself the cumulative effect of economic and ideological pressures upon artistic production. If SF developed within the set of artistic and commercial opportunities and constraints afforded by the emergence of mass culture, then understanding these constraints and opportunities is crucial to an account of how the genre came to be recognized and practiced. We should expect to find that genre construction both follows the channels of least resistance and registers the traces of collective desire.

To assert that SF is organic to mass culture is also to highlight the way constructing, maintaining, and contesting the category of SF actively intervenes in promoting the distribution of a certain kind of fiction. It names that fiction, in the first place, bringing it into visibility and constituting it as an object. The generic category subsequently acts as a matrix for communicating practices of writing and reading among artists, editors, and readers (modes of participation that overlap heavily in the culture of the SF pulp magazines), involving them in ongoing debates about the genre's boundaries and protocols that feed back into artistic practices while constructing the genealogies and canons of a "selective tradition" subject to continual reinvention.

The term "selective tradition" appears in quotation marks because I draw it from Andrew Milner's *Locating Science Fiction*, a book that in its project and ambitions seems to me quite consonant with this one. "Selective tradition" is a term Milner borrows from Raymond Williams, who explains it as "an intentionally selective version of a shaping past and a preshaped present, which is then powerfully operative in the process of social and cultural definition and identification" (Milner 39, quoting Raymond Williams, *Marxism and Literature*, 115). Milner argues in *Locating Science*

Fiction that because SF is a selective tradition it is therefore "essentially and necessarily a site of contestation" (39–40). But first it has to be the site of some agreement about generic identity; otherwise there would be nothing to contest. The key term for me in conceptualizing this basic agreement is the community of practice. As I will argue in chapter 1 and elaborate more fully in chapters 5 and 6, the genre of SF is the product of multiple communities of practice whose motives and resources may have little resemblance to one another.

Before explaining the plan of the book, let me acknowledge some of its limitations, however briefly. It is a sketch of the history of SF, but only a sketch and a very selective one at that. I am under no illusion that the several dozen texts I write about in this book constitute some sort of representative sample of the entire genre. My narrative focuses on English-language SF and mostly American SF. I do not think or mean to imply that the influence of mass culture or the dynamics of cultural prestige attached to literary traditions and popular entertainments in America is a model or prototype for the rest of the world. The book is entirely devoted to the analysis of print and film SF to the exclusion of digital media or games, even though I am quite aware of how important they have become both commercially and culturally. Similarly, although there are two chapters about communities of practice, I have hardly brushed the surface of what could be said about SF fan cultures or contemporary participatory cultures. I can only hope that scholars who know more than I do about other national traditions of SF, digital media, fan cultures, and the rest of SF's myriad array of venues and practices can make some use of my work in those areas of research.

Here, then, is the plan of the book. Chapter 1 is a minimally revised version of an essay published in *Science Fiction Studies* in 2010 under the same title. It is devoted to basic issues of genre theory in relation to the problem of defining the genre of SF. Chapter 2 picks up the theoretical issues of chapter 1 in order to elaborate a description of the mass cultural genre system as a whole. The rest of the chapters explore some problems in writing the history of SF based on the theoretical groundwork laid in the first two chapters. Chapter 3 takes up the question of generic origins by arguing that the genealogy of SF is better approached in terms of systemic changes than the influence of individual texts. Chapter 4 is devoted to the issue of SF's status within the traditional literary canon via an extended reading of the novels of Philip K. Dick. Chapters 5 and 6 turn to more recent SF to examine some of the effects of homogeneity and heterogeneity corresponding to the genre's mass cultural and subcultural communities of practice. Here, as in the chapter on Dick, I am also concerned with the kind of critical and anti-hegemonic power SF narratives often exercise. This critical power does not depend on SF's formal grammar, but rather on the way some narratives appropriate and recode the genre's resources. I am especially concerned in chapters 5 and 6 with their doing so in order to resist a given subculture's inclusion within, and often erasure by, mass cultural homogeneity. In the conclusion I offer a periodization of SF's history that attempts to support the claim, argued throughout the book, that the cultural and ideological power of SF is best understood when questions about it are set in the systemic context of its dialogue with other proximate genres and the tension between different genre systems based on their different venues and modes of publicity.

On Defining Science Fiction, or Not

Genre Theory, SF, and History

In his groundbreaking 1984 essay "A Semantic/Syntactic Approach to Film Genre," Rick Altman could accurately state that "genre theory has up to now aimed almost exclusively at the elaboration of a synchronic model approximating the syntactic operation of a specific genre" (12). Only a few years later, in 1991, Ralph Cohen announced that there had been a paradigm shift in genre theory, in the course of which its dominant project had changed from identifying and classifying fixed, ahistorical entities to studying genres as historical processes (85–87). Yet the impact of that paradigm shift on science fiction studies, while no doubt contributing to the predominantly historical rather than formalist orientation of most scholarly projects these days, has been neither so immediate nor so overpowering as to make entirely clear its implications for conceptualizing the genre and understanding its history. In this chapter I aim to help clarify and strengthen the impact of a historical genre theory on SF studies.

I start from the problem of definition because, although constructing genre definitions is a scholarly necessity, a historical approach to genre seems to undermine any fixed definition. The fact that so many books on SF begin with a more or less extended discussion of the problem of definition testifies to its importance in establishing a framework for constructing the history of the genre, specifying its range and extent, locating its principal sites of production and reception, selecting its canon of masterpieces, and so on.[1] Perhaps the scholarly task that best highlights the importance of genre definition is bibliography, where the choice of what titles to include necessarily has to be guided by clearly articulated criteria that often include such definitions.

Yet it seems that the act of definition cannot ever be adequate to the notion of genre as historical process. In his 1999 *Film/Genre*, Altman argues that "genres are not inert categories shared by all ... but discursive claims made by real speakers for particular purposes in specific situations" (101, quoted in Bould and Vint 50). Thus Mark Bould and Sherryl Vint argue, drawing on Altman's work, that "there is no such thing as science fiction," by which they mean that "genres are never, as frequently perceived, objects which already exist in the world and which are subsequently studied by genre critics, but fluid and tenuous constructions made by the interaction of various claims and practices by writers, producers, distributors, marketers, readers, fans, critics and other discursive agents" (48). The critical and scholarly act of definition seems reduced, in this conception of the "claims and practices" that constitute the history of the genre, to no more than one among many other "fluid and tenuous constructions." In fact, the only genre definition—if one can call it that—adequate to the historical paradigm would be a kind of tautology, an assertion that the genre is whatever the various discursive agents involved in its production, distribution, and reception say it is. And indeed statements of that kind consistently come up in discussions of the problem of defining SF, the best-known example being Damon Knight's gesture of dismissal toward the very attempt at definition—"Science fiction is what we point to when we say it" ("Science Fiction Adventures," 122; quoted in Clute and Nicholls 314).

In his 2003 essay "On the Origin of Genre," Paul Kincaid manages to render the tautological affirmation of genre identity into a thoughtful position. Basing his argument on the notion of "family resemblance" in Ludwig Wittgenstein's *Philosophical Investigations*, Kincaid proposes that we can neither "extract a unique, common thread" that binds together all science fiction texts, nor identify a "unique, common origin" for the genre (415). He concludes that "science fiction is not one thing. Rather, it is any number of things—a future setting, a marvelous device, an ideal society, an alien creature, a twist in time, an interstellar journey, a satirical perspective, a particular approach to the matter of story, whatever we are looking for when we look for science fiction, here more overt, here more subtle—which are braided together in an endless variety of combinations" (416–17). The usefulness of Wittgenstein's concept of family resemblance for genre theory will bear further discussion a bit later. For now, the important theoretical point with regard to Kincaid's argument is not only to agree that, according to a historical theory of genre, SF is "any number of things," but also to note and emphasize that this account of genre definition, like Altman's and Bould and Vint's, involves subjects as well as objects. As Jason Mittel argues with respect to television genres, it is not just a question of the properties of the textual objects referred to as "science fiction," then, but also of the subjects positing the category, and therefore of the motives, the context, and the effects of those subjects' more or less consciously and successfully executed projects: "Genres are not intrinsic to texts—they are constituted by the processes that some scholars have labeled 'external' elements, such as industrial and audience practices. We need to look beyond the text as the locus for genre, locating genres within the complex interrelations between texts, industries, audiences, and historical contexts" (9–10). Or to put it another way, the assertion that SF is "whatever we are looking for when we are looking for science fiction" does not mean anything much unless "we" know who "we" are and why "we" are looking for science fiction.

In what follows I propose to offer an account of the current state of genre theory as it applies to the attempt to say what SF is. The first section will concentrate on conceptualizing what sort of thing a genre is, or isn't. The second section will then return to the question of how to understand the collective subjects of genre construction. I am arguing, throughout this chapter, that the notorious diversity of definitions of the genre is not a sign of confusion, nor the result of a multiplicity of genres being mistaken for a single one. On the contrary, the identity of SF is constituted by this very web of sometimes inconsistent and competing assertions. The remaining chapters of this book will then turn to the question of what impact this understanding of genre formation should have on the project of writing the history of SF.

Genre as a Historical Process

I am going to make five propositions about SF, each of which could also be reformulated as a thesis about genre per se, constituting what I take to be a fairly noncontroversial but, I hope, useful summary of the historically oriented paradigm of genre theory announced by Cohen and elaborated by Altman, Mittel, and others. The sequence leads from the basic position that genres are historical processes to the point where one can effectively address the questions about the uses and users of SF that occupy the second section of this chapter. The five propositions are

- SF is historical and mutable;
- SF has no essence, no single unifying characteristic, and no point of origin;
- SF is not a set of texts, but rather a way of using texts and of drawing relationships among them;
- SF's identity is a differentially articulated position in a historical and mutable field of genres;
- attribution of the identity of SF to a text constitutes an active intervention in its distribution and reception.

Let me explain and defend these propositions one at a time.

SF is historical and mutable. Nearly all twentieth-century genre theorists before 1980 would have agreed that the "theory of genres is a principle of order: it classifies literature and literary history not by time or place (period or national language) but by specifically literary types of organization or structure" (Wellek and Warren 226). The newer paradigm, in contrast, considers generic organizations and structures to be just as messily bound to time and place as other literary historical phenomena, albeit with patterns of distribution and temporalities of continuity and discontinuity that may differ quite strongly from those of national traditions or "periods" in Wellek and Warren's sense. A newer paradigm is not necessarily a better one, however, and the choice between these two alternatives remains a matter of first principles, where the evidence seems susceptible of logically consistent explanation from either point of view. That is, if one considers SF to designate a formal organization—Suvin's "literature of cognitive estrangement" has of course been by far the most influential formal definition—then it makes just as much sense to find it in classical Greek narratives as in contemporary American ones; and, in addition, it makes sense to say, as Suvin did, that much of what is conventionally called SF is actually something else. But the newer paradigm holds that the labeling itself is crucial to constructing the genre, and would therefore consider "the literature of cognitive estrangement" a specific, late-twentieth-century, academic genre category that has to be understood partly in the context of its opposition to the commercial genre practices Suvin deplored. Suvin's definition becomes part of the history of SF, not the key to unraveling SF's confusion with other forms.[2]

Strong arguments for the logical superiority of the historical over the formal approach to genre theory have been advanced from the perspective of linguistics and on the grounds provided by the vicissitudes of translation.[3] Beyond that, I would argue, the historical paradigm is to be preferred because it challenges its students to understand genre in a richer and more complex way, within parameters that are social rather than just literary.[4] Confronted, for example, with the controversy over whether such acclaimed pieces as Pamela Zoline's "The Heat Death of the Universe" (1967) or Karen Joy Fowler's "What I Didn't See" (2002) are SF or not, a formalist approach can only ask whether the story is or isn't a legitimate member of the genre. Does it accomplish "the presence and interaction of estrangement and cognition ... [in] an imaginative framework alternative to the author's empirical environment" (Suvin 375)? Is it a "realistic speculation about possible future events, based solidly on adequate knowledge of the real world, past and present, and on a thorough understanding of the nature and significance of the scientific method" (Heinlein 9)? Is it "modified by an awareness of the universe as a system of systems, a structure of structures" (Scholes 41)?[5] Does it explore the impact of technology or scientific discovery on lived experience? And so on. A historical approach to genre would ask instead how and why the field is being stretched to include these texts or defended against their inclusion; how the identification of them as SF challenges and perhaps modifies the accepted meaning of the term (so that questions about form also continue to be part of the conversation, but not on the same terms); what tensions and strategies in the writing and publication and reading of SF prepare for this sort of radical intervention; and what interests are put at stake by it.[6]

SF has no essence, no single unifying characteristic, and no point of origin. That SF has no point of origin or single unifying characteristic is the Wittgensteinian position Kincaid proposes in "On the Origin of Genre." The application of Wittgenstein's thought to the notion of genre that is crucial to Kincaid was first proposed in 1982 in Alistair Fowler's *Kinds of Literature* (41–44), an impressively erudite book whose central thesis is that genres are historical and mutable. As Fowler saw, Wittgenstein's notion of "family resemblance" is enormously suggestive for genre theory because it conceptualizes a grouping not based upon a single shared defining element. In the language game that constructs the category of games, for example, Wittgenstein says, "these phenomena have no one thing in common which makes us use the same word for all,—but . . . they are *related* to one another in many different ways. . . . We see a complicated network of similarities overlapping and criss-crossing: sometimes overall similarities, sometimes similarities of detail." We extend the concept "as in spinning a thread we twist fibre on fibre. And the strength of the thread does not reside in the fact that some one fibre runs through its whole length, but in the overlapping of many fibres" (31–32, sections 65–66).

Another conceptual model for the shape of a genre that has no single unifying characteristic is provided by the notion of the fuzzy set (see Attebery, *Strategies*, 12–13). A fuzzy set, in mathematics, is one that, rather than being determined by a single binary principle of inclusion or exclusion, is constituted by a plurality of such operations. The fuzzy set therefore includes elements with any of a range of characteristics, and membership in the set can bear very different levels of intensity, since some elements will have most or all of the required characteristics, while others may have only one. In addition, one member of the set may be included by virtue of properties a, b, and c, another by properties d, e, and f, so that any two sufficiently peripheral members of the set need not have any properties in common. It thus results in a conception of the shape of SF very similar to one based on Wittgenstein's concept of family resemblance. Either model allows SF the kind of scope and variety found in John Clute and Peter Nicholls's *Encyclopedia of Science Fiction*.

It seems worth remembering, however, that something like such a fuzzy set was precisely the target of Suvin's influential intervention in the history of definitions of SF. What Suvin opposed to the wide range of texts included in the category of SF was a precise concept of the genre ruled by what Roman Jakobson called a "dominant": "the focusing component of a work of art ... [that] rules, determines, and transforms the remaining components" (Jakobson 82). The categorical entity constituted by a fuzzy set or family resemblance, from this point of view, simply allows any number of incompatible versions of the textual dominant to operate silently, side by side, producing in the guise of a narrative genre a motley array of texts with no actual formal integrity. That, according to Suvin, was the state of science fiction studies when he proposed his own rigorous formal definition, which directed itself powerfully against the illusion of integrity in a generic field that had allowed itself to be delineated in such a loose manner.

I think that the conceptualization of SF as a fuzzy set generated by a range of definitions remains susceptible to this formalist criticism of indiscriminately lumping together disparate subgenres under a nominal umbrella because it is still ruled by the logic of textual determination, albeit in a far more diffuse way than that demanded by Jakobson's notion of the textual dominant. A thoroughgoing theorist of the fuzzy set, rather than being pressed to identify the dominant that commands the operation of inclusion or exclusion from the generic set, would face the daunting task of enumerating the range of characteristics that merit inclusion, including not only textual properties but also intertextual relationships and paratextual functions like "labeling." Such a task would indeed be encyclopedic in scope, but I want to suggest that it would also be futile, because the quasi-mathematical model of the fuzzy set can never make itself adequate to the open-ended processes of history where genre formation and reformation is constantly taking place. In this respect, Wittgenstein's thinking is better attuned to the historical approach to genre than the notion of the fuzzy set, because "the term 'language-*game*' is meant to call into prominence the fact that the *speaking* of language is part of an activity, or of a form of life" (Wittgenstein 11, section 23, emphasis in original). Categorization, in this view, is not a passive registering of qualities intrinsic to what is being categorized, but an active intervention in their disposition, and this insistence on agency is what most decisively distinguishes the historical approach to SF from a formalist one.

The term "family resemblance" has its shortcomings, however, when it comes to thinking about the problem of generic origins. Historians of SF are all too fond of proclaiming its moment of birth, whether it be in Mary

Shelley's *Frankenstein* (1818), H. G. Wells's *The Time Machine* (1895), the first issue of Hugo Gernsback's *Amazing Stories* (1926), or elsewhere according to one's geographical and historical emphasis; and the term "family resemblance" encourages the construction of the history of SF as some version of a family tree of descendants from one or more such progenitors.[7] It is not quite enough to argue, as Kincaid does, that there is no "unique, common origin" for the genre (415); the collective and accretive social process by which SF has been constructed does not have the kind of coherent form or causality that allows one to talk about origins at all. Even without reference to Wittgenstein's antiessentialism, the historical approach to genre proposed in Hans-Robert Jauss's reception theory exposes the logical problem with identifying the moment of origin for a genre insofar as, for Jauss, the notion of genre is based on repetition and is strictly opposed to his notion of originality. In Jauss's reception theory, there cannot be a first example of a genre, because the generic character of a text is precisely what is repeated and conventional in it. A text can violate established generic expectations, but it can only be said to have established new expectations when other texts, in imitating its strategies, solidify them into the features of a genre. In order for a text to be recognized as having generic features, it must allude to a set of strategies, images, or themes that has already emerged into the visibility of a conventional or at least repeatable gesture. Genre, therefore, is always found in the middle of things, never at the beginning of them.

A model that helps to better conceptualize the absence of origins in a historical approach to genre is Gilles Deleuze and Felix Guattari's notion of the rhizomatic assemblage.[8] What Deleuze and Guattari call a "collective assemblage of enunciation" (22) is constituted by "lines of articulation or segmentarity, strata and territories; but also lines of flight, movements of deterritorialization and destratification" (3). It has no center, no "hierarchical modes of communication and preestablished paths, [but rather] the rhizome is an acentered, nonhierarchical, nonsignifying system ... without an organizing memory or central automaton, defined solely by a circulation of states" (21). The most important feature of the rhizomatic assemblage in relation to genre theory is that it is an "antigenealogy" that "operates by variation, expansion, conquest, capture, offshoots.... It has neither beginning nor end, but always a middle (*milieu*) from which it grows and which it overspills" (21). The movement of texts and motifs into and through SF does not confer a pedigree on them, then, but instead merely connects one itinerary to another. The paths that connect those itineraries are not given in the "acentered, nonhierarchical, nonsignifying" structure of the genre, but rather have been and must be constructed by writers, publishers, and readers out of the conjunctures they occupy and the materials at hand.

The notion that SF's history is one of "variation, expansion, conquest, capture, offshoots" rather than a lineage of ancestors and descendants is nowhere more important than in the study of what, following the hint in the title of Everett Bleiler's indispensable bibliography, *Science-Fiction: The Early Years*, I would call early science fiction. Studying the beginnings of the genre is not at all a matter of finding its points of origin but rather of observing an accretion of repetitions, echoes, imitations, allusions, identifications, and distinctions that testifies to an emerging sense of a conventional web of resemblances. It is this gradual articulation of generic recognition, not the appearance of a formal type, that constitutes the history of early SF. Thus, rather than sorting out true SF from the genres in its proximity or trying to find its primal ancestors, it is far more useful to take stock of the way SF gradually comes into visibility in the milieu of late nineteenth-century fantasy, imperial adventure fiction, the romance revival of the 1880s and 1890s in England, the boy scientists of the American dime novel, utopian writing, the future war motif, and so on.[9] One is not looking for the appearance of a positive entity but rather for a practice of drawing similarities and differences among texts, which is the point further elaborated by the third proposition.

SF is not a set of texts, but rather a way of using texts and of drawing relationships among them. All those involved in the production, distribution, and consumption of SF—writers, editors, marketing specialists, casual readers, fans, scholars, students—construct the genre not only by acts of definition, categorization, inclusion and exclusion (all of which are important), but also by their uses of the protocols and the rhetorical strategies that distinguish the genre from other forms of writing and reading. John Frow, at the beginning of his excellent and concise 2006 book on genre theory, writes: "I understand genre as a form of symbolic action: the generic organization of language, images, gestures, and sound makes things happen by actively shaping the way we understand the world.... Texts—even the simplest and most formulaic—do not 'belong' to genres but are, rather, uses of them" (2). The fact that genre requires "symbolic action" rather than being inherent in the form or content of a text can be illustrated by the way generic difference can reside within verbal identity. Consider the example offered by Samuel R. Delany of applying realist versus SF protocols to the sentence "He turned on his left side," where the realist reading understands that someone has changed the position of his body, but the SF reading might mean that he has activated the left side of his body by turning on a switch ("Science Fiction and 'Literature,'" 103). My point is not so much that the SF reading exploits the grammatical and semantic possibilities of the language in a different and richer way, as Delany argued, as that the second reading depends upon the reader's familiarity with and use of SF conventions—in particular, here, the expectation that the distinction between organism and machine is going to be blurred or violated. Both the writer and the reader of the sentence in its SF sense are using the genre to actively shape their understanding of the world—that is, the world depicted in the text in question, and its relation to both an empirical environment and to other generically constructed worlds (the world of fantasy, the world of comedy, and so on).[10]

The distinction between a text's using a genre and its belonging to it also changes the relationship between the individual text and the genre, so that it is no longer one of simple exemplification, where the text stands as a metonym or synecdoche of the genre. The character of genre as "symbolic action" implies that genre is one of the many kinds of codes that, as Roland Barthes pointed out so relentlessly in *S/Z*, a text activates. Generic hybridity is not a special case, then; any narrative longer than a headline or a joke almost inevitably uses multiple generic conventions and strategies. Distinctions between SF and fantasy typically, if tacitly, acknowledge this fact, since they so often turn upon the status afforded to realist conventions in relation to the rest of the narrative. Because of the way that multiple genres play upon and against one another in individual texts, pigeonholing a text as a member of this or that genre is much less useful than understanding the way it positions itself within a field of generic possibilities.[11]

SF's identity is a differentially articulated position in a historical and mutable field of genres. Frow, after postulating the thesis that texts use genres rather than belong to them, goes on to say that the uses of genre in a text "refer not to 'a' genre but to a field or economy of genres, and their complexity derives from the complexity of that relation" (*Genre*, 2). To speak of an "economy of genres," as Frow does here, means to think of the generic codes activated in a text or by a reader as a matter of making choices with values attached to them by virtue of their difference from other possible choices. Such an economy depends crucially on the system of genres in play at a given time and place. Genres—like phonemes and words in Saussure's lectures on linguistics—are here considered values that signify by virtue of their difference from the other values in their field, and may change or lose their meaning if transposed into a different system. Thus, as Tony Bennett puts it, generic analysis must always take into account "the system of generic differences—conceived as a differentiated field of social uses— prevailing at [a given] time in terms of its influence on both textual strategies and contexts of reception" (108), because every generic choice constitutes what Pierre Bourdieu calls a position-taking with respect to the positions and values that structure the contemporary field of choices. Understanding the dynamics of genre in a given text depends upon being able to understand the field that offers the writer or reader its range of generic possibilities and determines the values attached to them.

Problems of generic economy are absolutely crucial to SF studies in two ways, the first having to do with questions of prestige and the second with writing the genre's history. Roger Luckhurst has written very entertainingly about SF's "death wish," which is to say its desire to stop being SF and become "literature." The source of that desire is the way positions and values line up in the contemporary economy of genres to produce the negative connotations often attached to "genre fiction": "The paradigmatic topography of ghetto/mainstream marks a border on which is transposed the evaluations popular/serious, low/high, entertainment/Literature.... The only way, it is proposed, to legitimate SF is to smuggle it across the border into the 'high.' And for the genre as a whole to become legitimate paradoxically involves the very destruction of the genre" (Luckhurst, "Many Deaths," 37–38). The conceit of the death wish actually refers to something rather different from an instinctual drive, of course—the fact that, although one can make choices (in this case, about genre), one can choose only from the options that history makes available. Many scholars (and editors, writers, and readers) of SF would like to have their SF and their literature too, but that is an option that the distinction between high and low culture has tended to foreclose.

The obsession with definite boundaries that once abounded in discussions of genre rested not on a widespread desire for precision in making genre distinctions, but rather on the effects of prestige attached to positions in the contemporary genre system; and this is the source of the recurrent drawing and redrawing of SF's borders that Luckhurst writes about. The fact that genre boundaries are so frequently described as prescriptive and constricting derives, similarly, not from their really being that way, but rather from the fact that in modern Western artistic practices more prestige accrues to violating these boundaries than to conforming to them. Hence the concept of "literature" as such has repeatedly been formulated as the category where every work constructs its own unique genre (e.g., by Friedrich Schlegel, Benedetto Croce, and Maurice Blanchot; see Frow, *Genre*, 26–27, and Altman, *Film/Genre*, 4–7). What this understanding of "literature" puts at stake is much less the prescriptive force of generic boundaries than the play of expectation and surprise in a text's handling of them, as in the stark opposition in Jauss's reception theory between innovative strategies and the understanding of genre itself as a set of predictable and eventually worn-out conventions. Yet, although distinctions between high and low modes of narrative can be expected to exist wherever class differences attach themselves to the production and distribution of narratives—which is to say throughout history—the particular way that high and low are connected in contemporary genre practices with innovation versus imitation is a more recent and specific development. The peculiar sense of "literature" as the category whose members defy categorization is an integral part of the history of the sense of "genre" that is one of SF's conditions of existence. Thus writing the history of SF has to involve, at a minimum, attending to the historical change in genre systems that produced that distinction.

The way generic terms and choices signify in relation to other terms and choices is constantly in flux. Thus, as Fowler says, "It is neither possible nor even desirable to arrive at a very high degree of precision in using generic terms. The overlapping and mutability of genres means that an 'imprecise' terminology is more efficient" (130). Such overlapping and mutability also make necessary the practice of retro-labeling in order to trace the lineaments of emerging genre categories (hence, "early science fiction"). Nonetheless, attention to the history of genre systems ought to foreclose the option of transposing the category of SF wholesale onto early modern or classical texts. If Shelley's *Frankenstein* was not SF when it was written (see chapter 3), neither, a fortiori, were Swift's *Gulliver's Travels* or Lucian's *True History*. The important point is that the emergence of SF has to do not with the first appearance of a certain formal type, nor with when the term "science fiction" was first used or by whom, but rather with the appearance of a system of generic identities that articulates the various terms that cluster around SF (scientific fiction, scientific romance, scientifiction; but also horror fiction, detective fiction, the western). Clearly Gernsback did not initiate this system of generic identities when he published the first issue of *Amazing Stories* in 1926. But just as clearly, the milieu of mass-marketed periodical publications is one of the historical conditions for SF's emergence as a distinctive genre, and that milieu carries with it its hierarchical opposition to a specific version of the realm of "high" culture.

I propose that understanding the positions and values of SF within past and present economies of genre, or how the history of this shifting and slippery subject, science fiction or SF, fits into the larger context of changes within the system of genres, is the frame in which to put the question, What difference does it make when "we" point to a text and say that it is SF?

The answer to that question from the perspective of genre theory is that *attribution of the identity of SF to a text constitutes an active intervention in its distribution and reception*. Here we should speak of labeling itself as a rhetorical act. One of the most bustling areas of genre theory in recent years has been that explored by rhetoricians focused on the pedagogy of composition, rather than critics and scholars of literature (Frow, "'Reproducibles,'" 1626–27). In an important early contribution to the new rhetorical approach to genre, Carolyn Miller wrote in 1984 that a "sound definition of genre must be centred not on the substance or the form of discourse but on the action it is used to accomplish" (151). Miller is primarily concerned with "the '*de facto*' genres, the types we have names for in everyday language," because these genres "tell us something theoretically important about discourse" by "tak[ing] seriously the rhetoric in which we are immersed and the situations in which we find ourselves" (155). Although her analysis is therefore more concerned with genres like the letter of recommendation or the inaugural speech than with drawing distinctions between different types of storytelling, Miller's approach to genre might well lead one to ask why distinctions between types of story are drawn and insisted upon at all. How can one explain this "mutual construing of objects, events, interests, and purposes that not only links them but makes them what they are: an objectified social need" (157)? What action does it accomplish to attribute the label, SF, to a narrative?

Whatever protocols of interpretation or formal and thematic conventions the label refers to, the labeling itself often serves to position the text within the field of choices offered by the contemporary genre system in quite material ways: how it will be printed, where it will be sold, by whom it is most likely to be read. Generic attribution therefore affects the distribution and reception of texts—that is, the ways they are put to use. It is a way of telling someone how to read a text, and even more a kind of promise that the text can be usefully, pleasurably read that way. The attribution does not just classify the text; it promotes its use by a certain group of readers and in certain kinds of ways (e.g., with a high level of seriousness, or a lack of it). When "we" point to a story and say it is SF, therefore, that means not only that it ought to be read using the protocols associated with SF but also that it can and should be read in conversation with other SF texts and readers.

Such acts of labeling, by assigning texts a position and a value within a system of genres, entangle them within both a synchronic web of resemblances and a diachronic history of generic "variation, expansion, conquest, capture, offshoots" (Deleuze and Guattari 21). A history of genre systems attentive to the power that genre attribution exercises upon distribution and reception would not be one structured primarily by the appearance of literary masterpieces, but rather one also punctuated by watersheds in the technology of publication, the distribution of reading material, and the social production and distribution of literacy itself. In the second chapter of this book I will attempt a description of the formation and topography of the mass cultural genre system within which the category of science fiction arose. But first I will turn back to the questions I raised earlier about the collective subject of SF genre formation. Those questions can now take an expanded form that should make their ramifications clearer. If SF is "whatever [in all its historical mutability and rhizomatic irregularity] we are looking for when we are looking for science fiction," what kind of a collectivity is formed by those who recognize the genre? On what terrain—that is, what system of genres, what regime of the production and distribution of literature and literacy—does the collective endeavor of "looking for science fiction" take place? What in the economy of genres or the dynamics of distribution and reception drives that collectivity to look for SF? And what kind of intervention in that economy is their saying they have found it?

Categorization and Communities of Practice

SF history and criticism afford two drastically different versions of the collective subject of genre formation. The list of "writers, producers, distributors, marketers, readers, fans, critics and other discursive agents" in Bould and Vint's "fluid and tenuous" construction of SF indicates an anonymous, disparate, and disunified set of people. The use of Knight's or Kincaid's pronominal "we" here would constitute a kind of grammatical mirage imputing collective intentionality to a process without a subject—or, to be more precise, a process involving so many and such disconnected subjects that they share only the nominal common ground of their participation in the production, distribution, and reception of SF. This anonymous and scattered sense of a defining collectivity stands in sharp contrast to the practice of referring the construction and definition of SF to a rather tightly knit community, a folk group who get to say what SF is by virtue of their shared participation in the project of publishing, reading, conversing, and otherwise interacting with one another about it: "'Modern' science fiction, generally dated as having begun in late 1937 with the ascent of [SF editor and writer John W.] Campbell, was a literature centered around a compact group of people.... There could have been no more than fifty core figures who did 90 percent of the writing and editing. All of them knew one another, most knew one another well, lived together, married one another, collaborated, bought each others' material, married each others' wives, and so on" (Malzberg 240). This sort of usage has the considerable merit of making a concrete history and set of motives underlying SF refreshingly clear. Yet an excessive emphasis on the community of writers, editors, and fans in the early pulp milieu encourages an illusion of voluntary control over genre formation that is certainly exaggerated. Even during the so-called golden age of Campbell's editorial influence, SF resided within a larger economy of genres whose shifting values and fluid boundaries no group, much less a single editor or publication, could control. Genre construction is intentional only in fits and starts, only as localized as the circulation of the narratives in question, and even then subject to the pressures of the entire system of publication and circulation in which it takes place.

Even worse, the peculiar situation of the pulps can be taken as normative for genres as such, as Gary Westfahl demonstrates in *The Mechanics of Wonder*: "If we define a genre as consisting of a body of texts related by a shared understanding of that genre as recorded in contemporary commentary, then a true history of science fiction as a genre must begin in 1926, at the time when Gernsback defined science fiction, offered a critical theory concerning its nature, purposes, and origins, and persuaded many others to accept and extend his ideas.... Literary genres appear in history for one reason: someone declares that a genre exists and persuades writers, publishers, readers and critics that she is correct" (8–12). If this conception of genre were correct, it could be so only with respect to modern genre practices. Certainly there is no body of contemporary commentary that illustrates a shared understanding of what constitutes the genres of the proverb, the riddle, the ballad, or the epic. But even if one stays within the field of genres occupied by Gernsback, one cannot locate a master theorist or "announcer" for the western, spy fiction, detective fiction, and so on. The more usual case with genres is surely the one described by Michael McKeon in *The Origins of the English Novel*, when he argues that the novel as a generic designation came to be formulated only when the process of its emergence was complete.

I suggest that it is possible to articulate the anonymous collectivity of the "complex historical process" of SF's emergence and ongoing construction, maintenance, and revision with the rich particularity of an account like Malzberg's by means of the theorization of categorization and its uses offered by Geoffrey Bowker and Susan Leigh Starr in *Sorting Things Out: Classification and Its Consequences* (1999). Bowker and Starr are concerned with the way classifications are constructed within communities of practice, emphasizing the ad hoc supplementation and renegotiation of official or institutional categories by those who make them work: "We need a richer vocabulary than that of standardization or formalization with which to characterize the heterogeneity and the processual nature of information ecologies" (293). They emphasize, too, the "collective forgetting" about "the contingent, messy work" of classification that unites members of a community of practice (299). Full-fledged membership in such a community involves the naturalization of its objects of practice, which "means stripping away the contingencies of an object's creation and its situated nature. A naturalized object has lost its anthropological strangeness" (299). As a result of its naturalization, it can be pointed to as an example of X with an obviousness that derives not from the qualities of the object itself, but rather from membership in the relevant community.

Objects and communities of practice do not line up simply and neatly, however, because people come in and out of such communities, operate within them at various levels of familiarity with their categories, and may at the same time be members of different communities with conflicting classification practices. Bowker and Starr therefore emphasize the importance of "boundary objects" as ways of mediating the practices and motives of overlapping communities of practice: "Boundary objects are those objects that both inhabit several communities of practice and satisfy the informational requirements of each of them.... The creation and management of boundary objects is a key process in developing and maintaining coherence across intersecting communities.... Boundary objects are the canonical forms of all objects in our built and natural environments" (297–307). To speak about a common ground of SF shared by writers, editors, publishers, marketers, fans, general readers, critics, and scholars might mean to identify the boundary objects that these various communities of practice share. The advantage of this conceptualization of classification is that the communities of practice do not disappear into anonymity, nor do the differences and tensions among their practices fall out of view, nor does whatever consensus settles among them embody the essence of the object. Boundary objects—for example the texts that make up the SF canon—are not by necessity the most important or definitive objects for any given community, but simply the ones that satisfy the requirements of several communities at once.

Using the concepts of communities of practice and boundary objects to sort out the complex agencies constructing SF implies at least three distinct ways of understanding the assertion that SF is "whatever we are looking for when we are looking for science fiction." First, the "we" who are looking for science fiction could refer to the members of the speaker's own community of practice; this is the sense it had when Damon Knight wrote that "science fiction is what we point to when we say it." Second, however, "we" could be taken to refer to all the different communities of practice who use the category, and "science fiction" to all the objects that all of them collectively point to. Any expectation of coherence here is obviously doomed to disappointment, but nonetheless this encyclopedic sense of the genre has the virtue of pointing toward the broad horizon of social practices where the history of genre systems can come into view. Third, science fiction could be taken as the set of objects that all the relevant communities of practice point to in common—that is, the boundary objects "we" communities share.

This third reading refers to a shared territory that is not a matter of giving up on arriving at a definition of the genre, but rather is precisely the product of the interaction among different communities of practice using different definitions of SF. The multiplicity of definitions of SF does not reflect widespread confusion about what SF is, but rather it results from the variety of motives the definitions express and the many ways of intervening in the genre's production, distribution, and reception that they pursue. A wealth of biographical and paratextual material can be brought to bear here, as in Justine Larbalestier's decision that "letters, reviews, fanzines, and marketing blurbs are as important as the stories themselves" in piecing together her detailed history of a riven and complex SF community in *The Battle of the Sexes in Science Fiction* (1). Brian Attebery's description of the shape of SF in *Decoding Gender in Science Fiction* also attributes that shape to the interaction of disparate communities: "Some outgrowths of the genre have so little in common that they hardly seem to constitute a single category. Yet if they share few features, all the myriad manifestations of SF may still be analyzed as products of a single process. All result from negotiated exchanges between different segments of culture" (170). Understanding the relations between its various communities of practice, whether of negotiation or conflict or deliberate noninteraction, is among the most important problems that genre theory poses SF critics and scholars.

Thinking of genres as categories wielded by communities of practice has one final advantage that can serve as the conclusion to this chapter and point our way forward to the rest. Bowker and Starr's analysis makes all definitions of SF appear in the light of working definitions, provisional conceptualizations suited to the purposes of a particular community of practice and, within that community, to the needs and goals of a specific project. Thus definitions may be necessary, even indispensable, and yet constructing and adhering to a single definition of the genre, far from being the goal of a history of SF, is more likely to be a way to short-circuit it. Definition and classification may be useful points of departure for critical and rhetorical analysis, but if the version of genre theory offered here is valid, the project of comprehending what SF has meant and currently means is one to be accomplished through historical and comparative narrative rather than formal description. I hope to contribute a few episodes to that narrative in what follows. But first we need to examine the concept of the genre system, and the mass cultural genre system in particular, more closely.

2

The Mass Cultural Genre System

Most genre theory has focused on the choices writers make when composing texts or that readers make, or ought to make, in interpreting them. But the practice of attributing genre to narrative fiction also clusters heavily in two institutional locations, commercial publishing and the academy. On these two sites, practices of reading dovetail with acts of selection, publication, and dissemination coordinated with complex and multiform motives. The relation between these two institutional locations is a feature of contemporary genre systems that most twentieth-century theory turned its back upon, failing to even notice it, much less ask about its significance or implications. Recent contributions to media studies like Altman's *Film/Genre* and Mittel's *Genre and Television* have begun to repair this neglect by elaborating theories of genre attentive to the practices of the Hollywood studios and corporate broadcast television. What I am attempting here is a more general description of the mass cultural genre system that proceeds on the premise that the commercial and academic genre systems will be better understood in relation to one another than either one in isolation. My account takes its point of departure from the emergence of mass culture in the late nineteenth and early twentieth centuries, and will pay attention throughout to the relations between the mass cultural and the academic genre systems. I begin by asking not what kind of definitional or conceptual work these systems accomplish, but what sort of organizational tasks they perform. How do they intervene in organizing the distribution and reception of narrative fiction?

While literary genre theory has for the most part related genres to one another by means of formal and thematic, or as Altman puts it, syntactic and semantic, criteria, an opening to the institutional functions of genre differentiation can be afforded by recent rhetorical approaches to genre theory, which have been exploring the ways that complex organizational tasks often involve an array of interlocking and codependent genres. For instance, the organization of an academic conference might involve calls for papers, proposals, abstracts, the exchanging of drafts and feedback, and many other formal and informal genres in the course of its affairs. Summarizing and elaborating on this work, Clay Spinuzzi sorts out several different sorts of assemblages that such rhetorically interlocking genres can form. By a "system" of genres Spinuzzi designates a group of genres that are related to one another through a community's use of them in a sequential and stable fashion to accomplish organizational or communicative tasks, like the organization of a professional meeting or the writing of a grant. More interesting to Spinuzzi, and more relevant to the sense of system I mean to explore here, are genre "repertoires," a concept which recognizes that genres overlap, change over time, and demand improvisation, and that they are not simply means of communication but also ways of mediating social interaction and managing "distributed cognition" (Spinuzzi 4). Most robust of all Spinuzzi's assemblages is the genre "ecology" (cf. the "information ecologies" of Bowker and Starr), which includes the properties of the genre repertoire but adds that within the framework of the genre ecology, "genres are not simply performed or communicated, they represent the 'thinking out' of a community as it cyclically performs an activity" (Spinuzzi 5). According to Spinuzzi, "genre ecologies are constantly importing, hybridizing, and evolving genres," and in the framework of the genre ecology he sees "genres as collective achievements that act just as much as they are acted upon" (6).

Although I choose to keep the term "system" rather than "ecology," the notion of a literary genre system proposed in this study resembles Spinuzzi's notion of a genre ecology in a number of striking ways. Both the mass cultural and the academic-classical systems are means of mediating distributed cognition. Not only do the genres in these systems overlap, change over time, and demand improvisation of their users, but both systems also import and hybridize genres, albeit with quite different temporal rhythms. One can certainly argue that the genres involved are collective actions that act as much as they are acted upon. Most intriguing of all is Spinuzzi's suggestion that the performance and communication of the genres within a genre ecology represent the thinking out of a collective activity. The mass cultural genre system plays a key role in organizing the production, distribution, and reception of storytelling within the milieu of mass culture, and although the activity of constructing narratives certainly does not exhaust the forms of verbal artistry, eloquence, and persuasion that are mediated by the mass cultural or the academic-classical genre systems, it would be difficult indeed to overestimate or overstate the importance of the collective activities and desires that are mediated and put at stake by storytelling alone.

But mass culture does not organize storytelling for storytelling's sake. It turns some stories into entertainment, others into news. The collective activities of buying and selling coalesce in mass culture with the rhetorical projects of publicizing and promoting, and this rhetorical-commercial matrix inevitably tangles itself in political relations as well. In what follows, I will argue that the commercial advertisement is the keystone of the mass cultural genre system, and that its calculated instrumentalization of the aesthetic pervades not only narrative production, both high and low, but also political discourse in the form of advertising's first cousin, propaganda. I will also be arguing, however, that this instrumentalization of the aesthetic is far from determining the quality or the critical power of all the products of the culture industry. I will borrow from Antonio Gramsci's *Prison Notebooks* the distinction between organic and traditional intellectuals in order to compare the work done by the mass cultural genre system, a form of intellectual activity that emerges spontaneously within advanced capitalist relations and is therefore organic to it, to the work done by the traditional genre system located and maintained in the schools. Finally, I will attempt to map out the topography of the mass cultural genre system in terms of the effects of seriality, stratification, and the formation of subcultures that characterize its terrain. I begin by returning to the problem of conceptualizing the organizational function of a system of genres.

Genre Systems and Institutional Practices

Attempts to describe a system of literary genres have not often approached this project as a question about organizing the social functions of narrative. The most influential twentieth-century formulation of a system of literary genres, Northrop Frye's *Anatomy of Criticism*, took no interest in questions about social organization. Frye's formal, thematic, and stylistic anatomy postulates an overarching, transcendent organization of literary types the principle of which is immanent in the logic and significance of literature itself. Thus his genre system has no clear historical boundaries and is not tied to any specific social milieu, an impulse echoed in Darko Suvin's contention that the "literature of cognitive estrangement" thrives in times of social disruption per se, rather than in any specific moment of political or historical change. In sharp contrast to Frye's grand sweep and universalizing impulses, which impose on the history of literature the synchrony of a kind of grand museum exhibition, Hans Robert Jauss's carefully historicized, meticulous study of the medieval genre system in "Theory of Genres and Medieval Literature" insists that historical contingencies have caused literary genres to be organized in different ways for different purposes according to different values at different times and places.[1] Jauss's approach does not explicitly tackle the organizing social function of the medieval genre system, but it opens the possibility of doing so.

As Jauss articulates the many differences between the system of medieval genres and both classical and modern ones, he argues that the development of literary forms is neither continuous nor teleological: "No perceptible historical continuity exists between the forms and genres of the Middle Ages and the literature of our present. Here the reception of the ancient poetics and canon of genres in the Renaissance unmistakably cut through the threads of the formation of tradition. The rediscovery of medieval literature by romantic philology produced only the ideology of new continuities in the form of the essential unity of each national literature" (108). Literary forms do not simply grow and develop out of one another, and the logic of form, content, and style is not adequate to account for the discontinuous terrain of their history. The notion of a system of genres is for Jauss inherent in the broader concept of the horizon of expectations that frames literary reception, so that "the relationship between the individual text and the series of texts formative of a genre presents itself as a process of the continual founding and altering of horizons" (88). These horizons of expectation are not exclusively literary: "the work of art is [to be] understood as a sign and carrier of meaning for a social reality, and the aesthetic is defined as a principle of mediation and a mode of organization for extra-aesthetic meanings" (108). Although Jauss assigns the impetus for the early modern reordering of the genre system to scholarly reanimation of the literature of classical antiquity, his attention to the ever-shifting horizons of expectation and the organization of extra-aesthetic meanings might just as consistently include the impact of the printing press or the changing relations of church and state in the transition from feudalism to centralized absolutist monarchies. Both contributed to the secularization of literacy, shifting it from a predominantly clerical to an increasingly aristocratic and capitalistic, financial and bureaucratic set of functions. The question might well be raised, then, of how changes in the system of genres responded to these shifting technological and social horizons of expectation.

Certainly the emergence of science fiction has often been explained as a response to the shifting horizon of technological possibility. One of the most frequently reiterated commonplaces about science fiction is that it concerns itself with the social effects of technological change and emerges in the context of industrial technological innovation, and no doubt the reason this is so frequently repeated is that it is so obviously correct. For instance, in Roger Luckhurst's recent history of science fiction he lists as one of the conditions of the genre's emergence "the context of a culture being visibly transformed by technological and scientific innovations" in the later nineteenth century (*Science Fiction*, 16). But Luckhurst lists three other conditions for the emergence of science fiction that are very much to the point in the present context: "1) The extension of literacy and primary education to the majority of the population of England and America, including the working classes; 2) the displacement of the older forms of mass literature, the 'penny dreadful' and the 'dime novel', with new cheap magazine formats that force formal innovation, and drive the invention of modern genre categories like detective or spy fiction as well as SF; 3) the arrival of scientific and technical institutions that provide a training for a lower-middle-class generation as scientific workers, teachers, and engineers, and that comes to confront traditional loci of cultural authority" (*Science Fiction*, 16). Luckhurst's second condition corresponds directly to the subject of this book. One of the major questions being raised here is how the new magazine formats "force formal innovation, and drive the invention of modern genre categories." But there is a prior question implied in this one, the problem of what encouraged the development of these new magazine formats in the first place. The changes in the distribution of print, the speed of communication, and the technology of broadcast media that made possible mass culture were a no less momentous redistribution of literacy and its effects than those caused by the invention of the printing press itself. The question is what role the new, mass cultural genre system might have played in organizing, or managing, this redistribution of literacy.

I propose to approach this question by examining the emergence of the mass cultural genre system in relation to the one that prevailed in the set of institutions traditionally and directly charged with the social function of organizing and managing the distribution of literacy: the schools. The first and the third of Luckhurst's conditions point to the expansion of the reading audience taking place on two levels of the educational system. Alongside the expansion of literacy at the most basic level of the ability to read, there is a more selective development in "scientific and technical institutions" of the specialized literacies required for technical and managerial tasks. Both the increasing number of people receiving primary education and the increased emphasis on technical training at the advanced level are part and parcel of "a culture being visibly transformed by technological and scientific innovations" insofar as these social phenomena respond to the needs of a growing industrial economy. While the growth of the reading public would seem to be one of the preconditions for the formation of mass culture in general, Luckhurst's emphasis on the training of technicians ("scientific workers") and engineers points more directly to the emerging audience for science fiction. That the younger readers aspiring toward this technical-managerial literacy composed a significant part of the reading audience for early science fiction seems a reasonable guess, given the didactic ambitions and extraordinary success of Verne's *Voyages extraordinaires*, and likewise fits well with the "Edisonades" and boy geniuses of the transition from the dime novel into the pulp magazines.[2] This relation to a specialized body of generic content seems typical of mass cultural genres. Just as science fiction specializes in the subject matter of science and technology, detective fiction focuses on law and police work, the western on the settlement of the American western frontier, and romance on the social and emotional dynamics of courtship and sexuality (Attebery and Hollinger xi). The way this specificity of content fits into the larger mass cultural genre system is an issue we will need to return to later. First, however, let me return to the relation of technical training to developments in the larger educational apparatus and the academic genre system.

The development of advanced scientific and technical training takes place within an expansion of higher education through the growth of the redbrick universities in the United Kingdom and the emergence of the first great state universities in the United States. More than just opening up new venues and less exclusive opportunities to attain higher education, this growth signals a modernization of the university curriculum that includes not just scientific subjects but also a shift in literary studies away from classical antiquity toward vernacular languages and national literatures. In this context the category of "literature," which had already developed from the designation of printed matter in general to a term that conferred upon selected texts the distinction of high quality and demanded the exercise of tasteful discernment in its use, became a kind of master genre, a boundary object that helped to rationalize curricular regularities in relation to the bureaucratic structure of the educational apparatus. What in the eighteenth century was a course of lectures in rhetoric and belles lettres would mutate into a panoply of courses on literary forms (the triad of poetry, drama, and prose supplying the overarching generic logic) and national traditions that, when entered upon a student's transcript, promised his or her exposure to a standardized regime of study that could be measured in credit hours, billed for tuition, and used by administrators to determine the allocation of institutional resources.[3]

In the shift from classical to vernacular languages, the category of "literature" thus helps adapt the academic genre system to the way, in Luckhurst's words, a "generation [of] scientific workers, teachers, and engineers . . . confront the traditional loci of cultural authority." John Guillory, surveying the changing historical forms of the literary canon, writes of this nineteenth-century development that "it is only vernacular writing that has the power to bring into existence the category of 'literature' in the specific sense of poetry, novels, plays, and so on. The brackets that close around a particular set of genres at this time increasingly distinguish it on the one side from philosophical and scientific writing, and on the other from scripture" (76). These generic enclosures within the academy would come to complement and reinforce the separation of "literature" from the mass cultural genre system as a whole throughout most of the twentieth century.

Guillory argues that the displacement of the classics by vernacular "literature" changed the canon of texts used in advanced literary pedagogy but retained a crucial element of that pedagogy's fundamental form, the phenomenon sociolinguists call "diglossia." In the strict sense of the term originally formulated by the linguist Charles Ferguson, diglossia refers to a hierarchical differentiation of functions between a common, spoken language and one "which is learned largely by formal education and is used for most written and formal purposes but is not used by any sector of the community for ordinary conversation" (quoted in Guillory 69). Guillory stretches the concept of diglossia to include the practice of preserving and disseminating a canonical body of writing in the schools in order to inculcate an advanced linguistic competency. Thus what was formerly a linguistic distinction becomes a generic one, and the displacement of the classics by national traditions as "loci of authority" in the university curriculum institutionalizes "different practices of the same language" that help to coordinate different levels of educational attainment with different class destinations (Macherey and Balibar 47, quoted by Guillory 78).[4] The ability to operate this genre distinction, then, is one of the specific disciplinary mechanisms by which the schools perform the function of "ideological state apparatuses"—as Louis Althusser called them in his most famous and influential essay. The ideological self-recognition associated with "literature" has to do with becoming a full-fledged human being regardless of class position (though of course one's facility with and discernment of literature are strong signals of class), while the discourses of the various technical competencies excluded from that category are "practical" and job oriented—hence direct determinants of one's economic status. It is easy to see how this dichotomy would come to dovetail with the rift between modernist experimentation and the more formally conservative methods of mass cultural artistry.

These developments are of course not isolated within the schools. Richard Ohmann usefully contrasts the "sacralization" of higher culture signaled in the second half of the nineteenth century in the United States by the founding of municipal art museums, symphonies, and opera companies with the burgeoning sphere of popular consumer culture in the same period:

> Elites carried forth the "sacralization" of art and culture: purging it of amateurism, widening the separation between creators and audiences, framing art as difficult and pure, divesting it of more accessible, popular elements. Barnum-like exhibits were distinguished from art museums; ragtime from the symphony. Vaudeville, dime novels, comics, the saloon and the dance hall, Coney Island and the nickelodeon, the ethnic club and the sports park drew more uniformly working class participants. Culture became a system that clearly signaled and manifested social class; refined and sacralized at the top of the hierarchy, pleasure-seeking and openly commercial at the bottom. (221)

Explaining the twentieth century's peculiar rearticulation of the long-standing European division of high genres and high style from low ones as a reordering of the distribution of literacy and the cultural competencies and privileges attached to it supplements and complicates the thesis concerning commercial narrative production proposed by Fredric Jameson in his essay "Reification and Utopia in Mass Culture." There Jameson proposes that the specter of commodification looms over high modernism just as much as over mass culture. Where the products of the culture industry are explicitly designed as commodities, and their production intentionally organized around commercial activity, the artifacts of high modernism are, according to Jameson, just as strongly determined by their rejection of commodity status. One needs to add, however, that the antithetical practices of high modernism and mass culture reiterate the generic and disciplinary division of literary study from technical and scientific training in the schools, and that what Jameson quite reasonably sees as a set of heavily constrained responses to the pressures of commodification might also be seen as practical, goal-oriented management of the linguistic resources corresponding to that division. The mass cultural genre system would from this point of view be engaged in what Spinuzzi calls "thinking out" the technical and instrumental character of advanced capitalist social interaction. But this "thinking out" takes place within the constraints of class, and the management of narrative in mass culture includes—as Jameson goes on to argue in "Reification and Utopia"—the way it negotiates the tension between the commercial status quo and class-based fantasies of liberation from that social order.

The relation between the genre systems generated in commercial publishing and the academy is not one of simple exclusion or straightforward hierarchy, then, but rather involves a distribution of the social functions of narrative across the fields of education, employment, and consumption. The tensions of class dominance and resistance pervade the entire field. As Theodor Adorno famously observed in a letter to Walter Benjamin dated March 3, 1936, both high modernism and mass culture "bear the stigmata of capitalism," representing the "torn halves of an integral freedom, to which, however, they do not add up" (*Culture Industry*, 2). Merely to condemn the "culture industry" as a debased form of more authentic traditional cultural practices enforces a false separation upon cultural analysis that encourages nostalgia and elitism. Yet to celebrate the mass cultural system as the realm of the popular, embracing the wider reading audience that the elitist practices of high modernism and the upper levels of academic literary specialization exclude, would be to confuse consumerism with democracy.

Nonetheless it is entirely appropriate to draw upon Gramsci's distinction between organic and traditional intellectuals to speak here of the confrontation of organic versus traditional genre systems. This opposition does not have to do with the political activities of the intellectuals involved but with the institutional locations where the genre systems are primarily enacted—in the cauldron, so to speak, of commodity production, on the one hand, and in the ivory tower of the academy, on the other. The academic genre system, organized around the category of literature, imports and hybridizes genre categories that emerged in previous social formations and mediates their ongoing impact upon the present. Its task is to help construct the meaning of tradition. The mass cultural genre system arises out of the distribution of cultural resources and the inextricably entwined commercial and cultural motives of practice organic to the contemporary social formation, and its task is to help coordinate these various resources and motives. Its emergence within the specific historical constraints of late nineteenth- and early twentieth-century American and British capitalism is the topic we turn to in the next section of this chapter. Among the issues that remain to be explored is whether and to what extent the mass cultural genre system participates in what Gramsci calls the ideal social and political function of the organic intellectual, to give a social group "homogeneity and an awareness of its own function" (5). It cannot be doubted, at the least, that mass culture relentlessly insists on telling us who we are, and who we ought to want to be.

Before turning to the emergence of the mass cultural genre system it is worthwhile to measure our distance from the situation I have been describing. The early twentieth century's antagonism between modernism and mass culture has faded into the early twenty-first century's postmodernist irreverence for the canonical and the ongoing disintegration of the prestige of "literature." In higher education the technical and managerial linguistic competence aimed at in composition courses has arguably overtaken and subsumed that embodied in the study of literature. This was John Guillory's judgment in 1993: "We know that fewer students are [nowadays being] routed through the curriculum of literature, although this is not a matter of numbers only—the center of the system of social reproduction has moved elsewhere, into the domain of mass culture" (80). In 1991 Michael Denning called the same situation the end of mass culture: "We have come to the end of 'mass culture'; the debates and positions which named 'mass culture' as an other have been superseded. There is no mass culture *out there*; it is the very element we all breathe" (267). It is not any coincidence that the paradigm shift in genre theory described in the first chapter corresponds closely in time with such calls to end the othering of mass culture, as testifies the fact that some of the most notable advances in the new paradigm have come in media studies devoted to mass cultural genre practices.

Two decades later, after the intervening explosion of digital media and the emergence of online social networking, the skills relevant to commanding "the center of social reproduction" seem even less likely to coincide with mastery of the traditional literary canon. Henry Jenkins, in *Confronting the Challenges of Participatory Culture: Media Education for the 21st Century*, argues for shifting the educational institution's conversation about the new media away from its obsession with technological access and toward the project of developing the cultural competencies and social skills necessary to play a full role in the emerging culture. The new literacies Jenkins adds to the list of traditional research, technical, and critical-analysis skills include such subjects as simulation, appropriation, multitasking, distributed cognition, collective intelligence, transmedia navigation, networking, and negotiation. None of these seems particularly focused on the traditional genre system, and most of them are likely to involve direct engagement with the mass cultural genre system. If, nonetheless, the hierarchical divide between the traditional and the mass cultural genres still has considerable force, there remains at this point no good reason to continue to defend the cultural divide between the two genre systems, or to take up partisan advocacy of one against the other, or to study one as if the other did not exist or were an embarrassment. On the contrary, there is every reason to give mass culture and the mass cultural genre system the best scholarly and critical attention possible.

Advertising and Serial Fiction

The opposition between the mass cultural genre system and the traditional genre system operating in the schools and the critical establishment plays a key role in organizing the social functions of narrative in twentieth-century U.S. and British society. The way that the modernist experimentation of writers like James Joyce or T. S. Eliot highlights the polyglot nature of Western tradition and renders the native tongue difficult takes its point of departure from the diglossia of literary education, which still depended heavily on the learning of foreign languages in the early twentieth century. Thus the prestige afforded to "literature" both originates in and depends upon its alignment with the cosmopolitanism and multilingual competency of the traditional intellectual. The organic genres of mass culture, in contrast, cultivate the lingua franca of homogeneous and contemporaneous national culture, the language of the news as well as of emerging technical disciplines. In what follows, I will argue that the key element of the mass cultural genre system's coherent organizational function, the binding agent, as it were, of whatever collective practices and subjectivities it sets in motion, is the commercial advertisement.

The best account of the emergence of mass culture is Richard Ohmann's in *Selling Culture*. According to Ohmann, mass culture consists of "voluntary experiences, produced by a relatively small number of specialists, for millions across the nation to share, in similar or identical form, either simultaneously or nearly so, with dependable frequency; mass culture shapes habitual audiences, around common needs or interests, and it is made for profit" (14). One index of its development in the nineteenth-century United States is the growing dominance of national over local news: the Associated Press wire service was founded in 1848; syndicated newspaper columns became common in the 1880s, syndicated comics in the 1890s. But more crucial to the "voluntary" and "habitual" nature of this emergent "homogeneous national experience" (21) is the fact that, starting in the 1890s, a few newspapers and magazines pioneered a business model in which these publications depended on advertising rather than sales for their main source of income. Their product, at this point, became not the news, journalistic features, or fiction they provided the public, but rather the attention of the public, which they sold to the advertisers.

Ohmann argues that this business strategy was a response to the recurrent economic crises of overproduction that beset the American economy from 1873 into the 1890s. It involved a shift of corporate "ingenuity, resources, and organizational energy" from production to sales, abandoning the free market "war of all against all, with its destructive bouts of price cutting and market cornering" for "more steady and reliable ways to maintain a market share and expand the whole economy" (74). These more steady and reliable ways centered on advertising.[5] Late nineteenth-century monopoly capitalism, as it is usually called, was above all "*marketing* capitalism" (74). The key was a shift from maximizing the extraction of labor from workers to a new emphasis on turning them into reliable consumers: "not only would they [the corporations] colonize the leisure of most citizens, as they had previously dominated work time; they would also integrate the nation into one huge market and market culture" (59). The new national culture being promulgated in the newspapers and magazines thus marched hand in hand with the promotion of national brands and increasingly equated social identity with consumer habits. As Ohmann sums it up, the magazines "located advertising . . . in the center of American cultural production, and it has remained there since," where it reinforces "the tight linkage of social identity with the purchase and use of commodities" (362).

One could therefore say that the commercial advertisement is *the* organic genre of mass culture. It is the keystone of the mass cultural genre system: all other genres necessarily take their position within the system in relation to it. This does not mean, however, that mass cultural genres necessarily resemble ads. The relationships at stake have more to do with practical proximity or distance than with formal similarity. The glossy magazines and newspapers of the 1890s interspersed advertisement into the news or into an editorial selection of features and fiction. The form impressed upon other genres by their proximity to commercial advertisements—a form so familiar today as to be almost invisible—is what Adorno, in one of his jeremiads against the culture industry, decried as the "variety act" (*Culture Industry*, 69). Adorno stresses the suspension of the work of art's finality, which gives way to the predominant quality of "expectation" where "waiting for the thing in question, which takes place as long as the juggler manages to keep the balls going, is precisely the thing in itself" (70). What I mean to emphasize is the transformation of every segment of the broadcast or magazine into an episode, discrete in itself, that may be preceded and followed by a variety of other episodes with no thematic or formal resemblance to it. For instance, there is no real logical or thematic unity to the news broadcast's or general interest magazine's sequence of political news, human-interest stories, the weather, sports, etc.; they are, as Adorno puts it, arranged as "episodes" rather than "acts" (69). But all of them are linked to one another through the connective tissue of the advertisements—which themselves have no internal sequential logic, their length and placement being determined instead by marketing strategies and costs. The news broadcast or televised narrative may represent the commercials as "interruptions" (if it mentions them at all), but from the point of view of the genre system as a whole, commercial advertisement is mass culture's most persistent and binding element. It is the other genres that "interrupt" this constant presence, even—or especially—when, as in feature films, there are no commercial interruptions.

The centrality of commercial advertisements to the mass cultural genre system does not mean, then, that the form of the commercial imposes itself on other mass cultural products directly, but rather that the market pressures and commercial goals that shape the commercial from the inside impose themselves upon other mass cultural products from the outside. One result is a generalized instrumentalization of the aesthetic. Consciously manipulating beauty's power to command attention in order to promote economic or political interests was hardly a new practice at the end of the nineteenth century, but the very urgency of proclamations of art for art's sake and of the disinterestedness of fine art at that time points toward an intensification of the manipulative powers of image and eloquence that finds its most deliberate, scientific expression in the emergent advertising industry. Ohmann argues that the work of the ad agencies, a new form of business enterprise that came into existence in the 1890s, was "to alter consciousness and deliver customers" in pursuit of "interests [that] were structurally very close to those of still more powerful businesses, and not very close to those of other citizens" (100). It is a short step from professionalized market research and the construction of advertising campaigns to the techniques of political propaganda. As Raymond Williams observed in a 1960 essay arguing that advertising had become "the official art of modern capitalist society," "The need to control nominally free men, like the need to control nominally free customers, lay very deep in the new kind of society" (*Problems*, 184, 180).[6]

The citizens of the mass cultural nation—and so the audiences of mass cultural genres—are first and foremost consumers, then, and the ideological force borne by the act of consumption is evident in the utopian aura it acquires. The world projected by advertising takes on a magical quality, as a 1909 *New York Evening Post* editorial wryly observes:

> What a reconstructed world of heart's desire begins with the first-page advertisement. Here no breakfast food fails to build up a man's brain and muscle. No phono record fails to amuse. No roof pane cracks under cold or melts under the sun. No razor cuts the face or leaves it sore. Illness and death are banished by patent medicines and hygienic shoes. Worry flies before the model fountain pen. Employers shower wealth upon efficient employees. Insurance companies pay what they promise. Trains always get to Chicago on time. Babies

never cry; whether it's soap or cereal, or camera or talcum, babies always laugh in the advertising supplement. A happy world indeed, my masters! (quoted in Ohmann 210)

The instrumentalization of the aesthetic conveys, not in spite but at the core of its calculation and manipulation, this utopian anticipation of a world of fulfilled desires. But the "crucial quality" of modern advertising as a form, Williams argues, is that its utopianism expresses itself by means of an all-abiding dissatisfaction or lack that the commodity never completely overcomes: "The material object being sold is never enough ... but must be validated, if only in fantasy, by associations with social and personal meanings which in a different cultural formation might be more directly available" (*Problems*, 185). That distance and lack are evident in the way the manipulation of spectacle cultivated in advertising tends to change beauty into glamour, transforming disinterested contemplation of the beautiful object (as in the philosophical tradition running from Kant to Bergson) into envious admiration of its owner (Berger). These tendencies toward glamour, fantasies of possession and consumption, and the concomitant projection of a world of abundance and fulfillment, radiate from the practices of advertising to encourage a kind of endemic otherworldliness in the mass cultural milieu. The glitter of the variety show, the nostalgia of the western, the exotica of horror or science-fictional narratives, or the erotic entanglements of romance all find a common reference point in the world of glamour and the fantasies of attaining happiness through consumption that drive the advertisement.

Thus are spawned a number of formal and thematic contradictions. The antithetical but codependent tendencies toward propaganda and utopian fantasy in commercial advertising match the incongruent goals of manipulating the audience to a specific end, on the one hand, and maintaining the atmosphere of leisure, on the other. These disparate aims foster within the content of the ads a tension between those elements that seek to provide information and those that offer entertainment, often by connecting information about a product with logically unrelated fantasies of gratification. This opens up a kind of vertiginous balancing act between the individual customer and the general public, which results, for instance, in the way that ads often adopt a familiar form of address, speaking to the audience in the second person as if to each individual one at a time, while at the same time they tend to resist identifiable settings in time or place. One can line all these contradictions alongside one another, perhaps, insofar as they all correspond to an ideological celebration of individuality being mediated by the homogeneity and impersonality of mass culture itself, where the consumption of national news and national brands, increasingly purchased by mail order and in chain department stores, pervades the domestic space of privacy and leisure.

The various contradictions internal to commercial advertising have no simple or straightforward impact on mass cultural serial fiction, however. It is clear enough that serialization per se is aligned with the same overriding rationality that Ohmann ascribes to mass culture in general, the project of "shap[ing] habitual audiences, around common needs or interests... for profit" (14). There is no better example than the newspapers' daily comics. However, the practice of serializing fiction was adapted to mass culture rather than developed by it. The serialization of novels was already common practice in the mid-nineteenth century. The short story, as a modern form, takes shape in conjunction with the needs of periodical magazine publication in the early nineteenth century, and so lay ready to hand later in the century for mass cultural media and venues of publication. That fiction should in the mass cultural milieu become both episodic and formally predictable fits very well with the part it was called upon to play as a "variety act" in the interstices between commercial ads. Insofar as the logic of encouraging habitual consumption, the raison d'être of advertising, guided editorial selection, it also influenced artistic practice. But serial fiction has a prior and separate history from its use in the glossy magazines of the 1890s and the other venues of mass culture that followed in their wake.

The tension between information and entertainment in advertising tends to split into the distinct genres of news and fiction in the mass cultural genre system, although the problematic motives of entertainment and distraction that persist in corporate news media become more and more obvious throughout the twentieth century. Mass cultural fiction, in contrast to the news, presents itself predominantly as pure entertainment and distraction, disavowing reference to real persons, places, and incidents in standardized disclaimers—disclaimers we all have learned when and how to ignore. For just as the commercial instrumentalization of the aesthetic entails a certain utopianism, the compulsory inoffensiveness of mass cultural fiction's aversion to explicit didacticism or pointed referentiality bears within it the inevitable traces of its class-specific and ideologically driven agenda. These once again are effects dependent upon editorial selection and policing of narrative content, so that they impose themselves upon fiction as external pressures rather than, like the ones just reviewed in connection with advertising, arising out of the tensions and goals of the act of storytelling itself. But this imposition of the internal contradictions of commercial advertising as external pressures upon the milieu of mass culture is precisely the way in which commercial advertising impresses its organizational power upon the mass cultural genre system as a whole.

These external pressures are not exerted in uniform fashion or with even intensity throughout the mass cultural milieu. On the contrary, they are very sensitive to differences of venue. It is therefore no accident that the mass cultural genre system so often encourages the identification of a genre with a venue, as in pulp fiction, Hollywood film, or network news. The differences among these three, for instance, correspond not just to diverse media but also to very different volumes of capital investment and distribution at each site of production. Large amounts of capital and large-scale distribution involve advertising and publicity more intensely in the production process, and therefore tend toward the "variety act" model, striving to enable the producer (whether magazine publisher, broadcast network, or film studio) to appeal to as many different consumer groups as possible. Rick Altman writes of the long-term effects of this tendency in Hollywood cinema, for instance: "When cinema was born, products determined publicity strategy; a century later, publicity determines product design" (132). According to Altman, the Hollywood strategy has for a long time been to hybridize genres, especially in pre-release publicity for films, trying to draw in as many different kinds of viewers as possible: "Hollywood's basic script development practice involves (a) attempts to combine the commercial qualities of previously successful films, and (b) the consequent practice not only of mixing genres but of thinking about films in terms of the multiplicity of genres whose dedicated audiences they can attract" (129). Niche market serial fiction, in contrast, perhaps constitutes the entrepreneurial and low-investment antithesis to such corporate practices. The niche market magazines that developed in the period between the world wars did not operate on the advertising-driven model of the mass-market glossy magazines. Advertising offered only supplementary income for them. They depended primarily on sales, and sales depended upon the ability of the publication to provide fiction that satisfied a well-defined set of habitual customers' expectations. The result was a narrowing of genre, where editors cultivated specialization in a certain mode of fiction rather than the calculated variety or hybridity of the larger mass market.

Ohmann, contrasting the active editorial interventions that encouraged the production of "formula fiction" for the dime novel and later the niche market magazines with the passive approach taken by the glossy magazines, which simply printed fiction that was as popular and risk-free as possible, argues that the "pertinent generalization" about the venues of formula fiction "is that the audiences they aimed at and satisfied lacked power and cultural authority. These stories targeted adolescents or women or uneducated people or people with little cash or audiences combining two or more of these attributes. Formula fiction offered entertainment, instruction, consolation, and pride to people whose lives were relatively limited. Perhaps mainly for that reason, this literature . . . drew condescension and scorn from arbiters of culture. It was escapist, it was immoral, it was trash, it was in a word not *literature* at all" (295). Thus the hierarchical distinction between mass-market and niche market fiction echoes that between "literature" and mass cultural fiction in general, despite the fact that niche market fiction shares with high modernism a specialized use of language and relative distance from the controlling power of advertising. The superior prestige of "literature" over mass culture is, after all, based on the more restricted audience with access to it, and art that targets only the highly restricted audience of other artists is, according to Pierre Bourdieu, the most prestigious of all. And it is very much the case, particularly in respect to science fiction, that the appeal to a restricted audience in niche market fiction can, as it does with the literary avant-garde, produce a subculture of devotees jealously protective of their insider status. But the fact that this structural homology between niche market fiction and the avant-garde does not absolve niche market fiction from its subaltern status is due, as Ohmann says, to the lower-class makeup of the niche market audiences.

The advertising that appeared in the niche market magazines clearly bespeaks the lower-class status of the audience. In contrast to the culture of identification by brand-name consumption fostered in the glossy magazine ads, advertisements in the pulps typically appealed to desires for self-improvement and the acquisition of supplementary income or of job qualifications so as to *become* a middle-class consumer. The April 1926 premier issue of Hugo Gernsback's *Amazing Stories* has often been scrutinized by SF scholars for Gernsback's selection of fiction and for his statement of editorial policies, but the selection of ads found in the issue is also worth noting. In one hundred pages of text, only four contain advertising (the inside front cover, the first page following it, and both sides of the back cover), and the fact that each page is entirely taken up by a single ad indicates both that advertisers were not abundant and that the ads were not expensive. The first offers readers the chance to "Be a Radio Expert" by enrolling in a correspondence course. The second offers lessons in self-confidence and elocution as a way to advance one's career. The third offers cheap, undeveloped real estate in "a newly discovered Florida dreamland abounding in opportunities," and the final one offers a twelve-week course in electrical training with the prospect of qualifying oneself to "Earn $60 to $200 a Week."

In a study of the relation of fiction and advertising in the hard-boiled detective magazine *Black Mask*, Erin Smith argues that this typical advertising agenda bears directly upon the content of the fiction: "Hard-boiled private eyes, with their monomaniacal dedication to work, anxiously overdone manliness, obsessive interest in clothing and interiors, and tough-talking machismo were the perfect salesmen for the products advertised in *Black Mask*—job training by correspondence, body-building programs, elocution lessons, and conduct manuals" (225). Perhaps. But it is quite clear that the same kind of ads don't accompany the same content in *Amazing Stories*, although it might be amusing to think of the hypnotic communications of Poe's "The Facts in the Case of M. Valdemar" (reprinted in the first issue of *Amazing*) as a pitch for a career in radio repair. It makes a good deal more sense, however, to observe that the ads and the fiction fit together precisely to the extent that advertisers succeeded in choosing to place their ads in magazines that were targeting the audiences they hoped to speak to.

To sum up, then, the division of mass-market from niche market fiction constitutes a large-scale cultural divide comparable to that between the traditional and mass cultural genre systems themselves. Niche market serial fiction is doubly marked for cultural subordination, by its commercial status in relation to the institutional literary establishment, and by its low-capital, niche market status in relation to the mass cultural nation. As a corollary to mass culture's consolidating the dominance of the standard vernacular, it renders silent or subordinate within its sphere the class, ethnic, and regional dialects, sociolects, and idiolects of communities excluded from or marginalized by the dominant national mass-market norm. The pulp-era niche markets did not typically represent these excluded communities directly so much as they served as a persistent symptom of the disunity obscured by mass culture's apparent ubiquity and homogeneity.

Yet it is a serious mistake to equate any given venue-genre combination with the whole practice of a given genre. Filmmaking is not confined to Hollywood studios, nor journalism to the network news. Thus, while it is no doubt true that the association of the pulp milieu with the genres of horror, science fiction, spy fiction, and so on contributed to the contempt in which these genres were long held by many members of the institutional literary establishment, it is a mistake to identify the genres themselves with the transient historical moment represented by the niche market pulp magazines. The pulps were an important site of genre specialization, but the genres elaborated at these sites have a larger history, one that pre-dates the pulps and expands beyond them. While niche markets are a significant site of genre specialization, especially during the period between the world wars, genre practices turn out to be more dynamic, and genre boundaries far more porous, than those who denigrate (or defensively idealize) the so-called genre ghetto seem to realize. One cannot write the history of the western without including Cooper and Wister, of detective fiction without Poe and Conan Doyle, or of science fiction without Verne and Wells. Furthermore, genre identification is hardly the monopoly of the producers and distributors of narrative. Readers and critics construct genres without any regard to commercial motives, even in the milieu of mass culture, as Altman has shown quite forcefully with respect to film. For example, science fiction did not begin to operate as a category in book publishing until after World War II, yet many of what were eventually recognized to be important science fiction novels were published in book form before that.[7] If we think of generic form as the effect of repetitive pressures upon the production *and* the reception of narrative, it seems better to try to understand how the topography of the milieu opens up paths of least resistance and pockets of opportunity than to expect generic form to reveal (or conceal) agendas of manipulation. The final section of this chapter therefore attempts a general, albeit brief, description of the topography of mass culture.

One last word about the niche markets before moving on: if it is wrong to identify the genres that flourished in the niche market magazines too strongly with this peculiar moment in their histories, it is equally mistaken to ignore the influence and importance of the niche markets within the mass cultural genre system and within the histories of the relevant genres. Niche market publishers, writers, and readers constituted important communities of practice, especially in the case of science fiction, where niche market fandom acted as an entry point for a number of influential writers, editors, collectors, and scholars. And perhaps even more to the point, the niche market genres did not die with the pulps, but rather have continued to develop, intersect, mutate, and adapt in the venues and media of the later twentieth and early twenty-first centuries.

Series, Strata, and Subcultures

I propose mapping the paths of opportunity and lines of resistance in the field of mass cultural narrative production, distribution, and reception along a set of three alliterative coordinates: seriality, stratification, and subcultures. By seriality I refer primarily to a set of mechanisms set in motion in the processes of production in response to market pressures. Stratification corresponds more directly to the terrain of distribution as it is unevenly determined by class and education. Subcultures, finally, direct our attention to the effects of reception, conceived as an array of active practices. Thus, to borrow a pair of terms made familiar by Stuart Hall's influential essay "Encoding, Decoding," seriality involves the encoding of texts, while the terrain of stratification and the formation of subcultures refer to processes of decoding, or, as we will see in chapter 6, recoding. All three of these terms have already played a part in this discussion, but the choice to organize a sketch of mass culture's topography around them is dictated more by their methodological impact on science fiction studies than by the demands of description. I am not proposing that these are the inevitable terms with which to delineate the shape of the mass cultural genre system, then, but rather that these terms will elucidate the impact on SF studies of the thesis that science fiction is an organic genre of mass cultural production.

Seriality is, in any case, as inevitable, inescapable a feature of mass culture as one could name. The goal of producing habitual consumers, mass cultural production's raison d'être, makes serial fiction the narrative form most strongly suited to and encouraged by it. While serial storytelling has a broad history that harks back to such venerable antecedents as the relation of frame to tale in *The Thousand and One Nights* or the storytelling contest of Chaucer's *Canterbury Tales*, the techniques of serial linkage, episodic rationing, and strategic interruption become dominant features of mass cultural narrative to a degree unmatched in any previous cultural milieu.

The major ramification of seriality for the study of science fiction is that it dictates the priority of repetition as an object of study. It is repetition, not individual distinction, that necessarily comes into view when one considers a text as a member of a series. As a consequence, textual integrity, attention to which typically orients interpretation toward authorial intention and artistic skill, tends to disappear under the scrutiny of procedures that decompose the text into an amalgamation of recombined elements or motifs. Vladimir Propp's work on the folktale and Claude Lévi-Strauss's work on myth offer sophisticated and powerful examples of this decomposing impulse.[8] In both cases it operates in alliance with the assumption that a kind of collective authorship unfolds itself in the collocation of the texts' repetitions and recastings of shared material, and that this level of textual significance reveals itself only in the collective, repetitive character of these motifs. At the other end of the spectrum of literary methodology lie close readings of masterpieces, the cult of genius, and the notion of literature as the anti-genre, the category made up of works that defy categorization. The function of the authorial signature within the mass cultural milieu is not to designate the charismatic authority of the artistic genius, however, but rather to guarantee the reliability of a brand. (This is not to say that close reading, appreciation of individual artistry, or the recognition of masterpieces should be ruled out of science fiction studies, but rather that such practices have too often been based on assimilating science fiction to the traditional academic genre system.) As a result, genres themselves, within the mass cultural milieu, attain a certain quasi-archetypal quality, so that "romance" or "the fairy tale" or "science fiction" come to operate as signifiers not so much of a category of fiction as of an imaginary realm, a domain of possibilities, a collective fantasy. Genres become worlds, not just in the sense John Frow ascribes to all genres—"a relatively bounded and schematic set of meanings, values, and affects, accompanied by a set of instructions for using them" (*Genre*, 85–86)—but also in a sense cognate with the utopianism of the commercial, an endemic otherworldliness that pervades mass cultural entertainment.

Thus any given story is liable to become an episode, any character can become the center of a new ("spin-off") narrative, any discarded plot possibility can fuel a revised version, since every story is already a kind of synecdoche for a generic cosmos. In SF studies this proliferating quality of the mass cultural genre system has long been recognized under the term of the SF "megatext," coined by Damien Broderick (*Reading by Starlight*), and its open-endedness has more recently been theorized cogently by Brian Attebery as the SF "parabola" ("Science Fiction, Parables, and Parabolas"). The principle of megatextual or parabolic proliferation is a crucial part of what makes generic difference in the mass cultural genre system depend upon content rather than form.[9] Attebery and Veronica Hollinger, in their introduction to the collection *Parabolas of Science Fiction*, briefly propose what might be expanded into a theory of the genre system as a whole: "Each [mass cultural genre] has its own version of a megatext and each continually renegotiates its relationship to that megatext. For the romance, that might be the current state of relations between the sexes and the institution of courtship and marriage. For the Western, it is the history of westward migration and settlement, which has been radically revised, since the creation of the fictional genre, within what is now called the new western history. For mysteries, the relevant megatext would include changing demographics of crime as well as evolving techniques of detection" (xi). What is not explicit but surely is to be understood in this very suggestive passage is that the relation of the generic megatext or cosmos to discourses such as the history of the U.S. western frontier or the changing demographics of crime is imaginary. The generic megatext is in dialogue with history, demographics, scientific innovation, and so on, but at the same time its commercial rationale is to *dis*connect the audience from the workaday world, to distract rather than to inform, or more precisely to envelop information in an atmosphere of distraction. Seriality, one could say, constructs a set of continuities in the generic world that simultaneously accentuate its discontinuity from other domains of experience. It establishes a periodicity that punctuates the other routines and duties of the mass audience by separating itself from them and asserting a life, or at least a temporality, of its own. Thus the topic of seriality leads from repetition to collective fantasy, on the one hand, and to the temporal rhythms of mass culture, on the other.

The drive toward repetition is always counterbalanced, of course, by more or less urgent demands for variation. The ephemerality of fashions and fads is as much a part of mass cultural temporality as the repetition of motifs, and the way successful strategies and motifs proliferate across media and cross genre boundaries means that adaptation, hybridity, and creolization ought to feature prominently in any analysis of the workings of mass cultural seriality. Emphasizing the repetition of generic motifs does not mean ignoring the specificity of the texts that perform the repetition, then, but rather directs our attention to the dialectical play between the typical and the individual. The question is what different kinds or degrees of value one assigns to individual texts and performances as opposed to types of texts and performances, which means working out how one positions individual texts, and oneself, in relation to the genre system or systems involved. This set of questions points toward the second of my three coordinates, the stratification of the field of cultural production.

By stratification I am referring to a number of things that have already been discussed: first, the differences in social prestige and institutional power associated with the mass cultural genre system versus the academic-traditional system, including the values and resources positioned in the culture industry versus the schools, "practical" technical discourses and training versus the study of literature, and the national vernacular versus the cosmopolitanism and multilingual training of the traditional intellectual; and second, the interior stratification of mass culture itself between mass-market and niche market products. These differences of institutional power and social prestige can be summarized by mapping them onto the "compass" proposed by Pierre Bourdieu's work on the field of cultural production, where the horizontal, east–west axis measures the volume of economic capital investment and the inversely corresponding degree of artistic control or lack of it over the cultural product, and the vertical, north–south axis corresponds to the volume of what Bourdieu calls the symbolic capital accruing to the institutions that sponsor cultural production, the traditions that inform it, and the groups that practice it. A map of the mid-twentieth-century American field of production would look something like figure 1.

The overriding question concerns how the relation between high art and popular culture, or between the dominant and hegemonic culture and marginalized or subaltern ones, changed with the emergence of mass culture. The mere facts of class differentiation and ruling-class hegemony persist, but in an altered and complex new form. For instance, the cultural authority of "high" modernist art seems to be contradicted by the quantity of wealth invested in mass culture and the class power that investment represents and exercises, even if modernism's anti-commodity status (cf. Jameson's thesis in "Reification and Utopia") is ultimately belied by the economic value conferred upon it by its canonization or, as Bourdieu puts it, consecration in academies and museums. It would seem that, rather than a clear correspondence between class origins and prestige—for example, the art of an aristocracy or a bourgeoisie versus that of a peasantry or a working class—considerations of abundance and scarcity take precedence, and may produce, among other things, an odd homology between the avant-garde elite and niche market fandom.

The first point to make about science fiction in relation to the stratification of the field of cultural production is that the genre is produced and

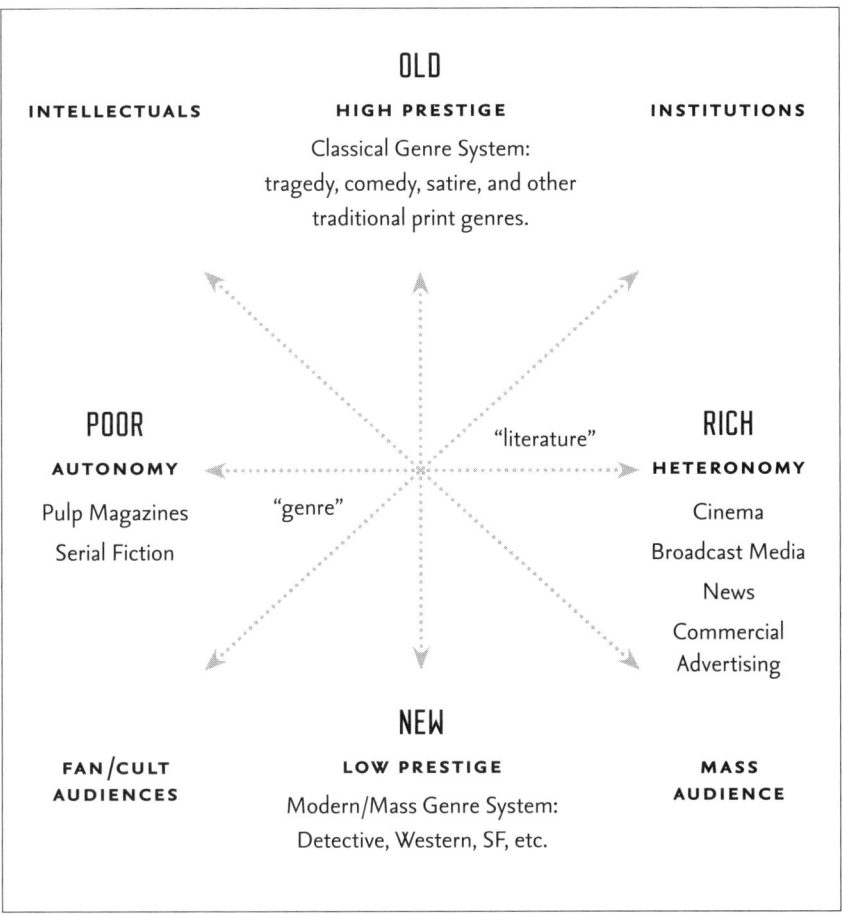

FIGURE 1. The mass cultural genre system in the field of cultural production

circulates across the entire range of cultural locations in question; it is not and never has been confined to or defined by the limits of a "genre ghetto." Nonetheless there is no doubt that the uneven distribution of literacy and of access to it determines an unevenness in the modes and venues of reception that has a powerful impact on the history of science fiction. What is at stake are the different forms of publicity—the different publics, and the different practices and rituals by which texts are made available, evaluated, and responded to—in the schools, the mass market, and the niche markets.

The problem of canon formation can serve as an example. Andrew Milner has described quite well how the price of admission to the academic canon is the detachment of a text from its mass cultural genre identity: "The boundary between the SF field and the canonical 'literary' field takes a form loosely analogous to that of a membrane—that is, a selective barrier, impermeable to many but by no means all elements—located in the overlap between the SF restricted field and institutionalized bourgeois SF. From the canonical side, this impermeability tends to allow SF to enter the canon, but not to return to SF; from the SF side, movement is normally permitted in both directions" (67). This, at least, is the way literary study worked in the twentieth century, and it strikingly represents the dynamics that shape Suvin's exclusionary definition of SF and his defense of SF from contamination by its neighboring, non-"literary" genres. The recognition of an SF text as worthy of close reading, as even perhaps a literary masterpiece, typically meant assimilating it to the traditional genre system, reading it as satire, romance, or utopia, and Suvin's intervention opened a space for SF within this structure of exclusion that arguably did more than any other critic's work to procure a footing for SF studies within the academy. But twenty-first-century SF studies ought to take on the stratification of reception directly—both by challenging it and by making it a crucial topic of study—rather than continue to search out ways to assimilate SF to the traditional genre system.

Canon formation also brings into view questions about the status of the text that follow from those raised by seriality and repetition. Just as the topic of seriality involves sighting the SF text from the dual perspectives of its individuality and its typicality, the topic of stratification puts the canonical text's representativeness into question. The question of whether a masterpiece epitomizes a genre or is precisely the sort of text that escapes generic determination is badly put, I would argue, because it leaves out of consideration the agency that makes the text canonical. One needs to ask instead what those who form canons are looking for in the texts that they choose. What use is the canon, and to whom? Here again no simple answer is possible because there is no single agent involved and no single set of motives at work. The literary canon is determined by the selection of texts that serve the purposes of literary education. But, as Mark Bould has argued forcefully with respect to fantasy, if we are to study SF as SF, not as the blessed few pieces of "literature" that transcend the genre, the SF canon cannot be made up of literary masterpieces ("Dreadful Credibility"). SF studies needs to also pay attention to the canonization carried out in nonacademic venues—for instance, the editing of commercial anthologies, the awarding of prizes, and the compilation of "best of" lists, especially those based on fan surveys. One way to move forward would be to confess that there are different canons that are formed for different reasons, interrogate each one on its own terms, and then proceed to make comparisons and try to understand the more general terrain they share and the different positions they occupy on it. Another, complementary alternative would be to ask why some texts seem to attain a canonical status that crosses these boundaries. I have already argued that the category of "literature" acts as a boundary object that integrates the needs of teachers, students, and administrators within the schools. Thinking of canonical texts, too, as boundary objects that are characterized by their fitness to serve the purposes of several communities of practice at once offers, at the very least, a useful check on any temptation to assume that because a canonical text is canonical it is therefore an exemplar or formal paradigm of the genre.[10]

The diversity of reception among different communities of practice brings us to the third of our three coordinates, the formation of subcultures. With this third coordinate I refer not just to subcultures but to an array of effects of homogeneity and heterogeneity associated with the distribution and reception of mass culture. A good starting point here is Benedict Anderson's thesis in *Imagined Communities* concerning the role of the novel, the newspaper, and print capitalism in the formation of the "imagined communities" of nationalism. The "homogeneous national experience" (21) that according to Ohmann is one of the major expressions of mass culture could be thought of as the fully developed form of the "vernacular" nationalism that Anderson associates with print capitalism. Anderson's suggestion that novelistic form helped establish the hegemony of a national, homogeneous temporality is made a good deal more solid and credible in the terms given the argument by Ohmann, where what is crucial is not literary form but the patterns and modes of mass cultural distribution, which more and more displaced local and regional rituals and entertainments with national products and events tied to nationally distributed publicity and eventually to broadcasting. The national imaginary community thus depends not only upon serial temporality—the daily ritual of the news, the seasonal rituals of sporting events, the annual ritual of elections—but also on linking together a series of spectators, readers, and consumers into a collectivity based on their common participation, at various distances, in national politics, economy, and culture. A homogeneous national culture forms not only out of an imaginary relation to the real conditions of mass marketing and mass distribution, then, but also out of a serial relation to them.

However, the imaginary homogeneity of the nation is shot through with real demographic heterogeneity. Myriad local, regional, ethnic, and class communities are more or less submerged within, and more or less resistant to identification with the nation. The niche markets form around such pockets of difference, based in the case of science fiction partly upon the technical discourses of science and engineering, but also, in much pulp practice, on age and gender—that is, on appealing to young males. In the case of 1930s pulp science fiction, a very important and influential fan subculture forms within the niche market, and other fan subcultures later form around, for example, the *Star Trek* franchise. In the case of the Futurians and of *Star Trek* fandom alike the subculture becomes a site of production and recoding of generic conventions.[11] What better example is there than *Star Trek* "slash" fiction to illustrate the energy and creativity with which such subcultures can assert their resistance to assimilation into a homogeneous, in this case especially to a heteronormative, social order? One of the fundamental instabilities of capitalism here asserts itself. Its master category, exchange value (money, financial credit), must inevitably, at some point in its circulation, be embodied in the concrete use value of a commodity, and as use value it falls under the control of laborers and consumers and so eludes the calculations of the corporate accounting sheet. Thus, where mass cultural production and dissemination are driven by the capitalist imperative to dissolve all qualitative differences in the quantitative determinations of exchange, subcultural resistance responds with irreducibly qualitative appropriations of cultural products' use. By the late twentieth century this bifurcation of the dominant, commercially driven versions of SF from subcultures of resistance becomes one of SF's most important features.

Science fiction's participation in imaginary social homogeneity and its use in subaltern recodings and resistance to hegemonic ideologies is certainly an international, not just a national phenomenon. Recent work on Latin American science fiction can serve as an illustration. In Rachel Haywood Ferreira's *The Emergence of Latin American Science Fiction*, she holds up the ninety-plus works in her bibliography of "Primary Texts of Latin American Science Fiction through 1920" (257–66) as evidence that SF "has been a truly global genre from the earliest times of [its] formation" (220), but at the same time emphasizes the regional and national peculiarities of Latin American SF. Latin American writers, she says, "did not feel described" by Northern SF, and so "they produced their own" SF, which "gave greater emphasis to reflections on politically charged issues of national identity and national composition" (220–21). She notes, furthermore, that this nineteenth- and early twentieth-century situation resembles the present state of affairs described by Gabriel Trujillo Muñoz in his *Biographies of the Future: Mexican Science Fiction and Its Authors*: "Now we have a historical consciousness of belonging to a global movement and, at the same time, we respond to this world science fiction movement with our own characteristics, with notable antecedents and with distinctive, complementary aspirations" (355, quoted in Haywood Ferreira 219–20). Whether the globality of SF refers to its penchant for imagining world travel, world conquest, worldwide disasters, a unified world state, and so on, or to the international circulation of publishing phenomena like Verne's *Voyages extraordinaires* or George Chesney's "The Battle of Dorking,"[12] Haywood Ferreira's observation that Latin American writers did not feel described by Northern SF betrays their sense of uneven participation in, or marginality to, the project of modernization. That is to say, the global character of SF before the 1920s has a lot to do not just with the worldwide diffusion of modern scientific and technological discourses, but just as importantly with different local and regional articulations of modernization's ideological allure and its attendant mapping of the world into zones of unevenly distributed progress and development.

The role of mass culture in the international political economy becomes all the more important with the dissolution of the early twentieth century's imperial and colonial system. In the arsenal of advanced weaponry that procured and sustained American international hegemony after World War II, the products of American mass culture were arguably among the most potent. The global dissemination of American films, broadcast entertainment, and commercial advertisements supplemented the worldwide U.S. military presence—and its threat of nuclear holocaust—by relentlessly attempting to assimilate foreign desires into an American economic and ideological framework. If American science fiction played at best a minor role in the real onslaught of Cold War–era mass cultural globalization, nonetheless it has certainly continued to explore and play variations upon fantasies of global unity as well as the practice of cultural imperialism. The tension between the universalizing imaginary of modernization and the material, place-bound exigencies of literary production and reception demands of us, then, an attempt to articulate the national, regional, and global histories of SF and the broader historical themes of colonialism, imperialism, and postcolonialism with the dynamics of local, subaltern recoding and appropriation of the genre.

Genealogies of SF

I argued in chapter 1 that genres have no origins, for two reasons: first, because genre is always intertextual; and second, because it is always systematic. A genre cannot have an original member, because genres consist of relations between texts, so that texts do not belong to genres but rather use them. This use is not generated from the developmental logic posited by an origin, but rather emerges in the course of practices of imitation, echoing, allusion, parody, and so on, in the production of texts as well as practices of categorization, generalization, periodization, and so on, in the interpretation of texts. To say that a text originates a genre attributes a false agency to it, since this origination is wholly dependent upon later texts' interpretation and revision and repositioning of the earlier one. Thus a corollary to the thesis that genres have no origin is Jason Mittel's critique of the "textualist assumption" that genre is determined solely by the formal or thematic properties of a text rather than in concert (or tension) with acts of classification and positioning, what Mittel calls the social construction of genres. The social construction of genres entails the positioning of texts within a field of values, and hence points to the second reason for refusing the notion of a generic origin, the determining force of the genre system. To confuse a genre with a set of formal properties is like confusing a word with a sound. The formal properties of a text, like the sound, are necessary to sustain the genre, but the sound becomes a word, or the text an example of a genre, only by virtue of its articulation with other sounds or texts within the linguistic or generic system. Furthermore, to confess the limits of the analogy, a new genre is less like a new word than like a change in usage or grammar (say, a grammatical "mistake" that over time establishes itself as a convention), something that cannot be recognized on the basis of a single example but only as a pattern of established practice.

To say that a genre has no origin is not to say that we cannot talk about its beginnings, however. By a beginning I do not mean an origin but rather a turning point, not an event that establishes a paradigm but rather one that introduces a discontinuity. Beginnings are plural, and their significance is determined less by what they are than by what is made of them. In this chapter I propose to take up the topic of the intertextual and systematic character of SF's beginnings. My points of departure will be two texts that scholars have nominated as origins of SF: Mary Shelley's *Frankenstein* and the initial, April 1926 issue of Hugo Gernsback's *Amazing Stories*.[1] The role I propose to adopt is not that of a seeker after origins but rather of a genealogist in the sense that Foucault applies to Friedrich Nietzsche. According to Foucault, Nietzsche rejects the search for origins "because this search assumes the existence of immobile forms that precede the external world of accident and succession." Instead of the secret of the essence of things, the Nietzschean genealogist finds "the secret that they have no essence or that their essence was fabricated in a piecemeal fashion from alien forms" (142). Investigating the process of the piecemeal fabrication of SF will not lead us into Victor Frankenstein's "workshop of filthy creation," but rather into the milieu of the "Gothic" in relation to *Frankenstein*, and of niche market serial fiction in relation to *Amazing Stories*. My thesis is that the impact of these two remarkable texts on the fabrication of SF is better approached in terms of changes in the relevant genre systems than in terms of individual invention.

Frankenstein and the Gothic

When in 1973 Brian Aldiss designated Mary Shelley's *Frankenstein* "the Origin of the Species" he established what has become a critical commonplace in SF criticism. However, as might be expected, the formal and thematic features of *Frankenstein* that twentieth-century scholars most often designate as crucial to its generic innovation—its "rejection of the supernatural" (Alkon 2), its "*epistemological* radicalism" (Freedman, *Critical Theory*, 4), its transformation of the Faustian bargain with the devil into a failed laboratory experiment (Rieder, "Mad Scientist," 165)—were not part of the language of genre recognition for early nineteenth-century readers.

The status of Victor Frankenstein as a scientist (a term that did not yet exist in 1818) and the location of his project in an experimental laboratory became crucial generic elements of the story in the late nineteenth century, due in general to the shifting social horizon of expectations concerning experimental science and professional scientists and more particularly to the intervention of Robert Louis Stevenson's 1886 *The Strange Case of Dr. Jekyll and Mr. Hyde*, which may or may not have been influenced by Shelley's novel, and H. G. Wells's *The Island of Dr. Moreau* (1896) and *The Invisible Man* (1897), which certainly were. But the distinction between alchemy or black magic and modern science in the novel is not a prominent feature of the stage adaptations of the 1820s, and Mary Shelley herself ignores or at least obfuscates the scientific character of Frankenstein's project when, in the 1831 preface, she calls him a "student of unhallowed arts."

If we consider *Frankenstein* as a beginning of SF, the questions we ought to ask about it do not concern its power to predict the forms and themes that would become characteristic of SF in the later nineteenth and early twentieth centuries. Rather we should ask what it is about this novel that accounts for its astoundingly rich and complex reception history. What novelty or oddness did its contemporaries recognize in it, and what generic codes did it conform to or challenge? How and when did the generic codes change so that it became associated with an emergent SF? What explains *Frankenstein*'s protean capacity to inspire hundreds of adaptations and imitations? Why did this technically flawed novel become, in the later twentieth-century and early twenty-first-century academy, one of the most written about novels of its period, in spite of its obvious unevenness of style and characterization? The answers to these questions have to do with *Frankenstein*'s position at a set of historical and generic cruxes. A full account of *Frankenstein*'s reception history could easily become a monograph in itself (see Baldick, Glut, Lavalley). The briefer sketch that follows will focus on three moments in that history, each time emphasizing the novel's position in relation to shifts in the contemporary genre system: first, its reception from its first publication in 1818 to the publication of the revised 1831 version; second, its reception within the context of the late-Victorian Gothic; and third, the later twentieth-century entry of *Frankenstein* into the academic literary canon.

Upon its publication in 1818 *Frankenstein* received mixed reviews, ranging from the conservative John Wilson Croker's calling it "a tissue of horrible and disgusting absurdity" (382) to praise of its "originality, excellence of language, and peculiar interest" in an anonymous review in *La Belle Assemblée* (140). The one thing all the reviewers agree upon is their association of the novel with William Godwin, taking their cue from the inscription of the novel to "William Godwin, Author of *Political Justice, Caleb Williams,* &c." on the back of the title page. Complaints about the novel's lack of a moral or its pointlessness correspond reliably to the reviewer's dislike and distrust of the school of Godwin, and commendation of its interest and promise to political leanings in Godwin's direction.[2] With one notable exception, the reviewers have little to say about the novel's genre other than to complain about its implausibility (interestingly, the most consistent target of these strictures is not Victor Frankenstein's assembly of the creature but the manner in which the creature learns to speak and read).

The notable exception to these reviews is Walter Scott's "Remarks on *Frankenstein, or the Modern Prometheus*" in *Blackwood's Edinburgh Magazine* in March 1818. Scott focuses immediately on the topic of *Frankenstein*'s genre: "This is a novel, or more properly a romantic fiction, of a nature so peculiar, that we ought to describe the species before attempting any account of the individual production" (611). Scott then proceeds to delineate several subdivisions of "the class of marvelous romances": one in which the narrators believe in their material, a second in which the marvelous is deployed for its own sake, and third, "that class in which the laws of nature are represented as altered, not for the purpose of pampering the imagination with wonders, but in order to shew the probable effect which the supposed miracles would produce on those who witnessed them" (611). Scott's example of the second sort is the tale of Tom Thumb, and of the third Gulliver's adventures in Brobdingnag (612). Scott takes his cue from Percy Shelley's unsigned preface, quoting the argument in its opening paragraph that the central event in *Frankenstein*, "however impossible as a physical fact, affords a point of view to the imagination for the delineating of human passions more comprehensive and commanding than any which the ordinary relations of existing events can yield."[3] Scott thus stresses psychological plausibility as the key to the novel's effectiveness, and in this respect he finally compares Shelley's novel to William Godwin's *Saint Leon*, separating himself from the other reviewers by stressing Godwin's formal achievement rather than his political or religious positions.[4]

It remains the case, however, that Scott does not lay any importance at all on the absence of the supernatural in *Frankenstein*, nor does he see the novel as a "great leap away from the Gothic" (Alkon 6), likening it instead to Godwin's most Gothic novel. Scott's efforts are concentrated on discerning *Frankenstein*'s position *within* what scholars now call the Gothic revival of the early nineteenth century, which at the time was commonly referred to as the revival of romance—hence, the class of "romantic fiction" or of "marvelous romances."[5] Scott's sense of "romance" is related to a long-term shake-up in the academic literary genre system, dating back to the mid-eighteenth century. As Stuart Curran describes it in *Poetic Form and British Romanticism*, "the sudden recovery of lost literatures" in the eighteenth century led to "new examples of the romance" becoming a "conspicuous testing ground for the received generic paradigms." As a consequence the medieval paradigms that had been ousted by Hellenistic models in the Renaissance returned in the eighteenth century "to crack the veneer of neoclassical niceties" (6). This led to a "competition of values, a subversion of precursors" that undermined "the hegemony of neoclassical rules" (8). Curran locates the beginnings of this shift in the publication of Thomas Percy's *Reliques of Ancient English Poetry* in 1765 and Thomas Warton's *History of English Poetry* in 1774, 1778, and 1781, noting that "it is only after Percy's and Warton's researches begin to take cultural effect that romance enters into the list [of standard, academically recognized genres] with a formal lecture by Hugh Blair devoted to it in his *Lectures on Rhetoric and Belles Lettres* (1783)" (25). Romance emerged into new visibility, then, as part of the construction of a national literary tradition counterposed to the classical Greek and Latin canons. It therefore lies at the beginning of that set of developments that would install vernacular "literature" at the center of literary education in the universities by the end of the nineteenth century.

The term "Gothic" participated in the "competition of values" between classical and national traditions, and has in the twentieth century come to designate one important strain of a more widespread set of generic developments that included, among other things, the ballad revival, "graveyard school" poetry, and the reinvigoration of the sonnet. Fred Botting articulates the scholarly consensus about the cultural struggle enacted by the Gothic's anticlassicism: "The projection of the present onto a Gothic past occurred... as part of a wider process of political, economic, and social upheaval: emerging at a time of bourgeois and industrial revolution, a time of Enlightenment philosophy and increasingly secular views, the eighteenth-century Gothic fascination with a past of chivalry, violence, magical beings and malevolent aristocrats is bound up with shifts from feudal to commercial practices in which notions of propriety, government and society were undergoing massive transformations" ("In Gothic Darkly," 3). Although the Gothic revival was far from an artistically or ideologically uniform phenomenon, it is reasonably accurate to say that the reviewers of *Frankenstein* were expressing their positions toward the "massive transformations" of contemporary society via their antipathy to or allegiance with the school of the arch-radical William Godwin, and that this political position-taking carries over into aesthetic evaluations of the genre of the marvelous romance.

The anticlassicism of the Gothic is certainly associated with a new articulation of literary values and authority. As Botting says, "Between 1790 and 1810 critics were almost univocal in their condemnation of what was seen as an unending torrent of popular trashy novels" (*Gothic*, 21–22). The underlying causes of such condemnation may be elucidated by E. J. Clery's thesis, in *The Rise of Supernatural Fiction, 1762–1800*, that the commercialization of book publishing underlies the growth of supernatural fiction in the late eighteenth century and that this fiction reflected cultural anxieties rooted in the growth of consumerism. Classicist attacks on emergent commercial practices hark back to John Dryden's *MacFlecknoe* and Alexander Pope's *Dunciad*, inspired, as Pope's fictional editor Martinus Scriblerus tells his readers, by living "in those days, when (after providence had permitted the Invention of Printing as a scourge for the learned) Paper also became so cheap, and printers so numerous, that a deluge of authors covered the land" (344). Maggie Kilgour tells the same story with a different emphasis in *The Rise of the Gothic Novel*: "The spread of literacy, the growth of a largely female and middle-class readership and of the power of the press, increased fears that literature could be a socially subversive influence. Prose fiction was particularly suspect: romances, for giving readers unrealistic expectations of an idealized life, novels for exposing them to the sordidness of an unidealised reality" (6). Jerrold E. Hogle, similarly, sees the Gothic as the site of an ideological clash between high and low cultural practices. He describes Horace Walpole's choice of the Gothic as a label for what he was doing in *The Castle of Otranto* (1765) as "a marketing device designed to fix a generic position for an interplay of what was widely thought to be high cultural writing (epic, verse romance, tragedy) with what many still regarded as low by comparison (servant-based comedy, superstitious folklore, middle-class prose fiction)" (8).

The ideological tensions freighted in the genre of marvelous romance reached a crisis in what Robert Miles calls the 1790s "effulgence" of the Gothic in association with controversies over the significance of the French Revolution.[6] Miles argues that among the most profound aftereffects of the 1790s popularity of the romance

> was the development of a certain kind of literary snobbery, which for many years blinded critics to the obvious fact that many of the decade's canonical texts were first and foremost tales of terror. Such snobbery was undoubtedly connected to the material fact that for the first time women, at least as readers, were associated with a form that challenged (or was perceived to challenge) traditional literary authority. In other words, much of the tension between "high" and "low" literature which has pulsed through the institutionalization of "literature" over the last 200 years is first generated by the effulgence of the 1790s tale of terror. ("1790s," 60)

If "traditional literary authority" was aligned with what Jürgen Habermas theorized as the emergent bourgeois public sphere in eighteenth-century England, the Gothic's anticlassicism and popularity are symptoms of the actual heterogeneity of the bourgeois reading public and a response to the exclusions inherent in the hegemonic construction of civil society.[7] Thus by 1818 the marvelous romance was associated with challenges to traditional upper-class cultural norms launched variously, and with different effects, from the positions of women (Ann Radcliffe), non-heteronormative aristocrats (Horace Walpole, Matthew G. "Monk" Lewis), and ideologically subversive intellectuals (the school of Godwin).

The marvelous romance performed this role more by providing a location for the mixing of generic codes than by establishing a strict formal paradigm. In fact, mixing genres rather than aiming at purity is one of the key elements of the Gothic challenge to what Curran calls "neoclassical niceties." In the early adaptations for the stage of *Frankenstein*—an episode in the reception of *Frankenstein* that would prove far more consequential than the early reviews—generic mixing is everywhere apparent and of the foremost importance. The first stage adaptation, Richard Brinsley Peake's *Presumption; or, The Fate of Frankenstein* (1823), advertised itself on its title page as "a melodramatic opera"; John Kerr's *The Monster and the Magician; or, The Fate of Frankenstein* (1826) as "a melo-dramatic romance"; and Henry M. Milner's *Frankenstein; or, The Man and the Monster* (1826) as "a peculiar romantic, melo-dramatic pantomimic spectacle" (Wierzbicki 251–53).[8] From the beginning mixing the novel's horror and tragedy with comedy and song, the adaptations moved in short order to parody and farce with Peake's *Another Piece of Presumption* (1823), where Frankenstein turns into Frankinstitch, a tailor who murders his apprentices and then stitches them together, and the anonymous *Frank-in-Steam; or, The Modern Promise to Pay* (1824), where the monster turns out be the bailiff pursuing Frankenstein for his debts. Peake's *Presumption* and Milner's *Frankenstein*, the most successful adaptations, establish the creature's muteness, basing their treatment of him on the stock pantomime character of the Wild Man (James).[9] They also establish the character of Frankenstein's assistant, a low and comically fearful character in Peake's *Presumption*, and in Milner's *Frankenstein* a garrulous charmer who adds an adventurous, swashbuckling subplot to the tragic main plot. The creation scene and the finale both become opportunities for spectacular stage effects, including pyrotechnical display.

If all of this sounds quite familiar to anyone who knows twentieth-century cinematic adaptations of *Frankenstein*, it is equally typical of contemporary theatrical adaptations of the Gothic (Radcliffe's novels were repeatedly adapted to the stage during the period, and Lewis's supernatural stage thriller *The Castle Spectre* was in 1797 just as popular as his notorious novel *The Monk*). For the purposes of the present argument, the crucial point is that in these adaptations, Victor Frankenstein's non-supernatural, scientific dimension is hardly emphasized over the novel's association of Frankenstein with alchemy.[10] The way that horror, special effects, pantomime, melodrama, and comedy cluster in these adaptations has little to do with any generic innovation accomplished in the text of Shelley's novel. It is not the text but the milieu that determines these associations, and if it is significant that *Frankenstein* was so enthusiastically adapted into the melodramatic and spectacular theatrical milieu, it is because that milieu forms an important precursor to the mass cultural entertainment industry and clearly prefigures some of the generic affinities of what would later coalesce into the mass cultural genre system. At the same time the novel presents other thematic possibilities that the stage adaptations neglect to develop, such as its important and extended allusions to Milton's *Paradise Lost* and Coleridge's *Rime of the Ancient Mariner*. It is yet another set of such possibilities that elicits a new set of responses to *Frankenstein* in the milieu of the late nineteenth century. It is not as a formal paradigm, but as an extraordinarily rich matrix of opportunities for response, that *Frankenstein* plays its part in the beginnings of science fiction.

After *Frankenstein* was released in 1881 from the restrictive copyright attached to the 1831 edition, the novel sold four times more copies in the next decade than it had in its previous history (St. Clair). Whether because of these increased sales, or for the same reasons that fed the novel's popularity, it is at this time that the scientific character of Victor Frankenstein's "workshop" becomes a dominant element of the story's reception. Stories of Frankenstein-like scientists become commonplace in the late-Victorian period, some of them pointing quite directly to the precedent of Shelley's *Frankenstein*, while others seem simply to have picked up on one or the other of the plot conventions of reanimation of the dead, construction of artificial humans, or an ambitious experiment going horribly wrong.[11] The setting of the laboratory acquires the sort of conventional inevitability in these stories that it would retain on the cover illustrations of the science fiction pulp magazines of the 1930s through the '50s. The stories often dwell on technical details of the experimentation in a way that is at once quite foreign to Shelley's novel and equally indicative of the emergence of a genre of fiction attuned to mimicking, popularizing, and sensationalizing the discourses of experimental science.

Isolating such generic elements tells only part of the story of the impact of *Frankenstein* on emergent science fiction, however. The shifting social horizons of the late-Victorian period elicit responses to *Frankenstein* that resonate across and employ the resources of a cluster of interrelated genres. The emphasis on science and scientists coheres with a new visibility of other modern social practices as well. I've suggested elsewhere that "the sf topoi of the mad scientist and the failed experiment derive their power and durability from the way Shelley's plot speaks to the project of modernity, that is, the way it explores the project of reason or enlightenment and its limits. Shelley's novel explores the institutional framework of reason in the laboratory and the university, its methodological framework in the experiment, and its narrative framework in the plot of education and the professional career" ("Mad Scientist," 173). What I would like to emphasize here is that where in the early nineteenth century the novel's association with the school of Godwin pointed to the crucial importance of the theme of education (or miseducation), in the late-Victorian context the association of the "mad" scientist, his unconventional or illicit experimentation, and his monstrous creature with an array of Gothic hero-villains points to the crucial importance of the professional career and the tensions generated by pursuing it. While the *professionalism* of these late-Victorian hero-villains directs our attention to the way the status of science and scientists changed between the 1820s and the 1890s, their *Gothic* character points to the thematic and generic continuity of a set of figures and strategies that have persisted in the popular imagination over the last two and a half centuries and that connect inextricably the genealogies of science fiction, horror, detective fiction, and Gothic romance.[12]

What opens *Frankenstein* so richly to late-Victorian figures of monstrosity is the Gothic strategy of doubling or splitting exemplified in the tortured relation of Victor Frankenstein and his creature. The notion that Victor Frankenstein's creature is a split-off double of Victor is a commonplace of Shelley criticism, and it is equally commonplace to connect Gothic doubling and *Frankenstein* itself to such exemplary late-Victorian Gothic texts as R. L. Stevenson's *The Strange Case of Dr. Jekyll and Mr. Hyde* and Oscar Wilde's *The Picture of Dorian Gray*.[13] The fact that in all these cases one of the doubled figures is the other's hidden, dark secret suggests a splitting into public versus private selves that points back to such a figure as Ambrosio, the publicly sanctimonious and privately murderous and incestuous title character of Lewis's *The Monk*, and forward to the popular twentieth-century genre of the Gothic romance, the most famous example of which is Daphne du Maurier's *Rebecca* (1938). The Gothic romance is based on an elaboration of the fundamental opposition in the Radcliffean Gothic between the good lover and the dark one—between Valancourt and Montoni in *The Mysteries of Udolpho*, for instance—into a single, split individual. Joanna Russ, in her essay "Somebody's Trying to Kill Me and I Think It's My Husband," quotes editor Terry Carr's opinion that "the basic appeal" of the genre "is to women who marry guys and then begin to discover that their husbands are strangers. . . . Most of the 'pure' Gothics tend to have a handsome, magnetic suitor or husband who may or may not be a lunatic and/or a murderer" (32).

The way love and aggression line up alongside the shown and the hidden in all these versions of the Gothic proliferates further into a dichotomy that sets sexual reproduction in opposition to an exclusively male regime of technical reproduction in *Frankenstein*, *Jekyll/Hyde*, and *Dorian Gray*. This technical regime, in all three cases the site for the construction of the monster, can turn toward the construction of alternative gender and kinship relations (as in Bram Stoker's *Dracula* as well as Wilde's *Dorian Gray*), toward a critical or parodic rendering of the biblical account of Adam's creation by Jehovah (as in Wells's *The Island of Dr. Moreau*), or toward a questioning of the ethics of scientific investigation itself (as in *Moreau* and Wells's *The Invisible Man*). All these possibilities are suggested, albeit unevenly developed, in *Frankenstein*, and all three resonate far more powerfully than they did earlier in the century in the late-Victorian contexts of, respectively, an emergent science of sexuality (see Haggerty), Darwinian science, and the contemporary arms race.

Before looking in more detail at Wells's appropriation of the scientist-monster pair, we need to observe that the way the technical realm stands opposed to the normative sex-gender system parallels an opposition between careers pursued in male-dominated professions and what one might call the emotional careers of courtship and family life. The husband-murderer of the later Gothic romance is an embodiment of this professional-versus-emotional opposition from the perspective of the woman excluded from the male professions. The splitting of public and private selves results in both of them taking on the aspect of a mystery from the perspective of the other—the mystery of the man's world and its ways, or the mystery of women and their ways. Once again this suggests possibilities that resonate strongly with *Frankenstein* but are not particularly well developed there, since Victor Frankenstein's obsession with his experiment is a temporary aberration rather than a dedicated career. Still Frankenstein becomes an insoluble mystery to his family, and the creature's murders an unsolved string of crimes.

Let me suggest, then, that the relation of the professional career to the splitting of the public and private selves links late-Victorian horror and emergent science fiction to another genre with Gothic ancestry destined to play an important part in the mass cultural genre system, detective fiction. This is perhaps most obviously the case in Stevenson's *Dr. Jekyll and Mr. Hyde*. The tension between respectability and criminality, between a life devoted to duty and one ruled by desire, between the exercise of reason and submission to instinct, and between the guidance of law and the compulsions of addiction that divides Jekyll and Hyde into their sequestered halves is very much an opposition between two careers pursued in two contiguous but antithetical realms. Furthermore the plot of *Dr. Jekyll and Mr. Hyde* turns on the progressive exposure of the connection between the two careers. The underlying unity of the monstrous Hyde and the bourgeois Jekyll is the mystery the entire narrative works to solve. The plot of the gradually unfolding mystery, the character of the monstrous villain, and the central role of the scientist and of scientific apparatus is a triad that weaves together Gothic doubling with detective fiction, horror, and science fiction in Bram Stoker's *Dracula* as well. In *Dracula* the careers of Count Dracula and Van Helsing collide in a battle over the person of Mina Harker, who operates the technical equipment that records Van Helsing's investigation while at the same time recording the effects of Dracula's rather different investigation on her body itself. Count Dracula is the murderous counterpart of Mina Harker's legitimate spouse, Jonathan, of course, who therefore could be regarded as Van Helsing's primary client. And the same sort of tensions underwrite the career of the most popular of late-Victorian scientific detectives, Sherlock Holmes. Holmes, a master of scientific reasoning and technical manipulation who like many a detective after him (and some before him, especially Poe's Auguste Dupin) pays for his genius by being an emotional cripple, dwells in the borderland between the police and the criminals, the heteronormative and the perverse, the realms of public law and private desire.

Returning to Wells, whose debt to Shelley is deeper and more explicit than any of the other examples that have been mentioned here, one of the main things that sets Moreau and Griffin, the invisible man, apart from Victor Frankenstein is the context of the professional career. Both Moreau and Griffin exhibit the same addictive or workaholic dedication to a bizarre experimental regime as Victor Frankenstein, and both share Frankenstein's ethical and emotional tunnel vision in pursuit of their projects. However, unlike Shelley's Frankenstein but like many of his cinematic progeny, both Moreau and Griffin are renegades from their profession. They are criminals in a way that applies neither to Victor Frankenstein nor even to his murderous creature. The religious context that Shelley both supplies and questions via the creature's reading of *Paradise Lost* is supplanted by a professional code of ethics. Thus the secrecy with which Moreau conducts his research has been forced upon him by public outrage concerning the cruelty of his experiments, while he himself maintains that the ethics of scientific investigation should lead the experimental scientist to disregard such considerations in the pursuit of nature's amoral and merciless truths. The narrative's engagement with the discourse of science therefore takes on an entirely different cast than it did or could have done in *Frankenstein*, which is to say that the late-Victorian context supplies Wells with a generic possibility that was unavailable to Shelley. Shelley's text does not supply the generic possibility. Its status as one beginning of science fiction depends upon its appropriation by Wells and his contemporaries to the context of professional science.

In *The Invisible Man* Wells combines another critique of professional scientific ethics with a closer exploration of the scientist's class position and social function. *The Invisible Man* once again adapts Shelley's scientist-monster pair to the figure of the renegade and to the dynamics of secrecy. Griffin is, like Victor Frankenstein, a student who has a stroke of genius and pursues its consequences in experiments carried on in solitude while he is prey to a fixed idea based on a fantasy of power. The similarly disastrous consequences of his success result in his enforced estrangement from the community. Although he makes himself invisible in order to achieve power and freedom, his invisibility paradoxically turns out to be highly visible, forcing him into elaborate disguises and hardships in order to carry on even the most basic normal routines without exposing his condition to unwanted scrutiny. Thus the unintended consequences of his experiment join the scientist to his creature even more intimately than Jekyll is joined to Hyde. Like Frankenstein's creature, Griffin is an outcast, hidden, a parasite, and eventually the object of both mob and organized communal attack. But Wells affords Griffin none of the sympathy that Shelley gives Victor Frankenstein and his creature. The splitting of professional and domestic careers that produces the emotional crippling of Sherlock Holmes becomes in Griffin a pathological absence of normal attachments and responsibilities. Griffin's narrative, formally echoing the creature's narrative in *Frankenstein*, reveals him to be effectively a parricide, even though he is only indirectly responsible for his father's death, and without any sense of guilt or responsibility. More than merely an expert at rationalization, he is so narrowly self-interested and void of compassion as to become a study in criminal insanity. In the narrative's final turn he proceeds to outright murder and then proposes a "Reign of Terror" as the appropriate strategy for exploiting his invisibility.

What makes this rise to the level of Wells's best fiction is the way Wells connects Griffin's individual defects to the social position of the scientist. The setting in which the invisible man's fantasies of power are acted out is key. The portrayal of the village and villagers in the first half of the novel and the almost burlesque quality of the initial struggles and changes deflate Griffin's power fantasy and render his career thoroughly petty, a descent from the realm of the professional scientist into the lower-class settings of London and eventually the rural settings of the Coach and Horses Inn and Iping village. Griffin is finally the victim of his own class prejudice, which leads him to assume that his narratee, a local medical man, Kemp, will become his willing ally. Kemp instead listens to his story in horror and turns him over to the local police. The novel's subtitle, *A Grotesque Romance*, refers at least partly to the scope of the struggle between Griffin and everyone else being so localized, so small, mean, nasty, and brutal compared to the height of Griffin's ambitions.

This in turn is how the novel addresses itself to the social function of science, particularly the scientific development of weaponry, in the 1890s. *The Invisible Man* can be read as an ironic, subversive response to the plot of the renegade scientist who has developed a superweapon, like Verne's Captain Nemo with his submarine or like the far less well known mad scientist in William Rhodes's 1871 story "The Case of Summerfeld," who threatens to set fire to the world's oceans unless he is given a million dollars, or the one in Robert Duncan Milne's 1891 "A Question of Reciprocity," who threatens to destroy San Francisco with a bomb unless he is given twenty million dollars.[14] In contrast, violence in *The Invisible Man* occurs on a wholly human scale, without any of the military fanfare or technological wonder associated with it in "The Case of Summerfeld" and stories like it or, more importantly, in the polemical future war stories that proliferated during the decades of the world's first industrial arms race (see Clarke). The interplanetary scope of Wells's *The War of the Worlds* is his most famous revisionary appropriation of the plot of future war, but *The Invisible Man* is its counterpart in the sphere of the private individual. Finally, as with *The Island of Dr. Moreau*, *The Invisible Man*'s debt to *Frankenstein* is very much an element of Wells's "piecemeal" fabrication of his scientific, Gothic, marvelous, grotesque romance out of the intertextual, generic resources at his disposal.

When science fiction became a clearly delineated niche market genre in the late 1920s and 1930s, the influence of Wells certainly far overshadowed that of Mary Shelley. *Frankenstein* was best known in the mid-twentieth century via its adaptations to horror cinema in the Universal Studios cycle of the 1930s and the Hammer cycle of the 1950s and '60s. Hence when Brian Aldiss nominated *Frankenstein* as the origin of SF, he could write accurately that Mary Shelley's reputation had "been too long in eclipse" (37). That would change drastically in the ensuing decades, as Shelley's novel was reissued in numerous scholarly editions and became the object of intense critical scrutiny. Some of the reasons for *Frankenstein*'s academic resurrection are clear: feminist criticism's interest in writings by women, for one, and cultural studies' shift away from emphasis on literary masterpieces toward an analysis of literature's cultural impact, for another. A sophisticated academic discourse on the Gothic and the reorientation it effected on the scholarship of British romanticism followed a bit later. The academic canonization of Mary Shelley's novel has in its turn transformed literary and dramatic adaptations of *Frankenstein* in such work as Theodore Roszak's *The Memoirs of Elizabeth Frankenstein* (1995) and the National Theatre's production of Nick Dear's *Frankenstein* in 2011. In this most recent phase of *Frankenstein*'s reception, the importance of the novel to SF has been at best a minor factor. Nonetheless the question of what accounts for *Frankenstein*'s rich reception history, including its privileged position in the genealogy of SF, remains.

The answer begins with *Frankenstein*'s intertextuality. Its power has to do with the way it uses the resources of the marvelous romance to pull together the biblical account of creation with high literary allusions to Milton, Coleridge, and Wordsworth, dialogue with Percy Shelley and Lord Byron, and topical engagement with contemporary science and exploration as well as with the politics of education and criminal justice. I would agree with the majority of the novel's scholars and critics that above all this heady mixture endures so vigorously because of the way it addresses itself to gender ideology and the construction and social allocation of personhood. What I hope to have rendered plausible is a proposition about *Frankenstein*'s powerful intertextuality: that it is, for all the novel's peculiarity and individuality, fundamentally dependent upon the shifting sets of generic possibilities and positions that offered themselves to those who adapted and reinterpreted it. These possibilities participate in and draw much of their energy from the Gothic's "'carnivalesque' mode for representation of the fragmented subject" (Miles, *Gothic Writing*, 4). The scientist-monster pair belongs to an intertextual and inter-generic matrix that includes private detectives, vampires, and husband-murderers, and Frankenstein's endurance has everything to do with this proliferation of Gothic doubling-by-splitting throughout nineteenth-century popular fiction and twentieth-century mass cultural narrative. Although *Frankenstein* clearly is one of the important beginnings of science fiction, its power and appeal are not at all generically specific, as its numerous adaptations into horror and comedy make clear. Its influence on science fiction has much less to do with generic innovation than with inter-generic connectivity—that is, with its usefulness as a resource for later writers positioning the scientist, the laboratory, the experiment, and the monster within the generic articulations of the emerging mass cultural genre system.

Amazing Stories and the Pulp Milieu

There can be no doubt that H. G. Wells's *The Time Machine* marks a significant beginning or point of discontinuity in the history of SF. Even if the American niche market had never developed, or had developed differently, and a genre called "science fiction" had never come into being, the remarkable series of novels that Wells wrote in the late 1890s—*The Time Machine, The Island of Dr. Moreau, The Invisible Man, The War of the Worlds, When the Sleeper Wakes,* and *First Men in the Moon*—would still be read and studied and written about as constituting an important episode in the history of generic innovation and would no doubt still have inspired and influenced writers such as Olaf Stapledon or Karel Čapek who stood outside and independent of the American niche market context. Nonetheless Wells's influence on SF cannot, as things actually turned out, be separated from the reception of his work in American pulp fiction, and especially from its republication in Hugo Gernsback's *Amazing Stories*, the first twenty-nine issues of which each contained a reprint of a story or novel by Wells.[15] It is in Gernsback's *Science Wonder Stories*, too, that the term "science fiction" comes to name the genre.[16] Thus there is a good deal to be said for the case that, as James Gunn puts it, "Before Gernsback there were science fiction stories. After Gernsback, there was a science fiction genre" (Gunn, *Alternate Worlds*, 128, quoted in Landon 54). Gernsback did not invent science fiction, but, as Gunn says, he provided the space where it achieved recognition as a genre.

What needs to be added, however, is that Gernsback by no means created the conditions under which his magazine could assume the position of presenting a new genre to the public. The best available account of science fiction's emergence within the pulp milieu is John Cheng's *Astounding Wonder: Imagining Science and Science Fiction in Interwar America* (2012), where he argues that the genre's emergence was "accidental, the result of industrial shifts within early twentieth-century magazines that reorganized pulp publishing and, more specifically, of editors' opportunistic efforts within its revised fiction factory to invent and reinvent magazines and stories featuring science fiction. Their successful circulation ... tapped into a broader cultural impulse that imagined, celebrated, and considered modern science" (15). This conjunction of industrial shifts in publishing and the broader cultural significance of science resulted in the creation of a thriving SF subculture. In what follows I want to reiterate Cheng's thesis concerning editorial opportunism and the emergence of an SF subculture while supplementing his narrative from the perspectives of genre theory and literary history. This will entail arguing that Gernsback's theorization and promotion of science fiction do not constitute the "true history" of the genre, as Gary Westfahl argues in *Mechanics of Wonder*, but rather that the genealogies of SF are multiple. Gernsback's intervention does not originate or invent science fiction but rather is crucial to an eventful *splitting* of SF into three separate practices that operated in tension with one another: an emerging niche market SF, an emergent mass cultural SF alongside but by no means identical to it, and a preexisting literary practice of SF that registered and resisted the effects of niche and mass cultural practices from afar.[17]

The literary practice of pre–World War I SF is an international affair, including, in addition to the international impact of Chesney's future war and Bellamy's utopian fiction, such figures as Villiers de l'Isle-Adam, J.-H. Rosny aîné, and Gabriel Tarde in France; Kurd Lasswitz in Germany; and the Russian and Latin American traditions that have been the subject of recent studies by Anindita Bannerjee (*We Modern People*) and Rachel Haywood Ferreira (*The Emergence of Latin American Science Fiction*). In the national context of the UK, however, it can be identified as the genre Brian Stableford calls the "scientific romance," the term Wells himself chose to refer in retrospect to the series of breakthrough novels that started with *The Time Machine*. The scientific romance, as Stableford has shown, mainly comprises novels published in one volume (as opposed to the Victorian triple decker), but many of those novels—including all the Wells novels mentioned above except for *The Island of Dr. Moreau*—were initially published as serials in magazines. The two most important of these magazines were *Pearson's*, where *The War of the Worlds* first appeared, and the *Strand*, the original venue for *First Men in the Moon*. Both *Pearson's Magazine* and the *Strand* are general-interest publications that resemble "slicks" like *Ladies Home Journal* in the United States. Neither magazine includes advertising in the 1890s, although the *Strand* would soon begin publishing an annual supplement around Christmastime consisting entirely of advertising. There is no recognition in these magazines of the scientific romance as a genre, or of the generic peculiarity of Wells's novels. Roger Luckhurst writes of the "hybrid and 'impure' spaces" that constituted the ground for Wells's genre mixing, but the venues where Wells's work originally appeared were, in sharp contrast to the generic enclaves crafted by Gernsback, so deliberately heterogeneous as to obscure, if not nullify, Wells's own peculiar generic originality (Luckhurst, *Science Fiction*, 31).[18]

The War of the Worlds appears in *Pearson's* in April through December of 1897. The contents of the magazine in 1896 and 1897 show a marked interest in both imperial and scientific issues that resonates strongly with *The War of the Worlds*. There is, for example, a series of articles on "The Gates and Pillars of the Empire" running from April to November of 1896. The fiction includes Kipling's *Captains Courageous* beginning in 1896 and overlapping with *War of the Worlds*; Wells's own "The Rajah's Treasure" in July 1896; Mayne Lindsay's "The Mystery of Sada Sukh" in December 1896; Arthur Conan Doyle's "Tales of the High Seas" beginning in January 1897; and C. J. Cutcliffe Hyne's "The Adventures of Captain Kettle" beginning in February. Articles about science include a piece on Camille Flammarion titled "The Christopher Columbus of Mars" in July 1897, pieces on the Greenwich observatory and on the discovery of "Röntgen Rays" later in the year, and on the Yerkes observatory ("The Greatest Telescope on Earth") in August 1897.[19] Nonetheless the contents of the magazine are on the whole quite miscellaneous. Following the first installment of *War of the Worlds* there are articles on "The Queen's Dresses" and "Odd Musical Instruments"; following the second installment we find pieces on

"Remarkable Rocks" and "The Making of Cricket Bats." There is no editorial commentary or announcement of coming attractions that in any way recognizes the generic distinctiveness of Wells's novel (or of any of the other fiction).

The same combination of thematic resonance and general miscellany prevails in the *Strand*. The first installment of *First Men in the Moon* (November 1900, volume 20) is accompanied by a piece on "The First Moon-Photographs Taken with the Great Paris Telescope," by François Deloncle (493–97), and there are other articles during the run of Wells's novel on the Paris exhibition of 1900, "Science in the New Century," "Comets," and so on. But there are many more pieces on fashion, politics, and hobbies. There are colonial adventure stories like Walter Wood's "The Hero of the Drift" (21:66–72) and Alvah Milton Kerr's "In Front of the Stampede, A Story of the American Frontier Railroad and Plains" (21:73–80). But the only pieces of fiction that seem to command specific generic recognition are the fairy tales and children's stories that come at the end of each issue. The editor's ten-year anniversary message in December 1900 lauds the contributions of notable early SF figures Wells, Jules Verne, and Grant Allen (among many others) to the success of the *Strand* but does not suggest any generic affinities linking these writers to one another.

Thus, while the individual contributions in *Pearson's* and the *Strand* exhibit a thematic clustering and consistency in which one can see some topical and generic specialization, the magazines endeavor to cast their nets widely, fishing for as diverse an audience as possible. In this context the promise of serial satisfaction is bolstered primarily by the author's established reputation, while any given piece's generic specificity participates in the magazines' scattered ideological appeal—to identification with the project of empire, the project of science, a notion of manliness or womanliness, or simply dedication to an occupation or a sport or a hobby. When, in March 1912, the *Strand* announces a new serial by its star author, Arthur Conan Doyle, the editorial description of *The Lost World*'s genre recalls the polemics of the fin de siècle romance revival: "In our next number will commence Conan Doyle's Great New Adventure Story, guaranteed to give a thrill to the most jaded reader of fiction" (43:360). The promise of serial satisfaction rests firmly upon the authorial signature, however: "*Good judges who have read this eventful chronicle are of opinion that in Professor Challenger, as in Sherlock Holmes, Conan Doyle has added a new, original, and permanent type to the portrait gallery of British fiction*" (emphasis in original).

This balance of the functions of genre and author would soon shift as the result of the changes in the organization of the American publishing industry that made possible Hugo Gernsback's impact on science fiction. The two key changes were, first, the appearance of the all-fiction magazines, beginning with Frank Munsey's *Argosy* in 1896 and *All-Story* shortly after, and second, the advent of the genre-specific fiction magazines, beginning with *Detective Story Monthly* in 1915, followed by *Western Story* in 1919, *Love Stories* in 1921, and *Weird Tales* in 1923 (Clute and Nicholls 979). The general-interest miscellany that still prevailed in the early all-fiction magazines was steadily atomized into groups of related titles each appealing to a specific generic desire. The elaboration of the pulp chains then takes the form of mini-systems of genre, clearly participating in the larger formation of identities within the developing mass cultural genre system. For instance, the *Thrilling* chain of the late 1930s included *Thrilling Love*, *Thrilling Detective*, *Thrilling Western*, *Thrilling Mystery*, *Thrilling Adventure*, *Thrilling Spy Stories*, *Thrilling Ranch Stories*, and *Thrilling Wonder Stories*, this last title being the post-Gernsbackian descendant of *Science Wonder Stories* (Cheng 35). The crystallization of science fiction as an enduring category, that is, the emergence and consolidation of what the Clute and Nicholls encyclopedia calls "genre sf," is an effect of this set of changes in the production and distribution of commercial fiction in the United States. It involves both the construction and stabilization of the niche market genre and the inauguration of science fiction as a properly mass cultural genre in the comic strip *Buck Rogers in the 25th Century* from 1929 on, followed by *Flash Gordon* and the cinematic serials of both in the '30s.[20] What role do Hugo Gernsback's magazines play in this transformation? How powerful a turning point in the history of SF is the April 1926 issue of *Amazing Stories*?

Whatever change *Amazing* gave birth to was incubating for at least fifteen years before. Gernsback's publication of futuristic fiction about science dates back to the appearance of his novel *Ralph 124C 41+* in his magazine *Modern Electrics* in 1911, and he continued to publish fiction here and there in *Modern Electric*'s later incarnations, *Electrical Experimenter* and *Science and Invention*, from then until 1923, when the inclusion of one piece of fiction per issue becomes his standard practice.[21] There is certainly something science fictional about many of the cover illustrations of these magazines, often executed by the same Frank R. Paul who served as the chief cover illustrator for *Amazing* and the *Wonder* titles. Futuristic weaponry predominates on the covers of *Electrical Experimenter* during the World War I years, and after the war futuristic vehicles of transportation are a frequent subject. In 1918 R. and G. Winthrop's "At War with the Invisible," a proto-space-opera descendant of Wells's *War of the Worlds*, appears along with editorial commentary describing it as an "intensely interesting story of the future" (*Electrical Experimenter* 5.11:759) and a "scientific story" about "an inter-planetarian struggle for supremacy" (819). In 1921 we find Charles S. Wolfe's "The Devil's Understudy—Scientific Fiction" in March and his "The Love Machine—Scientific Fiction" in April. Gernsback uses "scientific fiction" as a generic tag a few more times in the following years, especially to designate the special focus of the August 1923 issue, which also provides the sole instance of a *Science and Invention* cover illustration concerning a piece of fiction (G. Peyton Wertenbaker's "The Man from the Atom," illustration by Frank R. Paul), but his terminology is not consistent.

In fact, despite Gernsback's clear interest in crafting some sort of generic niche, the genre status of the fiction remains inchoate in these publications. The table of contents usually lists the fiction under the heading "Popular Scientific Articles" (the other headings in *Science and Invention* were Prize Contests; Automobiles; Electricity; Radio Articles; Chemistry and Electro-Chemistry; Constructor Articles; and Astronomy). But when Gernsback reprinted Wells's "The Star" in March 1923 (with no editorial commentary acknowledging it to be a reprint, much less a masterly example of an emergent genre), it appeared twice in the table of contents, under both Popular Scientific Articles and Astronomy. Ray Cummings's "Around the Universe—an Astronomical Comedy," in six installments beginning in November 1923, is listed under Astronomy in the first and third installments but under Popular Scientific Articles in the other four.

This confusion of categories only makes more obvious the absence of any place at all for fiction among the headings. Confusing "The Star" with an article on astronomy is perhaps symptomatic of the ideas about science fiction Gernsback would later spell out in the editorial sections of his fiction magazines, with his strong emphasis on accurate scientific information and the educational value of the fiction. But these ideas, probably derived at some distance from the program of Jules Verne and Pierre-Jules Hetzel in the *Voyages extraordinaires*, are inaccurate descriptions of the fiction he published at best, and laughably incongruous with it in many instances.

A similar lack of distinction for what we now recognize as early SF prevails elsewhere in the magazines from 1912 to 1923. The most frequent of all publishers of this type of story before *Weird Tales* was *All-Story*, where Edgar Rice Burroughs made his breakthrough into popularity with *Tarzan of the Apes* just months after publishing the first of his John Carter of Mars stories there in 1912, and where later A. Merritt would publish "The Moon Pool" and other stories. Upon its initial appearance in February–July 1912, Burroughs's "Under the Moons of Mars" is designated in the table of contents a "romance of a soul astray." In December of that year, following a remarkable outpouring of readers' letters praising *Tarzan* and asking for more of the same, the editor forecasts "The Gods of Mars" in terms that recognize it as a "yarn" using extraterrestrial settings and "scientific paraphernalia": "This yarn is a sequel to 'Under the Moons of Mars,' of never-to-be-forgotten popularity. The author's imagination again riots over the periphery of our terrestrial neighbor. Once more we play with thoats and snarks and so forth, and six-legged gents, and the scientific paraphernalia that can exist nowhere but Mars, where, as we learn form our savants, 'they do those things better.'" But as with Conan Doyle in the *Strand*, it is the author rather than the genre that is offered as a guarantee of serial satisfaction. Some kind of generic, rather than authorial, promotion is going on when Merritt's "The Moon Pool," in June 1918, receives the interesting designation "A 'Different' Novelette." The "different" story was indeed a regular feature in *All-Story* at this time. The editorial advertisement for "The Moon Pool" in the issue previous to its publication promises a story of "weird power" and "compelling mysticism" that is "an amazing flight of fancy—and fancy based on scientific fact at that." However, the variously supernatural and exotic stories that appear under this "different" designation do not have a consistently science-fictional cast.

If the editor of *All-Story* was groping for some new nonrealist genre category in the "different" stories, the appearance of the *Thrill Book* in March 1919 adds further evidence of the sense that a generic niche existed that had yet to be adequately identified. The editorial announcement in the first issue declares, "Little by little we became convinced that there were whole cargoes of good things being jettisoned because editors and publishers lacked the temerity to publish the unusual, the illogical, the bizarre, swiftly moving story... In THE THRILL BOOK, therefore, you will find interesting stories of every kind—stories of queer, psychological phenomena, of mystic demonstrations, weird adventures in the air, on the earth and sea, and under the sea, in that vast domain of the Fourth Dimension—and of things that men feel but cannot explain." The *Thrill Book* was not a successful venture, folding after its October issue. Its program of the queer, the weird, the mystic, the vast, and the inexplicable nonetheless pointed to a potential niche that was being satisfied piecemeal in *All-Story* and then would be addressed more directly in *Weird Tales* starting in 1923, the year that Gernsback made "scientific fiction" the focus of an issue of *Science and Invention*.

Weird Tales published a good deal of science fiction, but did not, like Gernsback, programmatically isolate it. The "weird" in the magazine's title, something like an expanded version of the "different" in *All-Story*, functioned more as a brand name than as a generic term.[22] The relation of *Weird Tales* to the Gernsback magazines brings out both the distinctiveness of Gernsback's ideas about the genre and the multiplicity of SF's genealogies. In broad terms, *Weird Tales* emphasizes SF's Gothic ancestry, while Gernsback combines a Vernean notion of the genre's pedagogical mission with a large dose of the American dime novel Edisonade. *Weird Tales*, like Gernsback, reprinted H. G. Wells, but in the context of a tradition including Nathaniel Hawthorne, Alexander Pushkin, Charles Dickens, Théophile Gautier, and Bram Stoker, as well as the inevitable Poe. Gernsback, in contrast, reprinted Wells, Verne, and Poe alongside Luis Senarens, author of the Frank Reade Jr. dime novels.[23]

Luckhurst concludes that "the very foundational moment of scientifiction displays the kind of impurity or hybridity that also marked the emergence of British scientific romance. Gernsbackian technocratic advocacy is in intimate dialectical relation with Lovecraftian 'cosmic horror'... and this symbiotic coupling persists to the present day" (*Science Fiction*, 64–65). The point I would like to emphasize is that Gernsback's scientifiction and science fiction not only gave the genre the all-important attribute of a name, but that these efforts were articulated within a system of genres that included not only supernatural fiction of the *Weird Tales* variety but also the successfully delineated niche market genres of detective fiction, the love story, the western, and so on. His opening editorial in the March 1926 *Amazing Stories* declares as much: "ANOTHER fiction magazine! At first thought it does seem impossible that there could be room for another *fiction* magazine in this country.... There is the usual fiction magazine, the love story and the sex-appeal type of magazine, the adventure type, and so on, but a magazine of 'Scientifiction' is a pioneer in its field." This articulation of scientifiction within a field of possibilities that it is *not* points to its "organic" status within a systematic transformation of the production, distribution, and reception of popular fiction in America.

Gernsback's positioning of science fiction in relation to other pulp genres also bears upon an ensuing split between science fiction's niche market and mass-market versions. Gernsback was at some pains not only to define the "Jules Verne, H. G. Wells, and Edgar Allan Poe type of story" but also to declare its difference from and superiority to its niche competitors:

> The past decade has seen the ascendancy of "sexy" literature, of the self-confession as well as the avalanche of modern detective stories.
> But they are transient things, founded on the whims of the moment.... No wonder, then, that anybody who has any imagination at all clamors for fiction of the Jules Verne and H. G. Wells type, made immortal by them; the story that has a scientific background, and is read by an ever growing multitude of intelligent people.
> ... Wise parents, too, let their children read this type of story, because they know that it keeps them abreast of the times, educates them, and supplants the vicious and debasing sex story. (*Science Wonder Stories*, June 1929, quoted in Westfahl, *Mechanics of Wonder*, 45, and Bleiler, *Science-Fiction: The Gernsback Years*, 580)

FIGURE 2. Buck Rogers and the cowboys in the mass cultural future (used with permission © and ® 2016 The Dille Family Trust; Buck Rogers is © and ® 2016 The Dille Family Trust)

In 1934, in founding the fan group the Science Fiction League, Gernsback proclaimed his intention to turn audiences away "from meaningless detective and love trash to the elevating and imaginary literature of Science Fiction" (*Wonder Stories*, May 1934, quoted in Westfahl, *Mechanics of Wonder*, 46). Nonetheless, as Westfahl observes, the dominant mode of writing in the Gernsback magazines remained that of the pulp milieu in general rather than what Gernsback called for or claimed to be publishing (*Mechanics of Wonder*, 148–50). This writing tended to transfer formulas and motifs from other niche genres into SF wholesale, nowhere more obviously, perhaps, than in the most properly mass cultural science fiction publication of the period, *Buck Rogers*, where the future is a smorgasbord of mass cultural genre figures (see figure 2). As John W. Campbell would write in 1946, "In the public mind, 'Buck Rogers' is the standard science-fiction character; the comic strip has tended to be accepted as representative of the field. It is—to precisely the extent that Dick Tracy is representative of detective fiction" ("Concerning Science Fiction," v, quoted in Westfahl 182).

The strain of elitism (or of flattery) in Gernsback's characterization of the SF reading audience would become more pronounced and extreme in John W. Campbell's descriptions of science fiction and its readers during the "golden age" of *Astounding*, where Campbell claims that "no average mind can either understand or enjoy science-fiction" (*Astounding Science Fiction*, March 1938, quoted in Westfahl, *Mechanics of Wonder*, 186). What is far more important than Campbell's or Gernsback's attitudes, however, is the growth of the SF subculture to which these comments referred and at which they were aimed. The story of the emergence of SF fandom has been told with excellent clarity, force, and detail by John Cheng in *Astounding Wonder*, as I said earlier. Cheng shows that the "interwar science fiction pulps created a vital, thriving, and outspoken subculture for popular science that within a few years outpaced the original intentions of editors, writers, and indeed most readers" (8). The crucial space for the congregation of this subculture was the "back yard" of the magazines, the letters to the editor sections, which often functioned to launch correspondence between readers rather than simply as the public forum provided in the magazines. It is the conversations begun there and then extended into fan organizations and their independent publications, the fanzines, that Cheng refers to when he concludes that "the social dynamics of its reading culture sustained science fiction as a cultural genre and public. If Hugo Gernsback introduced the term and an original concept for it, readers' conversations maintained that social recognition even as they added to, extended, and changed what it represented" (74).

The fan subculture that produced such key figures in the ongoing development of SF as Frederik Pohl and Cyril Kornbluth, Sam Moskowitz and Forrest Ackerman, Judith Merril and Damon Knight forms in proximate, neighborly opposition to the mass cultural practice of SF. The gradual aggregation of a distinctly subcultural SF megatext is visible, perhaps, in such a characteristic "beauty" of the genre as the use of neologisms. Rampant in the fanzines, neologism became ever more important as a way of giving efficient, unobtrusive clues to the "novum" lodged in the SF setting, as a group of increasingly dedicated, skilled, and professional writers formed around Campbell's editorship of *Astounding*, and as the young fans of the Gernsback years grew into mature, more discerning readers as well as writers, editors, collectors, and organizers. The sophisticated practice of neologism described by Istvan Csicsery-Ronay Jr. in *The Seven Beauties of Science Fiction* implies a treatment of the SF sentence that is the explicit subject of Samuel R. Delany's classic essay "About 5,750 Words" and Kathleen Spencer's analysis of SF as realist prose written for an imaginary audience ("'The Red Sun Is High, the Blue Low': Towards a Stylistic Description of Science Fiction"). Both Delany and Spencer are presenting analyses that are closer, more detailed, and better articulated with professional academic literary criticism than those offered by Campbell in the '40s, but Campbell already grasped the main point that "the best modern writers of science fiction have worked out some truly remarkable techniques for presenting a great deal of background and associated material without intruding into the flow of the story" ("Concerning Science Fiction," ix, quoted in Westfahl, *Mechanics of Wonder*, 182–83). As Westfahl puts it, these techniques concerned the way writers communicated the "materials [that] *precede and inform* the story while not fully presented in it" (183), with Robert A. Heinlein as the best practitioner. Attunement to such a distinctive handling of the setting had become a primary requisite for participation in a thriving, firmly established SF subculture.

By the later 1940s the splitting of SF into mass cultural, subcultural, and an older literary set of practices was complete. Subcultural SF was distinctly new and firmly rooted in the development of "genre SF" in the American niche market magazines. The style of writing and of handling setting that developed in the subcultural strain of American genre SF is not to be found in Wells or the scientific romance, and is absent from such a major exemplar of literary SF in the 1930s and '40s as Olaf Stapledon.[24] When George Orwell creates Newspeak in *Nineteen Eighty-Four*, it is not a response to the SF sentences of Robert A. Heinlein but rather a critical estrangement of the mass cultural discourses of news and propaganda. But by 1950 American mass cultural and subcultural SF had reached a point of visibility and cultural power such that literary practitioners exploring dystopic futures or other science-fictional material inevitably found themselves in dialogue with them. It is no accident that the end date of Brian Stableford's study of the British scientific romance is 1950. From then on, mass cultural, subcultural, and literary practices of SF spoke to and responded to one another, as they have continued to do ever since.

Philip K. Dick's Mass Cultural Epistemology

With the remarkable success of the Library of America's *Four Novels of the 1960s* by Philip K. Dick in 2007, Dick became the first writer of the American SF subculture to achieve a solid claim to recognition as a major literary figure. As Andrew Milner has observed, the passage from subcultural to canonical status *"tends to allow SF to enter the canon, but not to return to SF"* (67, emphasis in text), which means, to put it another way, that any SF text that achieves recognition as mainstream literature is said to do so only and precisely to the extent that it transcends its genre status and leaves its original niche market provenance behind. A typical example of this sort of thinking is Adam Gopnik's August 20, 2007, piece about the Library of America volume in the *New Yorker*, in which Gopnik finds much to praise about Dick, comparing his satirical imagination favorably to Jonathan Swift's at one point, but also denies Dick a place alongside Pynchon or Vonnegut in the hierarchy of midcentury American literature because he remained "a pretty bad writer" who "had a hack's habits" and shuffled the same few characters "from hand to hand and from novel to novel like a magician with a few mangy rabbits." I am not going to defend Dick's gifts as a stylist—others have done so quite ably (see Freedman, *Critical Theory*, 34–43)—nor am I interested in debating the stature of Dick versus Vonnegut or anyone else. Much has been written about Dick's fiction, no doubt more than about any other American SF writer, and most of it would take issue with Gopnik's admitting Dick to the literary canon only insofar as his satirical genius can be dissociated from his unfortunate commercial milieu.

I do want to ask what gives Dick's fiction its strength, however, and I will draw extensively on previous commentary in doing so. The questions that motivate this chapter have to do, first, with the suggestion I made earlier that canonical texts are boundary objects, and second, with the repetitiveness that Gopnik so deplores. If canonical texts enjoy that status because of their ability to satisfy the needs of several different communities of practice, what generic or social boundaries are joined or put into dialogue in Dick's fiction? I want to argue here that, far from transcending its subcultural provenance, Dick's best fiction relies for much of its success on the way it holds blatantly and sometimes self-mockingly subcultural SF conventions and the conventions and values of mainstream realism in productive tension with one another. As for Dick's repetitiveness, I want to assess it in the context of the theses raised in chapter 2 about mass cultural seriality. If by the 1950s the seriality of SF had produced a more or less predictable world of conventional expectations, how does Dick's fiction set that generic "science fiction" world into motion? What strength does he draw from SF's generic resources? What dialectic of typicality and individuality comes into play? My argument here explores the thesis that the seriality of mass cultural and niche market SF necessarily produces as one of its intertextual effects a certain metafictional content. Every text employing the genre protocols of SF becomes, to a certain degree, about SF, and, at the same time, about mass cultural seriality. I argue that Dick's fiction consistently achieves this effect to an unusually self-conscious and thematically significant degree. It does so, in fact, precisely by the way it positions itself on the border between SF and mainstream realism—which is to say, between the SF subculture and the literary establishment and between the mass cultural and academic-classical genre systems. In fact, the metafictional clash of SF and realism provides the epistemological underpinning of Dick's ethics and ontology, and at the same time generates a meta-generic and meta-systemic critique of mass cultural news, advertising, and propaganda.

This chapter represents a definite change of pace from the previous two, immersing itself in the career of a single writer rather than galloping across the decades. Part of the point is simply to demonstrate in practice that the sort of literary history I am advocating would continue to perform close textual readings that recognize the unusual importance and power of SF's best writers. I have concentrated on the major SF novels of Dick's middle period, not because I consider the short fiction or the other novels irrelevant to the topic, but for the sake of narrowing my materials to a manageable focus and clinging to whatever claims to brevity and concision I can muster.

The Shakespeare of Science Fiction

Fredric Jameson described Dick at the time of his death as the "Shakespeare of science fiction" ("Futurist Visions"). The conjuncture of traditional literary authority and mass cultural niche genre in Jameson's praise points precisely to what is interesting but also problematic about Dick's position, for calling Dick the "Shakespeare of science fiction" definitely cuts two ways. On the one hand, Jameson means to erase or at least lessen the distance between SF and the traditional canon, putting Dick's artistic success to the job of valorizing and legitimizing the genre. Yet on the other hand his strategy remains congruent with that of Stanisław Lem, whose scorn for the culture industry rivals or exceeds that of Adorno himself, when Lem called Dick "A Visionary among the Charlatans," or made him the exception promised in "Science Fiction, a Hopeless Case—with Exceptions." Dick's position in either case, as "Shakespeare" or as "Exception," is defined by the antithetical conditions of canonized genius and pulp anonymity, and his distinction is to have achieved a more or less contradictory synthesis of the two.

Dick was certainly not, as Shakespeare was, an active and crucial player at the heart of his artistic milieu. He more or less stumbled into the field of SF because of an extraordinary but ephemeral boom in SF magazine publishing in the early '50s (Sutin 66–67). SF was a way to earn a modest paycheck while working on his more serious writing projects, the series of seven realist novels he wrote but failed to publish in the '50s. The Dick of the '50s saw early SF fans as "trolls and wackos, ... terribly ignorant and weird people" (Sutin 82). He described himself as "not educated on SF but on well-recognized serious writing" such as the works of Proust, Pound, Kafka, and Dos Passos (Sutin 57). As late as 1981 he would call his exclusion from the literary mainstream the "long-term tragedy ... of [his] creative life" (Sutin 280). Nonetheless, no critic has ever argued that Dick's realist fiction is greatly superior to his SF, and many have argued the reverse.[1]

The shifting relation between Dick's realist writing and his SF is one way to delineate the phases of his career. During the early phase the two endeavors proceeded side by side, with the realist novels exerting little influence on the short SF of the early '50s or a Van-Vogtian novel like *Solar Lottery* (1955).² A crucial turning point is the combination of realism and SF in *Time out of Joint* (1959), which, unlike any of Dick's previously published novels, was not marketed as science fiction but as "a novel of menace" (Sutin 94). Dick's attempt at an experimental blending of SF and realist techniques continued in *We Can Build You* (composed 1962, published 1969) and *The Man in the High Castle* (1962), the breakthrough success of which in the SF community, alongside Dick's continued failure to get any of the "mainstream" novels published, launched Dick into the SF-dominant phase of his career from the early '60s to 1974. Here the multifocal narrative strategy of *High Castle* is deployed with remarkable success in more conventionally science-fictional settings in *Martian Time-Slip* (1964) and *Dr. Bloodmoney* (1965). SF motifs wildly proliferate around the staple plot material of failed marriages, mental illness, and political repression in novels like *The Penultimate Truth* (1964), *The Simulacra* (1964), *Clans of the Alphane Moon* (1964), *The Zap Gun* (1967), *Now Wait for Last Year* (1966), and *Do Androids Dream of Electric Sheep?* (1968), climaxing in the baroque narrative complexities of *The Three Stigmata of Palmer Eldritch* (1965) and *Ubik* (1969). SF continues to predominate in the less prolific period of personal crisis and drug addiction in the late '60s and early '70s. That period can be said to have come to an end with the intense hallucinatory episodes of February and March 1974 (referred to by Dick as the 2-3-74 experience), after which the bulk of his writing (much of it in the notebooks known as *The Exegesis*) was devoted to theological speculation and autobiographical rumination.³ Whatever one can say about the level of realism or (what is not the same thing) the grasp of reality evident in Dick's post-1974 writing, SF recedes into a subordinate generic element in *A Scanner Darkly*, *VALIS*, and *The Transmigration of Timothy Archer*.

All this is to say that the relation of Dick's career to SF is somewhat eccentric. Even his canonization as a major American writer of the mid-century did not emanate from within the SF community of writers, editors, or fans. Despite the Hugo awarded to *High Castle* (which hardly implies widespread recognition as a major writer), his reputation only began to gather any real momentum after the peak of his middle, SF-dominant phase, by which time the SF field itself was, in the United States, increasingly riven between an old guard for whom the genre's golden age was in the past and the American version of the British "New Wave." Dick's prestige increased in the '70s with the attention lavished upon his work by Jameson, Suvin, and others during the burgeoning of academic attention to science fiction in that decade, and reached an entirely different sort of visibility—accompanied by his first real financial success—with the Hollywood adaptation of *Do Androids Dream of Electric Sheep?* as Ridley Scott's *Blade Runner* in 1982.[4] *Blade Runner* would probably not have been able to command the production budget it did—nor the services of Harrison Ford in the lead—had not the prior success of the *Star Wars* films transformed SF for the first time into a major generic player in big-budget Hollywood production. Thus by the mid-'80s Dick's work found itself centrally positioned in both the academic expansion of interest in SF and in the Hollywood economy. If his involvement with SF began opportunistically, it ended fortuitously.

The tension between SF and "mainstream" genre codes and institutional values is just as evident at the textual level of his SF novels as in the career as a whole. Carlo Pagetti wrote in the 1975 special issue of *Science-Fiction Studies* devoted to Dick: "[Dick] is challenging the narrative and cultural values of SF not by denying them flatly, but by exploiting them to their extreme formal and ideological consequences. Dick is actually writing SF about SF" (25).[5] The only drawback to this acute observation is that it seems to imply a level of seriousness about breaking SF conventions, or not breaking them, that Dick clearly did not possess. His attitude toward SF conventions entails a cavalier disregard for any sort of scientific plausibility. The question of whether Ganymede could actually be inhabited by slime molds (*Clans of the Alphane Moon*), or Callisto by cuddle sponges (*Flow My Tears, the Policeman Said* [1974]) simply does not matter. His flying cars and interplanetary rockets are mere narrative conveniences for getting characters from one place to another, usually in about forty-five minutes. His autonomic taxicabs are a kind of running joke. The entire weird array of pulpish extraterrestrials living in Chuck Rittensdorf's disreputable condo building in *Clans*—"Lord Running Clam" the Ganymedean slime mold, "a molten metal life form from Jupiter called Edgar," "a wizbird from Mars," "a greebsloth from Callisto," and "a Venusian moss"—constitutes a comic alert to the reader that we are in the genre ghetto (39). If he stretches SF conventions it is not because he cares about breaking them (e.g., in rebellion against Campbellian SF, cf. Robinson x–xi) but because he does not care at all. SF conventions are playthings to Dick, and one of the best things about his SF (and one of the principal reasons so many readers prefer his SF to his realist work) is its playfulness, as in the parodic, over-the-top explanation of the scientific basis of the Ubik spray can in *Ubik* (*Four Novels*, 795). But this is not to deny that there is a serious side to this playing with generic conventions. Two of the most idiosyncratically brilliant aspects of his SF novels emerge from it: the comic vignettes, and their grim counterpart, what I will call Dick's narrative sublime.

Two of Dick's funniest and best-known scenes, Joe Chip's argument with his door in *Ubik* and Rick and Iran Deckard's argument over the proper use of the Penfield mood organ at the start of *Androids*, involve a comic confusion between persons and things. This melding of things and persons is perhaps the SF trope most inventively and variously exploited throughout Dick's SF, and we will turn back to it in the context of Dick's response to mass culture shortly. The relevant feature of the two scenes for the moment is their ludicrous juxtaposition of the banal, quotidian routine of waking up and getting ready for work with the SF devices of the robotic door and the mood organ. It is not merely comic talent but the calculated play of the realist and the fantastic upon one another in such scenes that justifies the frequent comparison of Dick to Kafka (and makes one wonder how much all of Dick's waking-up-for-work scenes owe to *The Metamorphosis*).

A less well-known comic vignette that depends not just on clashing genre codes, but on playing the mass cultural genre system itself against the traditional canon, occurs in *Palmer Eldritch*. It involves an accessory for Perky Pat Layouts, the Great Books animator. As Barney Mayerson explains it to those who are about to share the vicarious world of Perky Pat with him via their ingestion of Can-D, "You insert one of the Great Books, for instance *Moby Dick*, into the reservoid. Then you set the controls for *long* or *short*. Then for *funny version*, or *same-as-book* or *sad* version. Then you set the style-indicator as to which classic Great Artist you want the book animated like. Dalí, Bacon, Picasso . . . the medium-priced Great Books animator is set up to render in cartoon form the styles of a dozen artists" (*Four Novels*, 350–51, ellipsis in text). The Great Books animator is in fact a joke machine, like those in which one constructs absurd epithets by making random combinations from three columns of possibilities.[6] What is distinctive is not just Dick's satire of mass cultural adaptation reducing canonical texts to consumer-oriented formulas, but the bizarre choices that quickly show up: *The Meditations of Marcus Aurelius* as a full-length funny cartoon in the style of de Chirico, and Augustine's *Confessions* in the style of Lichtenstein. The turn Dick gives the joke, turning the meditative and the confessional texts of Marcus Aurelius and Augustine into cartoon comedy, works at several levels. Thematically, the debasement of Augustine and Marcus Aurelius is a metaphor for the degradation of the colonists' lives; the process of adaptation itself echoes the government propaganda encouraging colonization and the compensatory satisfactions offered by Perky Pat by translating private (meditative, confessional) desire and anguish into public and exploitable fantasy; and the theological allusion to Augustine reinforces Can-D's bitter parody of the Catholic doctrine of transubstantiation in the sacrament of Holy Eucharist. As metafiction, however, the Great Books animator also expresses Dick's ambivalence about SF. The classical and modernist allusions seem to ask the reader to think of *Palmer Eldritch* itself as a work of serious intellectual ambition like *Moby Dick*, and at the same time not to take this request too seriously since it is couched in the form of a joke.

Just as the commercial success of Perky Pat Layouts is fueled by the desperation of the colonists in *Palmer Eldritch*, Dick's comedy in general derives much of its power from being poised at the edge of despair. The Dickian sublime erupts into Dick's novels when the narrative ground threatens to give way to the abyss. Much of the best that has been written about Dick's fiction concerns the workings of this process and emphasizes its patterned repetition throughout his oeuvre, as in the entropic sublime Christopher Palmer connects to patterns of movement and stasis in Dick's fiction, or the turning inside out of reality that N. Katherine Hayles connects to Dick's anxiety-laden depiction of women (Palmer 44–64, Hayles

160–91). Another pattern of sublime moments in Dick's novels arises from the rupturing of narrative continuity, what Umberto Rossi calls Dick's technique of suddenly changing the rules of the narrative game to produce "ontological uncertainty" in the stories, and that Fredric Jameson aptly describes as those "passages, in which the narrative line comes unstuck from its referent and begins to enjoy the bewildering autonomy of a kind of temporal Moebius strip" ("After Armageddon," 27). These moments of pulling the rug out from under the feet of the reader sometimes involve a sudden dissolution of the "effect of the real," as happens to Ragle Gumm in *Time out of Joint* when a soft-drink stand falls into bits before his eyes and he is left holding in his hand a piece of paper with the words "soft-drink stand" on it; or a sudden shifting of referential worlds, as when Nobosuke Tagomi walks out of the alternative San Francisco of *High Castle* into the "tomb world" of our own San Francisco; or the destabilization of any sure connection to the prior narrative, as happens to Barney Mayerson after ingesting Chew-Z in *Palmer Eldritch*, or to Joe Chip after Pat Conley alters the past and he finds himself married to her in *Ubik*, or again to all the passengers aboard the Runciter Associates ship when the Stanton Mick bomb explodes a bit later in the same novel.

This species of the sublime has to do, first of all, with the epistemological dilemma that according to Fredric Jameson constitutes the "basic content" of Dick's fiction. In the moments of narrative rupture, says Jameson, "Dick's work transcends the opposition between the objective and the subjective," but that opposition, "our simultaneous presence in separate components of private and public worlds," remains the existential core of Dick's fiction, the situation that it is most committed to addressing ("After Armageddon," 27). I would qualify Jameson's observation insofar as Dick's narrative sublime does not transcend the gap between private and public worlds so much as it exposes it, in such a way as to undermine faith in the stability or reliability of either private perception or public accounts of the world. In the 1964 essay "Drugs, Hallucinations, and the Quest for Reality," Dick explains that his interest in hallucinatory drugs and schizophrenia is based on the notion that they represent not mistaken or merely distorted perception, but an excessive perception of reality: "rather than 'seeing what isn't there' the organism is seeing what *is* there—but no one else does" (*Shifting Realities*, 173). Unfortunately the schizophrenic's attempts to communicate this experience do not make sense to those for whom the accepted filters remain in place, and so the schizo becomes cut off from others. But this differs from normality only in degree, not in kind. The juxtaposition of the normal and the hallucinatory accounts of things undercuts both, exposing the incongruity that always already exists between what Dick would call the *idios kosmos* or private reality and the *koinos kosmos* or public one. Dick's narrative sublime happens when a narrative agent disrupts whatever conventions of continuity and coherence seemed to establish the referential status of the public reality ("the narrative line comes unstuck from its referent"), leaving nothing but competing, dissonant versions of privacy in its wake.[7]

Dick's ambition in setting up generic dissonances and playing generic conventions against one another is not to push SF conventions to the breaking point, then, but rather to explore questions about fiction per se—or rather, to explore questions about reality by the only means possible, our fictions about it. In his late essay "How to Build a Universe That Doesn't Fall Apart Two Days Later" Dick says that all his fiction was devoted to exploring two fundamental questions, one of them being "what is reality?" (*Shifting Realities*, 260). This turns out to be an epistemological and ontological question with a set of metafictional, meta-generic, and meta-systemic answers. Dick explores the question of reality most effectively not when he breaks SF conventions, but when he most radically subverts the realism inherent in SF. Dick's sublime SF moments are paradoxically enabled by his utter disdain for SF protocols of scientific plausibility and the absence in his work of any pretense of extrapolating a believable future, leaving him free to construct peculiarly effective nonrealist worlds that in the SF novels are always part realism, part SF, part allegory, part satire, and part farce. This heady brew wrestles, at its best, with the onto-epistemological question of reality and the ethical question of how to act in response to the fact that, as Rudolf Wegener says to himself in the final chapter of *High Castle*, "We do not have the ideal world, such as we would like, where morality is easy because cognition is easy" (*Four Novels*, 217). Dick's response to the question of reality is metafictional because only approximations to the hidden and incommunicable truth are available, and yet the notion of truth itself cannot be abandoned, since there is never any doubt as to the ultimate power of the real over the individual. His response is meta-generic and meta-systemic because mixing and clashing genres and canons of value are at the heart of his method.

Broadcasting and the Critique of Mass Culture in Dick's Major SF Novels

We are now in a position to explore the way Dick's subcultural position energizes his response to mass culture. Dick is quite direct in "How to Build a Universe" about the importance of mass culture to the question of what is real:

> We live in a society in which spurious realities are manufactured by the media, by big corporations, by religious groups, political groups—and the electronic hardware exists by which to deliver these pseudo-worlds right into the heads of the reader, the viewer, the listener.... So I ask, in my writing, What is real? Because unceasingly we are bombarded with pseudorealities manufactured by very sophisticated people using very sophisticated mechanisms.... It is an astonishing power: that of creating whole universes, universes of the mind. I ought to know. I do the same thing. (*Shifting Realities*, 261–62)

The mass production of the "pseudoworlds" that bombard individual consciousness is answered in Dick's fiction by the construction of worlds that are intended to fall apart, to "come unglued" in order "to see how the characters in the novels cope with this problem" (262). SF has been called the literature of technologically saturated societies, but for Dick what counts most of all is the semiological saturation of the environment produced by the technology of the mass communication and entertainment industries and the fetishistic signifying power of commodities, particularly as represented in advertisements. The condition of semiotic immersion and response to it is of course a central topic in Dick criticism. In his essay on paranoia in Dick's fiction, Carl Freedman argues that exchange value in general and consumerism in particular "saturate the [capitalist] social field with hieroglyphics to an extent unprecedented in all of human history"

("Towards a Theory of Paranoia," 114). As a consequence, he argues, conspiracies and commodities hold a privileged place in the consciousness of capitalist subjects: "If we are economically constituted as capitalists and workers who must buy and sell human labor that is commodified into labor-power, then we are psychically constituted as paranoid subjects who must seek to interpret the signification of the objects—commodities—which define us and which, in a quasi-living manner, mystify the way that they and we are defined" (113–14). He might have gone on to say that the most obvious examples of "quasi-living" objects in Dick's America were radios and televisions, and indeed Freedman does go on to say in his editorial introduction to the 1988 special issue of *Science Fiction Studies* that Dick's paranoia is particularly attuned to the "penetration of the American mind by television" ("Editorial Introduction," 148). If, in Dick's fiction, an excess of signification exudes from every surface, potentially turning every object into a pseudo-person, the material premise for this situation is not simply capitalism per se but the mass cultural media environment of Dick's America. What I want to emphasize here is not Dick's "preeminence in the production of paranoid ideology" ("Towards a Theory of Paranoia," 116), then, but rather his engagement with *publicity* as a social force.

Grand conspiracies of misinformation are of course part of the stock-in-trade of midcentury SF, with Orwell's Ministry of Truth in *Nineteen Eighty-Four* the best-known and most influential example, and Frederik Pohl and Cyril Kornbluth's *The Space Merchants* (1953), aimed at commercial advertising rather than government propaganda, its subcultural counterpart. A combined emphasis on mass culture and government propaganda, which is to say on ideological and repressive state apparatuses, is apparent throughout Dick's SF. In Dick's first published novel, *Solar Lottery* (1955), ads are considered the highest form of art, as they are in *The Space Merchants*, and there are two channels of televised advertising that parody the division of high-modernist versus mass or popular culture (42). At the same time the government's electoral process is a kind of enormous game show. The crafting of illusion is elaborated into the creation of an entire fake town in *Time out of Joint*, this time under the direction of the military, but with a serialized newspaper puzzle contest at its center. In *Martian Time-Slip* the android teaching machines in the Martian Public School are seen by the repairman, Jack Bohlen, as "like booths in an amusement park" that mask a rigid disciplinary regime: "The school was not there to inform or educate, but to mold, and along severely limited lines.... Perpetuation of the culture was the goal, and any special quirks in the children which might lead them in another direction had to be ironed out" (*Five Novels*, 63).

Dick's interest in conspiratorial publicity campaigns seems to peak during the mid-'60s, with *The Simulacra*, *Clans of the Alphane Moon*, *The Zap Gun*, *The Penultimate Truth*, and *The Unteleported Man* (1966; later redone in expanded form as *Lies, Inc.* [1984]) all composed within about a year of one another. The collusion between military and commercial power that pervades these novels at times turns into a kind of in-joke Dick seems to be telling himself. Thus while the "ak-prop" (acquisitions propaganda) specialists in *The Zap Gun* work on "plowsharing" the weapons of a fake arms race between Wes-bloc and Peep-East (repurposing a weapons guidance system into "a hollow body in which cigars or pencils can be stored," in the novel's opening epigraph), a skit on the Bunny Hentman Show in *Clans* involves turning plows into swords: "Four plows would guide themselves, at news of hostilities, into a single unit; the unit was not a larger plow but a missile-launcher" (26).

What unites all these versions of government and corporate power is an elite group's monopoly on sending messages that script an official version of reality, relegating the bulk of the society—the "tankers" in *Penultimate Truth*, the "pursaps" of *The Zap Gun*, the "Befehlsträger" of *The Simulacra*—to mere passive receivers, with the senders in a corresponding position of dangerous power. The resulting social structure is an exacerbated form of that compartmentalization into private and public experiences that Jameson sees as the core dilemma explored in Dick's fiction, with a "public" account of things imposing itself on the "private" by means of its ownership and control of the means of mass communication. Nicole Thibodeaux, the First Lady in *The Simulacra*, may very well and rightly say that "the true basis of political power is ... the ability to get others to do what you want them to do" (90). But Nicole herself is only an actress; the scriptwriters remain off-scene: "there's just the TV image after all, the illusion of the media, and behind it, behind her, another group entirely rules" (171). The "public" conceals within itself another "private" compartment, the secret and hidden face of power, a social relation sometimes echoed formally as the subliminal content of advertising, but represented most often in these texts by the blatant, conspiratorial falseness of the account of things foisted upon the unknowing public. Here the epistemological question of reality is overwhelmed by the effects of power attached to control over mass media; as Dick says of the manufacturers of pseudo-realities in "How to Build a Universe," "I do not distrust their motives; I distrust their power" (*Shifting Realities*, 262). A culminating example—worked out in the terms not of SF but of the conflict between work and home in the police drama—is the conflict between Bob Arctor and Agent Fred in *A Scanner Darkly* that literalizes the split between a "public" self ruled by the script of a high-surveillance police state and a "private" self reduced to something like the status of a "quasi-living" object by his role in that script, as Bob is literally rendered into a recording to be viewed by his "public" self, and eventually reduced by his drug addiction to little more than a recording device himself.[8]

The fate of Bob Arctor is one of the examples of the strong "interpenetration of consciousness and media technologies" in Dick's work analyzed by Anthony Enns in "Media, Drugs, and Schizophrenia in the Works of Philip K. Dick." Working from the network theory of Friedrich Kittler, Enns argues that "Dick frequently represents media technologies as 'discourse networks' or technological systems of inscription that establish 'the framework within which something like "meaning," indeed, something like "man," becomes possible'" (Enns 69, quoting Wellbery xii). Enns traces Dick's debt to and use of the neurological research of Wilder Penfield and the existential psychology of Ludwig Binswanger to arrive at his representation of "consciousness and memory as an interface between a perceptual apparatus and a recording device" (74). The split subject of Bob Arctor / Agent Fred "parallels the division of the subject introduced by sound and optical recording devices" (79). Enns connects telepathy, and ultimately the reception of broadcasts from the divine, to Dick's belief that schizophrenia involves an excessive rather than deficient perception of reality. Most importantly, perhaps, Enns contends that the quasi-sacramental status of Can-D in *Palmer Eldritch* and the television religion of Mercerism in *Androids* spring from debates over the social impact of television, with the escapist consumerism of Perky Pat Layouts conforming with the belief that "television programming was designed primarily to serve advertisers," while Can-D's sacramental status or the empathetic religion of Mercerism conform to "the inherently communal and even spiritual element of television... praised by theorists such as Marshall McLuhan" (81).

Indeed, relations of power between senders and receivers permeate Dick's SF, from the remote-controlled assassin Pellig in *Solar Lottery* to the final moment of *VALIS*, with Phil Dick hoping to catch "symbols of the divine" on the TV (*VALIS and Later Novels*, 384–85). The permutations of sending and receiving in *Dr. Bloodmoney* match those of the character system mapped out by Fredric Jameson in "After Armageddon," with the ultimate power struggle pitting Walt Dangerfield's live broadcasts against Hoppy Harrington's prerecorded imitations, putting at stake (as does the similar pair of Mercer and Buster Friendly in *Androids*) the role of the serial broadcast itself to pull together an "imagined community" of postatomic survivors. To an important extent, as the example of Bob/Fred/Bruce in *A Scanner Darkly* shows, individuals are constituted as subjects in Dick's fiction by their interpellation, as Althusser would say, into such relations of power. The vicissitudes of subjection encapsulate the epistemological and ethical issues epitomized in Dick's two questions, what is real? and what is authentically human? It is here, indeed, that they become, as Dick says, the same question (*Shifting Realities*, 263–64). As Enns has shown, an analogy to broadcasting is lodged in the very notion of consciousness in Dick's fiction, and as a result Dick's idiosyncratic use of SF broadcasting motifs opens into some of his most consequential explorations of power, ideology, and publicity.

One of the recurrent forms of SF receiving in Dick, the precog (or in *Clans* a camera that photographs the future), explores a privileged form of mass cultural knowledge that we will return to at greater length in the next chapter, prediction. In *The World Jones Made* (1956) the title character's precognition enables his meteoric rise to political power. At the center of the plot of *Time out of Joint* stands Ragle Gumm's predictive ability, an instrument of crucial military strategic significance characteristically masked in the novel as a daily newspaper puzzle. More typically precognition takes an economic turn, directing itself toward the movements of the market. Manfred Steiner's terrifying visions of the future play against the predictive game of real estate speculation in *Martian Time-Slip*. Barney Mayerson works as a pre-fashion consultant in *Palmer Eldritch*. The most interesting examples of precognition in the context of the present argument are those that take a self-reflexive and metafictional turn. The precognitive weapons fashion designers of *The Zap Gun* enter into a trance state that is first described as a "purely private world" in which, nonetheless, "a common Something dwelt" (16). It turns out that this common Something is not a mystical opening upon the future, as they believe, but rather a lurid pulp comic book, *Blue Cephalopod Man from Titan*. This comic inversion of the Great Books animator of *Palmer Eldritch* exhibits the same ambivalence about SF, as the hidden role of *Blue Cephalopod Man* both confesses Dick's playful allegiance to the pulp origins of niche market SF and at the same time caricatures Gernsbackian claims that based SF's value on its ability to predict technological innovation. A final, subtler example of Dickian metafictive precognition is the operation of the oracle in *High Castle*. One way to interpret the notoriously puzzling twist in the final moments of the novel, when Juliana Frink forces Hawthorne Abendsen to confess that the oracle is the true author of *The Grasshopper Lies Heavy*, is to conclude that the oracle is indeed the author not only of *The Grasshopper Lies Heavy* but also of that other alternative history, *The Man in the High Castle*—that is, that the oracle is a figure for Philip K. Dick himself. The strange fact that the oracle consistently announces the same hexagram to different people at the same time points to its congruence with the authorial consciousness that oversees and arranges the novel's startling array of alternative histories, science-fictional extrapolation, psychological realism, and hoaxes, all in the pursuit of the author/oracle's desire (as the oracle tells Juliana) to communicate an "Inner Truth" (*Four Novels*, 227).[9]

The final SF turn Dick gives to mass cultural subjection is the private counterpart of public campaigns of misinformation that subjugate entire classes of people: the invasive broadcasting that emanates from and targets individuals, usually either via telepathy or the mediation of a drug. The fake intimacy of the commercial advertisement serves as a kind of paradigm for this form of invasion. Dick expertly parodies fake intimacy in the hideously annoying Theodorus Nitz commercials in *The Simulacra*, which take the form of parasitic insects that invade private dwellings in order to insinuate their anxiety-laden messages into the ears of the inhabitants: "In the presence of strangers do you feel you *don't quite exist?* Do they seem not to notice you, as if you were invisible? On a bus or spaceship do you sometimes look around you and discover that no one, *absolutely no one*, recognizes you or cares about you" (108). This nightmare of anonymity becomes the plight of Jason Taverner in *Flow My Tears*, as he finds himself transformed from a TV celebrity into a nonperson with no history, acquaintances, or legal records in one of Dick's Kafkaesque waking scenes. It turns out, however, that he is still in some sense the star of the show, since his new world is actually a projected drug hallucination authored for him by Alys Buckman. The play of celebrity and anonymity thus turns into another version of the secrecy of power that mirrors even as it manipulates the perceptual isolation of private experience. It makes all kinds of narrative sense, then, that when Taverner is delivered from Alys Buckman's hallucinatory pseudo-reality it is to be handed over into a frame-up for her murder constructed by Felix Buckman, her twin brother and chief of police.

Jason Taverner's metamorphosis is actually part of a group hallucination shared up until the moment of Alys Buckman's death by the police and everyone else Taverner encounters. The combination of a group hallucination constituting a trap and the plot of escaping from it recurs often in Dick's SF (and would later, via such Dick-inspired films as *The Truman Show* and *The Matrix*, become a staple of Hollywood SF). *Eye in the Sky* (1957) pioneers the strategy, using a series of group hallucinations, each under the control of a different individual within the group, and each developing into a catastrophic mode of violent oppression, to map out the pathological self-righteousness of a range of American ideologies. The 1950s suburban setting of *Time out of Joint* is based on Ragle Gumm's retreat into a fantasy world that must then be reinforced, for military purposes, by an elaborate theatrical illusion from which Gumm eventually escapes, so that within the novel realism is assigned the status of delusion and SF stands for sanity. *A Maze of Death* (1970) depicts the group hallucination of the crew of a spaceship who are interconnected by "polyencephalic fusion," originally intended as "an escape toy to amuse [them] during [their] twenty year voyage," but transformed into a violent, endless nightmare because the ship has been accidentally locked into orbit around a dead star, the orbit itself providing a fitting metaphor for the hopeless reiteration of the crew's fantasy of escape (*VALIS and Later Novels*, 160, 163).

Dick's most powerful and complex treatments of group hallucination induced by invasive SF broadcasting events are afforded by *Palmer Eldritch* and *Ubik*.[10] In *Ubik* this ultimately involves the vampiric telepathy of the adolescent Jory Miller in the "half-life" environment to which the cast of characters is consigned after they are assassinated by their commercial competitor midway through the novel. But the invasion and protection of privacy are already the substance of the commercial competition between the Hollis organization's telepaths and precogs and the "inertials" of Runciter Associates. The ruling metaphor of the entire novel is of course the ubiquity of "Ubik," the brand name that advertises its manifold products in the epigraphs that open each chapter. Its reiteration establishes the immersion of the world of *Ubik* in the discourse of advertising with its mass cultural concomitants, the reduction of news to entertainment and celebrity gossip (the task of the telepaths) and the reduction of knowledge to prediction in the pursuit of market advantage (the work of the precogs). Aside from the brand name itself, the phrase most often repeated in the epigraphs is the injunction to take or use the product "as directed," varied at its most ominous to "Warning: use only as directed. And with caution" (*Four Novels*, 663). Joe Chip's argument with his door is all about being forced to consume a product "as directed" (in this case, by including the contractually stipulated fee for the door's services). And up until the appearance of the psychic cannibal Jory, the most disturbing and dangerous character in the novel is Pat Conley, who bears upon her the tattoo warning "Caveat emptor" (*Four Novels*, 630).

The group hallucinations in the half-life environment thus literalize the entrapment in unreality by immersion in untrustworthy signs that is the novel's historical, social premise. Jory Miller's desire to consume the psyches of his victims merely inverts the epigraphs' injunctions to consume commodities, while retaining the parodic ads' fundamentally acquisitive motives. In this context it makes perfect sense that the task forced upon the protagonists is to *interrupt* the ubiquitous invasions and injunctions of mass culture, from the work of the inertials to the reality-restoring aerosol spray that saves Joe Chip from Jory Miller. But interruption can easily become another form of invasion, as in Pat Conley's terrifying ability to interrupt the present by revising the past. What if interrupting the permutations of fakery and specious realism in the discourse of advertising and mass cultural entertainment delivers one into a no-more-substantial world of SF conventions, a world where reality can be twisted and reconstructed to suit one's desires with no more trouble or responsibility than the pseudoscientific explanation Ellen Runciter gives Joe Chip for the effects of the Ubik spray? Where is the boundary between resistance to oppressive convention and taking refuge in escapist fantasy? Perhaps this sort of self-doubt is what provides the pull toward an oracular option like that offered in the final epigraph, where Ubik announces itself to be a divinity compounded of New Testament logos and Old Testament Yahweh: "*I am the word and my name is never spoken*" (*Four Novels*, 797). Should one try to read this assertion of a theological foundation for reality as offering a measure of hope for a real escape from the prison of illusion, or should one read it as the culminating hyperbole of advertising's grandiose claims about its products and the ultimate illusory confusion of the social system with the inevitable nature of things?[11]

By way of suggesting that the second option is superior to the first, I turn to my final exhibit, the invasion of Barney Mayerson's and Leo Bulero's psyches by the Palmer Eldritch thing via the drug Chew-Z in *Palmer Eldritch*. The situation in *Palmer Eldritch* develops directly out of Dick's treatment of escapist entertainment in the elaboration of Perky Pat Layouts. The Martian colonists' shared back-to-earth fantasies via Perky Pat reiterate a motif of escape from harsh reality into regressive fantasy that is also key to the popular fad of the "babylands," re-creations of one's childhood environment, in *Now Wait for Last Year*. But the most important example of the regressive fantasy world in Dick's earlier fiction is the 1950s town in *Time out of Joint*, modeled upon Ragle Gumm's delusional escape from the stress of his military role. The crucial difference between the life-size theatrical illusion in *Time out of Joint* and the miniaturized Barbie-and-Ken-doll world of Perky Pat is the conspiratorial element. The plot of *Time out of Joint* takes the form of the unwilling participants' escape from an elaborately staged governmental hoax, so that the sublime ruptures in the realist fabric of *Time out of Joint* are eventually explained away via the protagonists' breaking out into the real (that is, SF) world of the 1990s. No such explanatory recuperation of the sublime narrative rupture is possible in *Palmer Eldritch*. Instead Mayerson and Bulero find themselves precipitated into what promises to be an endless series of illusory escapes and nightmarish reimmersions in Eldritch's subuniverse. The free-fall disorientation of the narrative rupture, instead of interrupting the plot, becomes its ruling mechanism. Their plight fuses the generic registers of SF, metaphysical speculation, allegory, and satire into collusion against a realism that nonetheless continually reestablishes itself in their determined efforts to return to some sense of an authentic self.

There is no better example in Dick's work of his making reality come unglued in order to see how his characters cope with it, as the novel's epigraph turns out in retrospect to have announced. Rather than pursuing Dick's ethical theme, however, let us restrict ourselves here to the metafictional, meta-systemic implications of Dick's narrative strategy. These have to do with destabilizing the boundary between *idios kosmos* and *koinos kosmos*, not so much transcending the opposition between public and private as rendering it inoperable, and thereby exposing its effects. Making the plot itself into a trap with no escape exposes the necessary basis of the escapism of P.P. Layouts in seriality. The escapist fantasy is made effective only by its being an interlude inserted within the more or less insupportable routine of daily life. Chew-Z, in contrast, forecloses the shuttling between public and private realms that is the indispensable premise of mass cultural entertainment-as-distraction. A dream from which one cannot awaken is no longer a dream. While even the half-lifers in *Ubik* have lines of communication to those outside their group hallucination, any such possibility is radically absent in *Palmer Eldritch*.

What do we make, then, of the fact that Eldritch's victims suffer this fate at the hands of a capitalist entrepreneur who himself has been ingested by an alien who might also be God, or at least what has been passing for God for the last few millennia, and who announces the ambition of becoming "everyone on the planet" (*Four Novels*, 405) for the simplest and most circular of reasons: to perpetuate itself (*Four Novels*, 424)? As capitalist, Eldritch could be taken as a figure for exchange value that has detached itself from any notion of use, profit reproducing profit for no other reason than to reproduce itself. To turn that figure of voracious consumption and self-replication into a version of divinity is consonant with the final epigraph of *Ubik* only if the epigraph's deification of the commodity is read as intentional blasphemy. If Palmer Eldritch figures forth an "inner truth," whether that of capitalism or of the cosmos, it is a truth that attains the condition of utter absurdity precisely in proportion to its being disentangled from illusion.

. . . . .

Debate over the interpretation of Dick's metaphysics and ethics is sure to continue as long as he retains the canonical status currently accorded to him. Although Dick's status as a major writer of the midcentury seems secure, it is also likely to remain controversial for several reasons, foremost among them the obsessive and at times pathological limitations of his depiction of women—an important and perhaps ultimately crippling limitation on the capacity of his novels to serve as boundary objects for a sufficiently large enough group of readers. Another issue that will likely continue to be problematic is the relative value of his late work compared to the middle period, and particularly the foreshortening of political perspectives by the predominance of theological and psychological ones in the late period (see Suvin, "Goodbye and Hello"). What I hope to have demonstrated here is that the conjuncture of literary prestige and niche genre in the "Shakespeare of science fiction" is not merely a result of Dick's having broken into publishing in the way he did, nor is it the result of a great writer accidentally finding himself operating in a genre ghetto. Dick drew his strength as a writer from the hybrid nature of SF. Playing both the predictability and the outlandishness of the SF megatext against the conventions and the epistemological assumptions of realist fiction is at the heart of the comedy and sublimity of his best work. Dick's significance as the first SF writer to have been recruited, as it were, from the SF subculture into the literary canon (as opposed to merely achieving best-seller status, like Heinlein) is the degree to which he drew his strength from SF's generic resources.

5

Communities of Interpretation (1)

Two Hollywood Films and the Tiptree Award Anthologies

The formation of communities of practice is bound up with the construction of narrative genre categories as both cause and effect. The enormous differences between national-corporate cultures and localized subcultures are both the basis for and the ongoing effects of the stratification of the mass cultural field of production between high and low capital investment, and between mass market and niche market distribution and consumption. In the history of American SF those shifting effects of stratification underwent a number of signal developments in the second half of the twentieth century, which included in the 1950s and '60s the commercial dominance of the niche market magazines giving way to a no less niche market economy of paperback publishing, a steady trend of increasing professionalization among the community of SF writers, and SF's becoming a significant, although still decidedly minor, film genre. The impact of the British New Wave's polemical integration of literary and subcultural SF contributed to generational conflicts that were exacerbated by the antiwar movement and the emergent youth counterculture. In that same intergenerational context, the growing presence of women writers and fans of SF was a major factor. All these developments have taken on a new importance, however, because of the crucial change in the status of mass-market SF as the result of the extraordinary financial success of SF blockbuster films from George Lucas's *Star Wars* (1977) to James Cameron's *Avatar* (2009). The blockbuster economy has not undone the niche market and subcultural status of a good deal of SF, but has instead effected an emphatic bifurcation of SF between, on the one hand, the high-budget Hollywood sector and the franchise fiction that it generates, and, on the other, the proliferation and diversification of subcultural SF practices accompanied by a steadily narrowing division separating SF subcultures from literary and academic, institutional communities and practices (see Wolf 134–38, and Westfahl, "Marketplace").

The last two chapters of this study turn their attention to this reconfiguration of American SF. In this chapter I will be examining SF narratives addressed to very different audiences in vehicles employing drastically different resources. *Source Code* (2011) and *The Cabin in the Woods* (2012) are multimillion-dollar projects supported by major film studios. *The James Tiptree Award Anthology* (three volumes, 2005–7) is a relatively small-press production based on an annual award that is itself funded partly by bake sales. Although the structural division between mass and niche products persists in these examples, I hope to show that the character of the subcultural communities of practice that support contemporary niche market SF is quite radically changed from its mid-twentieth-century version.

Seriality and Escapism in *Source Code* and *The Cabin in the Woods*

I suggested in chapter 2 that mass cultural publishing's propensity for serial repetition, based on its raison d'être of producing habitual customers, has a number of important methodological consequences that make intertextual borrowing and the play of repetition and variation into privileged objects for the cultural critic, precisely because they are already so for mass cultural audiences in general. Reading a piece of genre fiction as an installment in a series—even when this is not explicitly the case—emphasizes the anonymous and collective character of the generic world. One of the ramifications of this anonymous serial intertextuality is that any given piece of genre fiction will reveal, upon inspection, metafictional, meta-generic, and meta-systemic features, not merely as an effect of scholarly or critical attention, or because of the extraordinary, self-reflexive playfulness of a Philip K. Dick, but rather as a standard, ubiquitous property of mass cultural narrative.

This metafictional effect is inseparable from the fiction's predictability. The fact that commercial pressures tend to make stories set in the generic worlds of mass cultural entertainment more or less predictable has been one of the most persistent complaints lodged against genre fiction by the advocates of high culture. From that perspective it would be no defense of the skills and the joys of prediction among connoisseurs of genre fiction to suggest that those skills and joys are cognate with the dominant form of economic and political analysis in mass cultural news, where prediction of the movements of the stock market or the outcome of the next election substitutes for critical reflection on them, as if such events were only another form of that other mass cultural staple, the sporting event, and all of them more or less consubstantial with the weather. The withering effect of such reification upon political and economic discourses has been one of the core observations of ideology critique throughout the twentieth century, from Lukács to Barthes to Jameson. But considering prognostication as a form of cognition should also lead us to recognize that the habitual consumers of mass cultural genre fiction, like corporate economists, analysts of electoral politics, and oddsmakers in the sports betting industry, constitute communities of knowledge with highly specific skills and protocols of interpretation.

Perhaps the clearest example is the gamelike, puzzle-solving aspect of crime fiction. Predicting the outcome of a criminal investigation, which is certainly one of the pleasures that audiences of such fiction expect and demand, depends not at all on understanding police work, very little on exercising logical deduction, and very heavily on understanding the conventions of crime fiction. However, the way any given piece of fiction deploys these conventions, intertwining them with the personal lives and romantic involvements of the main characters or with the economic and social framework of criminality and the legal system, varies enormously. Hence the interpretation and evaluation of such narratives need to attend to the tension the text establishes between its own individuality and its conventionality, and this tension will depend upon the way its storytelling strategies engage and fulfill, refuse, or modify the generic worlds and systemic motives of its milieu.

A powerfully self-reflexive turn surfaced in the Hollywood SF of the

1990s, as suffocating, oppressive enclosure within the confines of a generic, metafictional world became a major theme, first with the success of *The Truman Show* (1998, director Peter Weir, worldwide box office approximately $264 million).[1] The plot, loosely based on Dick's *Time out of Joint*, involves the protagonist's escape from an elaborate theatrical illusion. His entire life has been lived within an enormous studio set constructed exclusively for the purpose of broadcasting a television show in which he is the unwitting hero, everyone else is a paid actor, and every day is much the same as the previous one. It is precisely the predictability and repetitions that begin to alert Truman (Jim Carrey) to the suspicion that he is being manipulated and lied to (the fact that his wife [Laura Linney] breaks into a commercial for coffee in the middle of a domestic argument strengthens his doubts). The conflict between Truman's attempt to break out into the real world and the claims of the director (Ed Harris) that the show's version of small-town America is far better than the so-called real world matches the tension between the audience's vicarious experience of an idyllically uncomplicated, "normal" life of work and family routines and their sympathetic desire to see Truman liberate himself from his virtual prison.

The plot of escape from an immersive illusion then achieved greater success and influence in the Wachowski brothers' trilogy *The Matrix* (1999, worldwide box office $463 million), *The Matrix Reloaded* (2003, $739 million), and *The Matrix Revolutions* (2003, $427 million). *The Matrix* trilogy is typical of Hollywood blockbusters in its generic hybridity.[2] It combines its Dickian metaphysical and conspiratorial elements with the cyberpunk trope of virtual reality and liberal doses of Gothic styling, Asian martial arts, and a romance subplot with a strong fairy-tale allusion to Sleeping Beauty, all of them assembled around the main plot of the messianic rise of Neo, the protagonist (Keanu Reeves), to the status of savior of the human race from the machine intelligences that have enslaved it. The key neo-Dickian element is the machines' projection of the cinematic audience's present as the illusionary virtual reality that enables the machine intelligences to use their bodies as an energy source—the fossil fuel of this dystopian future. The machines' use of the daily routines of the late twentieth- or early twenty-first-century world as panacea to its enslaved population therefore constitutes a kind of allegory of the ruling class or "the system's" present-day hegemony. The films' best line, "Welcome to the desert of the real," spoken in *The Matrix* by the John the Baptist figure, Morpheus (Laurence Fishburne), when he awakens Neo from the virtual 1990s into the real twenty-third century, thus epitomizes an undercurrent of popular resentment (if not outrage) at the sense that contemporary political and economic power hides its fundamentally exploitive and repressive nature in a near-impenetrable web of lies—most fundamentally, this study has argued, in the very form of the advertisement as a lie that proclaims itself to be a lie, but nevertheless establishes a rhetorical regime of opportunistic untruth that pervades the news and political discourse.

The plot of escape from an immersive illusion and the themes that typically accompany it persist in a pair of more recent mass cultural big-budget blockbuster films, Duncan Jones's *Source Code* (2011) and Drew Goddard and Joss Whedon's *The Cabin in the Woods* (2012). Both engage as explicit subject matter the workings of seriality, prognostication, and the formation of communities within the apparatus of mass culture. Their plots of escape inevitably reflect upon the escapism that seems endemic to their milieu. In the reading of these two films that follows I am exploring the tension between, on the one hand, the otherworldliness of the collective fantasies that provide a foundation for mass culture's "imagined communities," and, on the other, the way that the fiction self-consciously reflects both upon the mundane routines that are the premise of mass cultural entertainment and on the generic repetitiveness that forms part, but definitely not all, of its substance.

Source Code and *The Cabin in the Woods* (*SC* and *CITW*) proclaim their self-consciously metafictive, meta-generic, meta-systemic significance in the fact that each involves an elaborately constructed story within the story. The motives driving the production of this interior narrative and the relation of the actors in the story within the story to the outer narrative frame form the thematic core of each film. The sites of production in both films are control rooms located at a firmly separated distance from the foreground drama, and in both cases this distance and separation suggest and parody broadcast technology. Both of the control rooms dictate scripts to a set of foreground actors, some of whom are aware that they are acting a part in a scripted drama, but most of whom, unaware of the artificiality of their environment, mistake this carefully crafted, immersive illusion for reality itself. In both cases the actors must follow the control room's script in order to save the world, which in both cases means to preserve the status quo from violent disruption—and the status quo is firmly identified with the maintenance of the control room's power to dictate the script. In *SC* this control room is under the command of the American military, while the quasi-corporate control room in *CITW* coordinates its efforts with a suggestively transnational and global network of operations. Thus the apparatus of power in *SC* is straightforwardly a police force, while in *CITW* it somewhat more ambiguously resembles the corporate media and the entertainment industry, but also, as we will see, invokes the ideological authority of the law itself.

Repetition and predictability figure heavily into both films in ways that directly invoke mass cultural narrative production and reception. The narratives themselves rely crucially on mechanisms of repetition—in *SC* an eight-minute time loop that the hero must repeatedly renegotiate in the search for a mad terrorist bomber; in *CITW* a carefully orchestrated sacrificial ritual that parodies formulaic horror films. Prognostication figures into *SC* in the way the hero gradually masters and responds to the sequence of events in the time loop. In *CITW*, alongside a string of jokes about horror cinema formulas, the employees in the control room conduct a lottery concerning the choices the sacrificial victims will make as to the exact mode of their deaths. But the primary form of prognostication is the rigging of the entire situation for an outcome dictated by the control room's motives, and this does not turn out well for the control room in either film. In both cases the actors manage to partially elude the control room's script and assert a measure of command over their own destinies. The two films arrive at antithetical resolutions, however, with *SC* and *CITW* offering, respectively, a happy ending versus an apocalypse, heroic rescue versus spectacular slaughter, and romance and identification versus parody and distance. These diametrically opposed resolutions amount to something like the antithetical meanings of a primal word: escape.

The more or less deliberate (more in *CITW*, less in *SC*) commentary the two films end up making on their own fictional and institutional status turns upon the escapist function of mass cultural entertainment. As in

The Truman Show and *The Matrix* in their very different ways, the two stories within a story are traps set in place by the control rooms to manipulate the actors. The plots of the frame stories turn on the protagonists becoming aware of their entrapment and escaping from it. But the diegetic escape that happens within the narratives inevitably reflects upon the extra-diegetic escape offered by the narrative itself from the nonnarrative, everyday world of the actual cinematic audience. In the light of this form of escape it is crucial that, although the control rooms in *SC* and *CITW* present themselves as enacting the most noble and public-spirited of motives (saving the world), their motives are also exposed as rationalizations for the state's and the corporate media's self-interested manipulation of news and entertainment. Within this context, then, escape can signify either succumbing to the pleasures offered by the manipulative delusion or the act of exploding its illusory reality and extricating oneself from its conspiratorial mechanism—that is, either assuming the passive role of a mass cultural consumer or achieving some posture of critical or subcultural resistance to the culture's hegemonic codes and motives. The question, then, is how the films' antithetical conclusions negotiate these alternatives.

SC begins when the protagonist, Captain Colter Stevens of the U.S. military (Jake Gyllenhaal), finds himself mysteriously inhabiting the body of a schoolteacher, Sean Fentress, aboard a commuter train heading into Chicago's business district from the suburbs, and engaged in the middle of an incomprehensible conversation with an attractive young woman named Christina (Michelle Monaghan). At the end of eight minutes, the train blows up, and Stevens finds himself in another mysterious, sealed environment, this time in conversation via computer screen with an attractive female military officer, Colleen Goodwin (Vera Farmiga). We learn that the experience Stevens has just had on the train is based on residual memories in the brain of Fentress, who, like everyone else aboard the train, died that morning in the explosion. Stevens has been inserted into Fentress's dying memories via a new technology called "source code," so that, by replaying Fentress's experience, he can discover the bomber, communicate the bomber's identity to his superiors, and thereby prevent a second, much larger attack on the same afternoon that involves detonating a thermonuclear weapon in downtown Chicago. The film consists of eight successive replays of the train sequence, punctuated by Captain Stevens's interactions with the control room in between the replays—in effect shuttling between conversations with Christina and Goodwin and developing alliances with both.

The resolution involves Stevens not only discovering the identity of the bomber but also preventing the explosion on the train, which isn't supposed to be possible because the source code time loop is only a virtual reality. As the military command repeatedly tells Stevens, the explosion has already happened in real time, and the fate of his fellow passengers is irrelevant to his mission because they are already dead. But when Stevens prevents the bomb from exploding and thus releases the train and its passengers from the eight-minute time loop, the ontological status of the story within the story escapes its determination by the "real world" of the frame. The effect is one common to time travel stories, which, as David Wittenberg has shown in *Time Travel: The Popular Philosophy of Narrative*, often literalize and make into substantial plot events the purely formal way that the *fabula* or the underlying sequence of actual events assumed in a realist narrative is routinely violated by the *sjuzhet* or the act of storytelling itself. Stevens is thus able to elude the unethical control of the careerist scientist who has invented source code, Colonel Rutledge (Jeffrey Wright), by transforming Rutledge's high-tech control room into a "narratological laboratory" instead (Wittenberg 2). Stevens does not defy his mission orders to identity the bomber, whom he now arrests *before* the bomber can set off the first bomb in the train. Rather, he violates the boundary separating Rutledge's version of the *fabula* from his own *sjuzhet*, taking control of the story and rewriting it so that the scientist's role is quite literally removed from the loop.

Stevens's escape from Dr. Rutledge's laboratory is rendered problematic and even gruesome, however, by the fact that it involves Stevens's disembodied consciousness setting up permanent residence in the body of Fentress. This is a happy ending, even though it is formally similar to an invasion of the body snatchers (see chapter 6). Not only is Stevens himself, like his fellow passengers, considered officially dead because of massive injuries suffered in combat that left only his brain intact; but also Fentress has been chatting up Christina for quite some time but has not had the courage to ask her out. Endowing the timid schoolteacher with the alpha male consciousness of Stevens solves that problem, so that, in Stevens's rewritten story, when the commuter train arrives unharmed in Chicago, Fentress and Christina take the day off in order to spend it with each other. The romantic couple is united, and even though the question of who exactly is walking into the figurative sunset with Christina remains unanswerable, the generic demands of the film's romance plot are satisfactorily fulfilled. Nonetheless the resolution enacts the fulfillment of Sean's and Christina's romantic fantasy in a curiously gamelike fashion, as if Fentress finally wins his personal dating game by adopting Stevens as his avatar.

Stevens's repeated runs through the time loop are in fact very much like a game player learning his way through a set of obstacles.[3] The important thing is not simply that he masters the sequence of events, however, but that in his dealings with his fellow passengers he gradually extricates himself from the military protocol that commanded him to consider them irrelevant. The setting of the commuter train itself is crucial. Riding the train is of course a kind of ritual based on serial repetition. The passengers are exactly the kind of intimate strangers that form the imagined community of the nation, according to Anderson and Ohmann. The train journey shuttles between the passengers' private lives and their workplaces, mirroring or prefiguring Stevens's negotiation of the chasm between military command and civilian interaction. The exact moment of Stevens's winning the game—that is, the moment in his eighth and final run through the time loop when the bomb fails to go off and he is freed to pursue his budding relationship with Christina—is telling. It is set up by Stevens's bad relations with some of the other passengers during the earlier sequences, when he brutalized several innocent suspects and drew a number of derisive comments from one in particular, a dour and unhappy man who also, Christina informs Stevens, is a successful stand-up comic. During the final sequence Stevens bets the comedian all the money in his wallet that he cannot make everyone in the train car laugh. At the moment when the bomb does not go off, the camera pans in slow motion a freeze frame of all the passengers in the car laughing. The shot signals that this disparate group connected only by a common route on the train has been melded into something different, not the batch of suspects seen from the military perspective of the state or even the imagined community of the nation, but an audience.

But if the device of the freeze frame successfully emphasizes that this is the crucial moment of disconnection from the military *fabula*'s moment of doom, it also seems to confess that this fusion of a serial assemblage of people into a quasi-community is only an ephemeral moment stolen from the routine that assembles them. Their role as an audience is inserted into a sequence that includes their being passengers on the commuter train, shuttling between private and public domains. Their momentary escape from their dull daily routine only reinforces the codependence and supplementarity of the roles of citizen and consumer, their sequential connection within a coherent set of rituals and institutions. Even the Sean Fentress / Colter Stevens identity's private moment of escape, playing hooky from school in order to hook up with Christina, is entirely compatible with his military duty. Rather than defying the military, his actions correct a corruption in the system. He claims no more than an unobjectionable just reward or fair wage for his services, and his escape from the official *fabula* or "real world" is precisely that just reward. As a story about storytelling, mass cultural entertainment, and the nation, then, *Source Code* articulates precisely the way that "escape" remains wholly confined within and harmonious with the "real world." The Stevens/Fentress hybrid is outlandish and impossible, of course, because it resolves the contradictions between the public and the private, the imperatives of the system and the desires of the individual, and this contradiction—not Colonel Rutledge's ethical shortcomings or the fatalistic imperatives of his time loop—is the kernel of reality that can be evaded only by entering the realm of the impossible.

The role that escapist entertainment plays in protecting "the system" from its own contradictions is the explicit satirical target of *CITW*. The entire plot, including its apocalyptic ending, constitutes a running joke about the formulaic predictability of horror cinema. This meta-generic satire becomes meta-systemic in several ways. First of all, the film draws a clear analogy between the control room apparatus and the entertainment industry. Second, it draws an equally clear identification of the control room employees with the cinematic audience. Finally, the film transforms the idea that genre itself is a contract between producers and audiences into a bizarre and grotesque parody of the Hobbesian social contract.

The plot of *CITW*, in which five unsuspecting college students take a camping trip that is an elaborate set-up designed to reduce their behavior to a series of ritual transgressions and their identities to a rigidly defined set of types who must then be slain in the precise order demanded by the ritual, is first of all an amalgamation of allusions to horror films and a stream of jokes about their predictability. For instance, the girl who must be first to die, the Whore, has dyed her hair blond the morning they leave on the trip. Unknown to her, the control room's Chemistry Department has contaminated her dye with chemicals that raise her libido and lower her inhibitions and her intelligence; the dye is literally a formula for producing a Dumb Blonde. Other fetishistic details of the ritual obviously refer to other specific ways that horror formulas enact misogynistic gender ideology. The Blonde *must* expose her breasts before she can be slain. The Virgin *must* be the last one left alive, the Final Girl of slasher-film convention.

Portraying the standard horror film as a fetishistic sacrificial ritual of course raises the question of why audiences revel in such spectacular violence, but the film's satire directs itself to the routinization of violence rather than to any exploration of psychological motives. This becomes clearest in the film's handling of the topic of choice. A cardinal point in the ritual procedure is the necessity that the victims choose the mode of their punishment. As the five of them are lured into a cellar full of creepy objects, each of which, if picked up and manipulated by the curious students, will unleash a specific monstrosity upon them, the two managers in the control room explain to a newcomer that "they have to make the choice of their own free will. Otherwise, system doesn't work. . . . Yeah, we rig the game as much as we have to but in the end, if they don't transgress, they can't be punished" (Whedon and Goddard 78). While they deliver this speech, the managers are also counting up the money from an office betting pool regarding which monsters the students will unwittingly unleash upon themselves.[4] In contrast to the military devotion to duty espoused in the control room of *SC*, the whole operation is just a day at the office for the control room crew in *CITW*.

The most telling scene, in this respect, and in some ways the highlight of the entire film, is the wrap party celebrated in the control room when the crew thinks that all the ritual obligations have been satisfied. The Virgin or Final Girl is still alive, but all the rest are dead (they think), and the

Final Girl's death is optional. All that is necessary, the managers assure the newcomer, is that she suffer. And suffer she does, her suffering displayed on multiple screens in the background as the crew engages in an utterly banal office party in front of them, unaware that they are acting out yet another well-worn horror convention, the false ending. But quite aside from its play on generic conventions, what the party scene outrageously displays is the ethos of the control room in *CITW*, which is centered not on duty but disavowal. The employees in the control room dutifully participate in the routine of maintaining "the system," which is to say the ritual sacrifice of young adults to the ancient, bloodthirsty gods who demand it, but they somehow manage also to detach themselves from their participation, as if the consequences of what they do were somehow not real. Amid all the meta-generic and self-referential jokes, this attitude of habitual, taken-for-granted detachment of work from its consequences is the film's core satirical target.

The way the office workers substitute prognostication for critical reflection—betting on the victims' choices rather than contemplating their suffering or allowing their devotion to public duty to be disrupted by any sense of responsibility for that suffering—helps to sharpen the film's focus on the topic of choice. The systematic insistence that the victims of the ritual must exercise the choice to "transgress" connects it to the capacity to define transgression that is the unique authority of the law itself. The ritual then takes the shape of a parodic rendition of Hobbes's theory of the social contract, a means by which a state of ubiquitous violence (the reign of the ancient ones) has been overcome by transforming it into institutional state violence. "Transgression" paradoxically does not mean defiance of the law so instituted but rather its fulfillment, the victim's choice of one of the acceptable options for completing the ritual. Although the law's rationale is to maintain a certain kind of order, this is something quite different from the law's *desire*, which is to exact punishment. This desire rules the narrative logic of *CITW*, as it translates the law's ritual reenactment of a primal bloodlust into the narrative terms of a demand for serial repetition of horror formulas. The options that the victims can activate by their "transgressive" investigations in the cabin cellar amount to a veritable compendium of cinematic monstrosities. But just as Stevens manages to evade Colonel Stevens's *fabula*, two of the intended ritual victims escape the story within a story and find a way to alter the frame narrative. They do so by finding a way to violate the principle of repetition that rules the control room's plot construction, not by defying the logic of repetition but by overabundantly fulfilling it—that is, by choosing all the options on the menu at once. The film's final third then becomes a carnivalesque celebration of the horror megatext that turns horror cinema's spectacular violence into a kind of special-effects slapstick comedy.

The apocalyptic ending, too, turns upon the issue of choices and their limitation to a menu of prescribed options. In the final scene the Director of the anonymous corporation (Sigourney Weaver) informs Marty the Fool (Fran Kranz), whose survival has disrupted the ritual and prevented its satisfactory completion, that the only choice he has is whether to die *with* everyone else or *for* everyone else. Marty refuses to save the world by killing himself, and the ancient ones do indeed arise, bringing the world as we know it to an end. The final moment in the film shows a giant fist rising up out of the earth and smashing down on the camera's point of view, at which point the screen goes completely dark. One way to read its emptiness is as the end of the reign of prediction. If the barrier protecting private conscience from public responsibility depended upon ritual repetition to simultaneously sacralize and automatize the operations of a ruling elite's corporate power, demolishing that barrier might bring to an end the reified science of mass cultural prognostication where analysis always yields another version of the same. This would indeed be a more radical form of escape, but it is also where the film's purview ends. Within its celebratory send-up of the horror genre, wiping the menu clean of the prescribed options yields not something new but nothing at all, nothing to choose from. This blank, indeterminate evocation of impossibility is antithetical to *SC*'s withdrawal into private fantasy. It is an escape rendered in the wholly negative terms of the impossibility of imagining its details within the constraints of the present menu of possibilities. *CITW* does not venture beyond this threshold, but it does at least intimate its existence.

In tracing out their antithetical modes of escape, *SC* and *CITW* are not simply two stories about storytelling. They are high-budget, mass-market films that depict storytelling very much in the terms of blockbuster cinema, as a complex and sophisticated technological achievement aimed at the creation of an immersive illusion, represented in each film as a sealed environment into which a carefully managed flow of information is released in order to manipulate the beliefs and actions of those within it. This scenario does not resemble the way stories help to form and support beliefs in everyday life nearly so well as it resembles the way commercial advertising and political propaganda alike envelop information in distraction and disguise manipulation as entertainment. One could say that the meta-systemic bottom line of these two films' metafictive narratives is the instrumentalization of the aesthetic by the "control room," which takes the form in these films of a conspiratorial representation of the state and of big media. The predictability of the stories-within-the-stories functions as a symptom of the artificiality of the "worlds" constructed in the films' sealed environments and, at the same time, as a means for those trapped within them to come to know how they work and how to gain some kind of enhanced agency within them, especially by forming horizontal alliances against the vertical, top-down imposition of definitions of the lawful, the possible, and the necessary. The horizontal alliances in these films remain private and individual affairs, however, and there is an undeniably self-serving quality in their invitation to identify heroism with defiance of the control room even while the films emanating from such control rooms use the fantasy of resistance to "the system" to sell their product. In turning now to a set of texts produced from a very different position within the distribution of resources and constraints in the contemporary field of production, we pass from the mass market and its discontents to a set of horizontal and anti-hegemonic alliances formed by a thriving subculture: that comprised by the feminist SF convention WisCon as it is constructed in the series of anthologies exemplifying and celebrating the annual Tiptree Awards given at WisCon since 1991.

Positioning SF in the Tiptree Award Anthologies

> "Science fiction" has moved on, you know, with anthropologists
> and such writing it. Not many rockets now.—Alice Sheldon,
> letter to Rudolph Arnheim, January 1972

One of the most knowledgeable and acute scholars of SF's commercial publishing history, Gary K. Wolfe, makes a convincing case for the crucial role played by anthologies in the history of science fiction. According to Wolfe, a series of commercial anthologies, beginning with Donald A. Wollheim's 1943 *Pocket Book of Science-Fiction*, followed by Groff Conklin's *The Best of Science Fiction* (1946), *A Treasury of Science Fiction* (1948), and *The Big Book of Science Fiction* (1950); Raymond Healy and Frank McComas's *Adventures in Time and Space* (1946); and John W. Campbell's *The Astounding Science Fiction Anthology* (1952), transformed "science fiction" so designated from an almost exclusively niche market "set of [pulp] text-products" into "a widely recognized and identifiable genre" in the book publishing industry by the later 1950s (G. Wolfe 12–15). Because of these anthologies "finding their way into public libraries, . . . science fiction now had a more or less permanent set of reference texts from which to derive its lasting ideologies" (15). The role of anthologies in consolidating the "lasting ideologies" by which SF writers and readers self-identify might be further illustrated by the way Philip E. Wegner cites three landmark anthologies to illustrate his periodizing history of the three main phases of SF's development: "*Mirrorshades: The Cyberpunk Anthology* (1986) . . . [was] to postmodern science fiction what Ellison's *Dangerous Visions* [1967] was to the preceding modernist period, or *The Science Fiction Hall of Fame, Volume One, 1929–64* (1970) was, retrospectively, to an even earlier science fictional realism" (36).[5] The present argument has to do with the shifting demographics of SF's subcultures from the 1970s on, in which context the anthologies most notably performing the ideological task of identifying a selective tradition within SF and therefore convening a community of practice on the ground of a shared ideological recognition would include Pamela Sargent's three *Women of Wonder* anthologies (1975, 1976, and 1978), which established an alternative canon of women's writing in SF counter to the white-male-dominated canons of Conklin, Healy and McComas, Campbell, and the *SF Hall of Fame*; Sheree Thomas's two *Dark Matters* anthologies (2000 and 2004), which performed the same task for African American writers; and Grace W. Dillon's *Walking the Clouds: An Anthology of Indigenous Science Fiction* (2012). Alongside these programmatic anthologies one might well align such formally and generically ambitious compilations as *Feeling Very Strange: The Slipstream Anthology*, edited by James Patrick Kelly and John Kessel (2006), and *The New Weird*, edited by Ann and Jeff Vandermeer (2008).

Some questions one might pose about the *James Tiptree Award Anthol-

ogy (volume 1, 2005; volume 2, 2006; and volume 3, 2007) edited by Karen Joy Fowler, Pat Murphy, Debbie Notkin, and Jeffrey D. Smith, then, are what set of ideologies informs its selection of texts, what genre boundaries those selections reinforce or challenge, and what community of practice the anthology constructs in the process.[6] The obvious answer to these questions, that the three volumes document the practices and choices of the James Tiptree Award selection committees, only shifts the terms of the questions slightly. What then is the significance of this award? What community of practice has invented and nurtured it, with what historical precedents, and to what ends? These are in turn questions with obvious answers that the anthologies are eloquently and abundantly eager to answer. I want to pay all due attention to these answers, first, and then use them as a basis for understanding the peculiar and powerful position this anthology stakes out in contemporary genre practices—a position that has everything to do not only with forming horizontal alliances among people but also with drawing strength from connecting and hybridizing genres.

The Tiptree Award's origin, purpose, and methods of selection are set forth in the editorial introductions to each volume and in Suzy McKee Charnas's "Judging the Tiptree," an account in volume 1 of her own role in the first and subsequent Tiptree Award selection committees (1:93–104). The Tiptree Award, as many readers will already know, is the brainchild of Karen Joy Fowler and Pat Murphy, who concocted it, as Murphy puts it, "to make trouble" (1:ix)—specifically, to counteract what they saw as a misogynist backlash in the late '80s against the advance of women writers into the SF field in the '70s and '80s, by dedicating an award to writing that stirs up "gender trouble."[7] Hence the naming of the award commemorates not only an important woman writer of the '70s but also the literary and epistolary cross-gender performance of "Tiptree" by Alice Sheldon (the anthology includes two of Sheldon's letters [1:19–28 and 2:11–14], an account of the Sheldon archive by her biographer, Julie Phillips [2:3–10], and a short biographical piece on Sheldon by Joanna Russ [1:187–90]) and the notorious controversies fomented by its revelation *as* a performance. At that point, as L. Timmel Duchamp puts it in her posthumous letter to Sheldon, "when you lost the masculinity of the name, the worldliness of your work lost all credibility" (3:195). Fowler concisely summarizes the "conundrum" posed by the Tiptree event thus:

Is James Tiptree, Jr. a woman? Or is James Tiptree, Jr. a man made up by a woman? And if so which one of them, the man or the woman, wrote the stories?

Does it make a difference? Why? (1:xii)

All of this means, first, that a heavy emphasis ought to be put on the theatrical connotations of the word "roles" in the official language that, since the first selection committee formulated it, has described the award's intention to honor writing that "expands and explores gender roles" (1:94); and, second, that the whole topic of the cultural and discursive formation of subjects and identities—and the materiality of the bodies that support or suffer those identities—is very much a part of the anthology's concerns.

Charnas's account of the selection process spends a lot of its time listing the many questions that the first committee asked itself as it sought to define its purpose. The two most important sets of questions in the present context are those related to feminism and those related to genre. In the former instance, Is this really an award for feminist SF? If so, why not say so? If not, how is it different? In the latter, Should the award be restricted to SF and fantasy, or should it honor writing that explores and expands gender roles in any genre? These questions take much of their force from the provenance of the award itself in the feminist SF convention, WisCon, held annually since 1971, and since 1991 the site for the awarding of the Tiptree. Jeffrey D. Smith's introduction to the third volume gives an account of the development of these questions over the following decade and a half, pointing out that the award has not been restricted to feminist work, and detailing the ways the generic character of the winners and short-listed works has steadily moved beyond the boundaries of the SF and fantasy field to include mainstream realist novels, nonfiction, and slash fanfiction. At the same time he welcomes seeing other groups "emerge from the WisCon DNA soup," especially the Carl Brandon Society, "which looks at race and society the way we [the Tiptree Awards] look at gender" (3:xii). Altogether, then, the anthology's editorial apparatus represents the Tiptree Award as an institution and WisCon as the meeting ground for a community of practice that, beyond merely resisting identification of SF with the conventions and canons rooted in the mid-twentieth-century, male-dominated niche market, work actively to reposition the genre in a broader, more diverse set of literary possibilities as well as a non-heteronormative and antihegemonic set of cultural and political alignments.

This repositioning is embodied in a set of narrative texts—mostly taken from the most recent set of prize winners and short-listed pieces prior to each volume's publication, but supplemented in each volume by several carefully chosen earlier texts—that constitute as good an example of "the literature of cognitive estrangement" as one could wish for. But, as Rhys Williams concedes in his recent argument for salvaging what is best in Suvin's theory of SF, cognitive estrangement has nothing to do with purifying SF of contamination by noncognitive genres like fantasy or the fairy tale. The cognition at stake is not tied to disciplinary sciences, according to Williams, but rather to "an understanding of social reality and human possibility as being historically and materially contingent" (623). Phil Wegner likewise contends that it is SF's "deep and abiding materialism, its commitment to demonstrating both the mutability of our historical circumstances and our all too human agency in shaping that reality" that is at stake in Suvin's efforts "to distinguish science fiction from 'non-cognitive' practices of estrangement such as modern fantasy" (69). But the Tiptree anthology demonstrates that "the supreme science fictional operation Darko Suvin terms *cognitive estrangement*, teaching the reader or viewer, through the rigorous narrative production of an-other world, to look at their own situation in a new and critical light" (Wegner 206) is not uniquely science fictional, or even nonrealist, at all. What makes a realist depiction of the other world of someone suffering from dissociative identity disorder, like the protagonists of Matt Ruff's *Set This House in Order*, the 2003 Tiptree winner, any less cognitively estranging than SF depictions of the experience of a visitor to another planet or a resident in a future society? If the science-fictional stories in the Tiptree anthology release or exploit the generic resources of what Suvin called the novum, the totalizing realization of another possible world that reflects critically on the restriction of freedom and justice in our own, they do so by hybridizing rather than purifying the genre, by connecting the resources of SF to neighboring genres such as fantasy, the fairy tale, and popular romance. And they do so, to a significant extent, by also drawing upon the overlapping of academic and commercial interpretive protocols in the WisCon / Tiptree Award community of practice. What the fiction in the Tiptree anthology achieves is not the fulfillment of some sort of formal destiny inherent in SF but rather the performance of a set of ethically and politically charged narrative possibilities forged in an actively resistant dialogue with dominant gender norms.

The fundamental coherence of the fiction is of course based on the criteria of the award—exploring and expanding gender roles, or, as I said earlier, playing changes on the cultural and discursive formation of subjects and identities and the materiality of the bodies that support or suffer those identities. Some of the familiar SF plots include strangers in strange lands (for example, L. Timmel Duchamp, "The Gift"), alien invasions (Joe Haldeman, *Camouflage*), prosthetic reconfigurations of sexual reproduction (Geoff Ryman, "Birth Days"), and war between the sexes (Carol Emshwiller, "Boys"). Many of the settings involve imaginary sex-gender systems, sometimes within an anthropological framework of radical cultural difference (Ruth Nestvold, "Looking through Lace"), sometimes within a biological framework of species difference (Vonda McIntyre, "Little Faces"). Alongside these SF elements there is just as persistently a playing upon and twisting or queering of popular romance, ranging from fairy tale adaptations (Nalo Hopkinson, "The Glass Bottle Trick") to supernatural teenage sex comedy (Eileen Gunn and Leslie What, "Nirvana High"), to doomed, mutually destructive love affairs (Jonathan Lethem, "Five Fucks"). A fitting emblem for the way that imagining other worlds and promoting a politics of alliance complement one another in the anthology is Ursula Le Guin's "Mountain Ways," which portrays a closeted, cross-dressed homosexual and a closeted heterosexual helping one another to negotiate the demands of a sex-gender system based on compulsory bisexuality.

The generic mix leans most heavily toward science fiction, but only about half of the twenty-eight stories are easily classified as science fiction (fourteen if you count Fowler's "What I Didn't See," which won a Nebula Award but is realist in every formal respect). There is a significant thread of fairy tale and fairy tale adaptations, including Hans Christian Andersen's "The Snow Queen" and two adaptations of it (Kara Dalkey, "The Lady of the Ice Garden," and Kelly Link, "Travels with the Snow Queen"), Hopkinson's adaptation of "Bluebeard," Jaye Lawrence's "Kissing Frogs," and what one might call a meta–fairy tale, Margo Lanagan's "Wooden Bride." There is another set of stories that resist easy classification, forcing one to resort to labels such as slipstream or experimental nonrealism (Emshwiller's "Boys" and "All of Us Can Almost... ," Lethem's "Five Fucks," and Aimee Bender's "Dearth"). There are two or three fantasy pieces (three if you count "Wooden Bride"), two young-adult stories, two pieces of realist fiction (if you count Fowler). Adding to the anthology's generic diversity is the interesting mixture of nonfiction pieces—in addition to Duchamp's epistle to Sheldon and the other material already mentioned, a speech by Le Guin bemoaning the denigration of "genre fiction," an essay on the vast array of sexual differences in the animal world by Gwyneth Jones, an appreciative assessment of Octavia Butler's fiction by Dorothy Allison, and two partly autobiographical and partly polemical pieces, Nalo Hopkinson's guest-of-honor speech to the 2002 WisCon, "Looking for Clues," and Pam Noles's "Shame."

One of the important things about these nonfiction pieces is the way they signal the intersection of fan and academic communities in the WisCon/Tiptree ensemble. Hopkinson's and Noles's essays contain remarkably similar accounts of the experience of being adolescent nonwhite fans of SF and fantasy who were moved to tears by their first encounters with a figure in the field who validated their own racial identities—for Hopkinson, seeing a cover photo that let her know for the first time that Samuel R. Delany is black; for Noles, the discovery of black protagonists in Le Guin's Earthsea trilogy (2:116, 3:97). Both of them address themselves to fan communities in the present in which they write (1990 for Noles), and Hopkinson concludes her speech by graciously acknowledging the importance of WisCon itself: "I treasure more than I can say spaces like this, that make it possible for us to gather, to talk and argue about this literature that we all love, and to challenge ourselves to push its boundaries" (2:118). Alongside these addresses to the fan community that underlies the entire institution of the Tiptree Award, the editors of the anthology have selected a few decidedly academic pieces, including Dorothy Allison's essay on Octavia Butler and Gwyneth Jones's "The Brains of Female Hyena Twins," a paper originally presented at the conference of the Academic Fantastic Fiction Network in 1994 in which Jones extensively engages *The Differ-*

ences between the Sexes as it is explored in a volume by that title comprising the published proceedings of the Eleventh International Conference on Comparative Physiology. This overlapping of fandom and the academy in the anthology's addressees justifies putting special emphasis on the way that allusive or direct use of academic, disciplinary discourses in the fiction interacts with its deployment of popular romance and SF conventions.

A story that impressively gathers together a number of the different generic threads in the anthology is Le Guin's "Another Story or A Fisherman of the Inland Sea" (2:185–226). SF readers will immediately recognize not only that it is another installment in Le Guin's career-long-running series of Hainish stories (as is "Mountain Ways"), but also that it begins with a direct allusion to the most famous and influential of the Hainish pieces, *The Left Hand of Darkness* (1969), one of the five retrospective winners of the Tiptree Award: "I shall make my report as if I told a story, this having been the tradition for some time now" (2:185).[8] As in *The Left Hand of Darkness*, the story is presented as a report to "the Stabiles of the Ekumen on Hain" (1:185), and although the quasi-anthropological and ethnographic dimensions of this report are a good deal less pronounced than in *The Left Hand of Darkness*, the inclusion of a folktale from the narrator's home culture is an important framing device. However, instead of the invented myths and legends of *The Left Hand of Darkness* (or of *Always Coming Home* [1985], where Le Guin pushes the form of the fictional ethnography to its most complete realization in her oeuvre), the legend in "Another Story" is an actual Japanese folktale, the tale of Urashima, "The Fisherman of the Inland Sea." The story of the fisherman who is seduced away from home and family by an underwater princess, only to return and find his family long dead, is then recast as SF in the narrator's story of being seduced away from his childhood love by career ambition, falling out of temporal sync with her during his nearly-as-fast-as-light interstellar travel, and finally, in what all SF readers would recognize as a play on the well-worn convention of the time loop, finding a way to change his earlier decision, stay at home with his love, and thereby consign the entire world based on his previous decisions to a "crease" in the fabric of space-time. Thus Le Guin melds folktale, scientific report, time-travel paradox, and the fundamental romance plot into this masterly hybridized piece of SF.

The plot of anthropological investigation, obviously promising ground for the topics of the Tiptree criteria, produces another joining of quasi-academic and popular-romantic material in Ruth Nestvold's "Looking through Lace" (1:131–86). The key to this story, which is punctuated throughout by brief documentary reports of the "xenolinguistic" specialists of an "Allied Interstellar Research Association first contact team" (1:141), is contained in two successive translations of the same native legend. The first, informed by the research team's male-dominant gender ideology, is titled "the legend of the little lace maker" (1:144–45). The second, corrected by the female protagonist's understanding of the native culture's female-dominant cultural arrangements, is titled "the story of the young poet" (1:179). The protagonist's scientific triumph is ironically simultaneous with her erotic deflation, however, as she realizes that the budding romance she thought herself engaged in with an attractive male aristocrat is actually based on the conscription of a slave to provide her sexual service.

The strongest connection between fiction and academic form in the anthology comes in the two pieces cast in the form of mock-academic essays, Raphael Carter's "Congenital Agenesis of Gender Ideation by K. N. Sirsi and Sandra Botkin" (2:15–30) and Richard Calder's "The Catgirl Manifesto: An Introduction" (1:105–30). Both these stories interestingly mimic Tiptree's performance of a fictional author, since "The Catgirl Manifesto" is supposedly written as an introduction by "Christina X" to a manuscript titled "The Catgirl Manifesto" by Dr. Evgeny Reinhardt. Calder's, or Christina X's, essay presents a wild mélange of SF motifs and academic allusions. Described by Ms. X as being "fantastical in the extreme, and resembling nothing so much as pulp science fiction" (1:107), Reinhardt's manifesto describes an extraterrestrial invasion by a mutagen that causes young girls to exhibit "extreme degrees of exhibitionism; an overriding need to be admired and pampered; infantilism; hyperaesthesia; and a tendency to spite, deceit and treacherousness," all directed toward "a desire—as instinctive as the silky murderousness of a cat's—to drive human males insane with lust" (1:108). "The Catgirl Manifesto" thus picks up on the narrative premise devised by Alice Sheldon, writing as Racoona Sheldon, in "The Screwfly Solution" (1977), of hyperbolizing sexual aggressivity and misogyny to the level of apocalyptic violence, combining it with *The Night of the Living Dead*'s (1968, director George Romero) mysterious transformation of a certain group of humans (adolescent girls in "The Catgirl Manifesto," rather than Romero's corpses) into a new species of predators that take humans as their prey. The Reinhardt syndrome thus manages to simultaneously hyperbolize and estrange the "roles" scripted by heteronormative femininity, the genre of pornography, and the popular figures of the vampire and the zombie.

"The Catgirl Manifesto" also luxuriates in sending up the discourse of critical theory. In addition to Christina X's lengthy epigraph from Michel Foucault's *History of Sexuality*, academically informed readers will quickly catch allusions to deconstruction, the history of avant-garde manifestos including "the calls to arms of the Futurists, Dadaists, and Surrealists" (1:106), cultural studies pieces like Dick Hebdige's 1979 study of the punk movement, *Subculture: The Meaning of Style*,[9] and the theorization of postmodern hyper-reality by Jean Baudrillard, as the manifesto itself is attributed a power of "reverse-mimesis" owing to "the colonization of reality by the meta-virus, or meme, buried in the manifesto's heart" (1:110–11). This listing could go on at much greater length, but what is more important than rehearsing the details of Calder's hilarious pastiche is the common solution Calder and Carter have hit upon for what is arguably the most fundamental formal problem of writing SF: how to handle the exposition of the non-realist setting and reveal its premises and their effects on the world of the story. "Congenital Agenesis" and "The Catgirl Manifesto" both take the disarmingly simple approach of turning the entire story into an expository essay dedicated precisely to elaborating this formal requirement.

There is much more that could be said about the fiction in the anthology—for instance, about the use of meta-generic strategies to estrange romance from its conventional support of normative gender ideology in Lanagan's "Wooden Bride" and Lethem's "Five Fucks"; or about the critical examination of mass culture, advertising, and the reification of aesthetics in relation to gender and embodiment in two stories quite deliberately placed side by side, Ted Chiang's "Liking What You See" (3:113–50) and James Tiptree Jr.'s "The Girl Who Was Plugged In" (3:151–90); or about the impact of mass culture and advertising on gender ideologies in the educational ideological state apparatus in "Liking What You See" and

Gunn and What's "Nirvana High"; and the list could go on. But let me conclude this all-too-brief commentary on the Tiptree anthology's fiction by describing a story that represents a kind of formal, fan-directed antithesis to Carter's and Calder's academic parodies, Vonda McIntyre's resolutely feminist refashioning of space opera in "Little Faces" (3:199–237).

In "Little Faces," McIntyre weaves the usual space opera apparatus—adventurers, spaceships, weapons, and warfare—into the elaboration of a carefully imagined, radically alien system of sexual reproduction. The characters are symbiotic humanoid-spaceship pairs, the humanoids female, the ships also referred to as "she" and capable of giving birth to new spaceships, but not in any other way clearly gendered in anything like humanoid fashion. The humanoid females carry in their abdomens male "companions," which have to be donated to them by other females through the equivalent of sexual intercourse. As it grows in the abdomen of a donor, the companion is referred to as a "son-spot." These "companions" are little furry pricks with heads and teeth, and are only semi-intelligent. But the companion can produce the sperm necessary for the making of a daughter, and along with its genetic material it carries the life memories of the donor. The choice to use one of the companions to impregnate oneself is carried out in isolation from other humanoids but in symbiotic harmony with the spaceship, since a humanoid daughter can be born only with a ship's simultaneous birth of a daughter ship equipped with all the information and genetic material provided as gifts by those who attend the ritual celebration of an anticipated birth. Such a ritual celebration is the occasion for the events of "Little Faces."

The plot turns on a romantic encounter gone drastically wrong. The main character, Yalnis, has invited an older, highly respected woman-adventurer, Seyyan, onto her ship, and the invitation clearly implies the hope of a sexual exchange. However, Seyyan's first or dominant companion (the humanoid females carry multiple companions, the more the wealthier) attacks and kills Yalnis's first companion. This act is quite clearly portrayed by McIntyre in terms that are meant to recall rape, especially in that Yalnis feels guilty for it and Seyyan accuses her of having wanted it and invited it. The subsequent break between Seyyan and Yalnis erupts into a classic he said, she said type of confrontation during the party Yalnis has convened for the birth of a daughter pair to herself and her ship.

It is here that the feminized space opera motifs of warfare and weaponry really kick in. In anticipation of the confrontation, Seyyan and her ship have started a new "fashion" leading up to the party by extruding a brightly colored silk-like material that other ships and their occupants accept, copy, and decorate themselves with. It turns out that the material contains a kind of viral coding that, as the party fiasco escalates into a kind of civil war, literally subjugates Seyyan's fashion slaves to remote control by herself and her ship. Only those who take Yalnis's side and refuse all contact with Seyyan are saved from this viral invasion. In the battle that ensues, these allies are able to help Yalnis spin a web of allergenic material around Seyyan's ship that will imprison her for as long as the material lasts, which it seems will be a very long time indeed. The story ends with Yalnis using one of her companions to impregnate herself, giving birth to a daughter, and installing the daughter in the daughter ship that has been forming throughout the story. Then, in good space opera fashion, Yalnis and her ship agree it's time to take off on an adventure.

Read against its implicit background of the tropes of male-oriented space opera from E. E. Smith to George Lucas, this delightful fable might be said to explore the mutual complicity of warfare and rape as they underwrite the ethos of the adventuring hero of such fictions. Its rearrangement of the status of daughters and sons, with daughters bearing the default category of the human person and sons rather resembling domestic pets, is obviously a feminist joke that exaggerates traditional patriarchal property arrangements at the same time that it reassigns long-standing narrative roles regarding activity and passivity. Thus, in the same joking manner, all the warfare between the ships is carried on in terms of enveloping and consuming rather than penetrating—that is, by the use of vaginal and womblike weapons rather than old-fashioned space opera's notoriously penile ones. This is not merely a reversal of roles, however, with females ascending to the dubious superiority of the rapist and warrior. The erasure of any distinction between nature and culture in the symbiotic sex-gender system disarms the use of sexual identity as an alibi for rape-like aggression. At the same time it troubles the distinction between things and persons in such a way as to reiterate suspicions, reaching back to Mary Shelley, about how much control humans really have over technology's unintended effects on the formation of subjects and the distribution of power, responsibility, and rights. All these strategies imply a certain kind of reader, one both versed in SF tradition and attuned to a feminist sensibility, and the story therefore addresses a community of practice based on a set of horizontal alliances against the viral coding woven into a particular set of dominant fashions, a situation not unlike that of Yalnis and her allies.

Communities of Interpretation (2)

Afrofuturism and Indigenous Futurism

The niche market audience of pulp-era science fiction that formed the basis of the midcentury SF subculture was predominantly white, male, young, and technically oriented toward engineering and the natural sciences. But if the double subordination of niche market fiction within both literary and commercial hierarchies calls to mind the doubly marked status of women of color within gender and racial hierarchies, there seems to be a certain appropriateness to the steady displacement of the white male SF community's centrality to the SF subculture by more and more writers and readers marked by gender and racial difference.[1] Not that such displacement is a structural inevitability, for it has clearly not taken place for every organic niche market genre of the mass cultural genre system. The peculiar itinerary of SF within the mass cultural system involves SF's transformation from the mid-1970s on from a predominantly, almost exclusively, niche market and subcultural genre into one of the mass cultural genre system's most profitable generators of blockbuster films and their attendant fantasy-entertainment franchises. I contend that as the SF tropes of corporate franchises have become increasingly integral to the dominant American cultural vocabulary, the overall practice of SF has become increasingly bifurcated between its mass cultural expression and the resistant, non-hegemonic recoding of SF by groups like the Tiptree/WisCon practitioners examined in chapter 5. In a kind of antithesis to an emphatically white and whitewashed SF's becoming a much more prominent feature of the dominant vernacular, SF's subcultural recodings have been blended more interestingly and provocatively with the dialects and purposes of nonwhite communities.

The way some of these practitioners have been recoding SF in the artistry of those gathered together under the terms Afrofuturism and Indigenous futurism is the subject of this chapter.² As the homogeneous national experience that Ohmann describes as one of the principal effects of mass culture consolidates a standard vernacular, in the process it marginalizes or exoticizes nonstandard dialects and idiolects. Minority communities and their conventions, marked by their class, ethnic, and regional differences, stand out from the unmarked background of the dominant ethnicity and ideology (for instance as "local color" or ethnic stereotypes) even as they are consigned to the background of, if not simply erased from, most mass cultural narrative.³ But these marginalized, often subaltern communities can and do seize upon the dominant tropes of mass culture and aggressively recode them to suit their own purposes.

I will illustrate this process through readings of four SF invasion narratives. I begin with Don Siegel's 1956 film *Invasion of the Body Snatchers*, starring Kevin McCarthy and Dana Wynter, a powerfully told narrative (in my opinion one of the best American SF films of the '50s) that by virtue of its classic expression of American Cold War anxieties is all about whiteness and homogeneity. It therefore rehearses in a remarkably interesting way the dominant cultural vernacular that the following three texts respond to and react against. The second text is John Coney's 1974 film *Space Is the Place*, starring Sun Ra, in which the plot of invasion and the status of whiteness are radically revalued by the poetic and musical performance of an artist, Sun Ra, who is widely acknowledged as one of the most important early practitioners of Afrofuturism. *Space Is the Place* thus offers a very different version of the dynamics of assimilation and the reorientation of desire, based upon its radically opposed perspective on the internal discord of American society. The third, Tsilhqot'in director Helen Haig-Brown's 2009 short film *?E?ANX (The Cave)*, has much to tell us about the generic, discursive, and sociohistorical boundaries that define an audience's relation to a story. Indeed, I want to suggest that all three of these films are, at one level, about the constitution of publics and counter-publics. The final text is Andrea Hairston's 2006 novel *Mindscape*, winner of the 2006 Carl Brandon Parallax Award, an offshoot of the Tiptree Awards devoted to issues of race rather than gender. Here the matter of publics and counter-publics is taken up both in Hairston's startling portrayal of a future version of Hollywood and in her dense engagement with Afro-American and Native American histories. The main focus of my reading of *Mindscape* is Hairston's recoding of the American frontier, a topic that opens onto the historiographic underpinnings of the fortunes of the American western and the rise of SF to blockbuster status.

The main line of division separating Afrofuturism and Indigenous futurism from the rest of SF is of course race. It is certainly not the case that race has suddenly become a topic of concern within SF in the last few decades. Given the way race and racism pervade every aspect of North American culture, it has always, inevitably been an important element of North American SF. But the prevailing mode of dealing with race in pulp and golden age SF was to erase it by positing a postracial future where racial differences had become unimportant or simply disappeared. This postracial future might, on the one hand, reflect the nonscientific basis of racial categories, and throughout my discussion I take it as given that race always designates a political relationship rather than a biological identity.[4] On the other hand, however, Mark Bould argues convincingly that this strategy has been by and large a means by which "sf avoids confronting the structures of racism and its own complicity within them" ("Ships," 180; and cf. note 3 above), and Isiah Lavender III, in *Race in American Science Fiction*, has elaborated the "blackground" traces of the white-black binary in much twentieth-century SF. Those unconsciously inscribed traces of racism, elaborated in what follows by the analysis of *Invasion of the Body Snatchers*, form the premise for the counter-hegemonic recodings of SF invasion in *Space Is the Place*, *The Cave*, and *Mindscape*.

Three Invasions, Three Publics

The importance of the plot of invasion to SF is grounded in the historical relation of the genre to colonialism, in general, and in the particular cases of *Invasion of the Body Snatchers* and *Space Is the Place* to the specific history of U.S. imperialism. In the late nineteenth and early twentieth century, as American imperial ambitions shifted from expanding the country's western border across the continent to becoming an important player on the international scene, the key terms of its imperialist ideology were nation, race, and destiny. The integrity of the American nation, the superiority of the Anglo-Saxon race, and the manifest destiny of white American territorial expansion were the linchpins of imperialist rhetoric, whether in the speeches of Theodore Roosevelt, the reportage and editorial columns of national newspapers, or the bizarre fantasy constructions of "yellow peril" fiction.[5] With America's ascent to the status of global superpower in the aftermath of World War II, one might say that the vehicle of mass culture that had propagated these values overtook its content to become in some ways more powerful than the messages themselves. In post–World War II American political rhetoric, advancing the causes of freedom and self-determination on the international front blended in practical terms with commercial export of American products and entertainment. Anxieties about national integrity gave way to concern for the international economy, proclamations of racial superiority to the hegemony exercised by Western fashions displayed on white models, and the teleology of territorial destiny to the all-enveloping net of American mass culture. In the process of this decades-long transformation, stretching from the end of the First World War to the consolidation of American global dominance after the Second World War, the United States' exemplification of Benedict Anderson's national "imagined community" based on print capitalism turned into a global imaginary community based on film and broadcasting, and the "homogeneous national experience" that Richard Ohmann sees as the fundamental sign and effect of turn-of-the-century mass culture imposed itself abroad as the Americanization of foreign desires. Turning foreign subjects into American-like consumers bolstered the imperial fantasy that an "imagined community" of the American nation extends itself generously to all willing participants. Postwar American imperialism operated on the assumption that assimilation to American consumerism is both what is good for the rest of the world and what it really wants. Thus, while historical narratives of race and destiny continued to undergird American exceptionalism and the aggressive military policies it justified, the seductions of American mass cultural entertainment and its ever-more-ubiquitous central organizing genre, the commercial advertisement, were arguably far more effective agents of American cultural hegemony abroad.

Alongside the burgeoning importance of advertising and mass cultural entertainment as purveyors of American global dominance, we find a growth market in narratives fueled by anxieties about brainwashing, nightmare visions of the propaganda state, and the plot of foreign invasion by invisible psychic subversion—politically, in the conspiracy theories of Senator Joseph McCarthy, culturally, in popular works like John Frankenheimer's 1962 film *The Manchurian Candidate*. I argued in *Colonialism and the Emergence of Science Fiction* that from the 1930s on, the plot of invasion in American science fiction more and more often takes the shape of secret conspiracy or communicable disease because it reflects upon contemporary forms of cultural, rather than military, power. It is no accident that the alien invader in John W. Campbell's "Who Goes There?" (1938) exercises a kind of reverse telepathy on the scientific crew that discovers it. Rather than reading the thoughts of those around it, the alien broadcasts its own thoughts on a kind of subconscious wavelength, entering the psyches of nearby humans in the form of nightmares.

This motif of vampiric telepathy receives its classic formulation in the 1956 version of *Invasion of the Body Snatchers*. The absorption of human victims into the alien seed pods' collective takes place during the victims' sleep, as it substitutes for the active human subject a passive "blank" upon which the subject's memory is written but which no longer generates desire or independent will. This psychic takeover typically has been read as an expression of American Cold War anxieties about communist conspiracy, but the pod invasion is at best an ideological misrepresentation of communism that lodges the communist threat entirely in the power of propaganda while emptying it of any actual communist doctrine such as a critique of private property or an insistence on class struggle. Rather than converting its subjects to communism, the pod invasion erases ideology altogether. Its program is not a party line but a grotesque travesty of one, the simple absence of individual volition and drowning of individual desire in the collective will. This is persuasion as distraction, with self-alienation weirdly mimicking passionate commitment.

However, the pod takeover does transform and quite pointedly colonizes the local economy. One of the first signs of the invasion is the closure of a small farmer's produce stand. Later we see a restaurant losing its business. Finally a group of aliens conspires behind a Main Street–type storefront after one of them grimly turns the sign on the door from Open to Closed. What these emptyings-out and closures signify is an economy bent entirely on the production and distribution of seed pods. The colonizing economy is not attuned to the local needs that a produce stand responds to, but rather focuses solely on the single-minded propagation and export of its one and only crop. An imaginary struggle between capitalism and communism seems much less apparent in all of this than a threat being posed to the face-to-face neighborliness of local, small-town America by an impersonal, anonymous outside force—not so much like a political party seizing power as like a giant corporation turning Santa Mira into a company town.

The conspiratorial aspect that the invasion takes on during the film, visually represented so powerfully in the great scene of seed pod distribution at the town center, is not itself the threat but rather one of its effects. The threat itself, the aliens' contagious reorientation of Santa Mirans' desires, resembles the workings of mass culture, and specifically broadcasting, rather than political conspiracy. In a telling scene near the end of the film, Miles (Kevin McCarthy) and his love interest Becky (Dana Wynter), having just eluded pursuit by a mob of pod people, hear music that seemingly comes out of nowhere. Becky thinks it is the most beautiful thing she has ever heard. When Miles goes to investigate, he discovers that the music is a radio broadcast, amplified through loudspeakers at a factory-like farm devoted entirely to growing seed pods. When he returns to Becky, she has been taken over. This hint of an association between the illusory intimacy of broadcasting and the pods' vampirism resonates with much in the rest of the film, suggesting that the entire invasion represents not just a political and ideological but also a commercial and cultural homogenization of experience and co-optation of desire. That the alien others are a metaphor for America at large is then not merely suggested but screamed into the camera in the penultimate scene as Miles staggers against the grain of a traffic jam on the highway, wasting on unsympathetic ears his message: "They're already here!" (which is where the film should have ended).

If this reading is correct, *Invasion of the Body Snatchers* is a strangely convoluted and deeply self-contradictory film. Its quasi-communist alien conspiracy turns out on close inspection to look more like monopolistic corporate capitalism. The threat of the seed pods spreading beyond Santa Mira seems an inverted representation of the disappearance of regional difference into mass-cultural national homogeneity. The core of the film's contradictions, however, is its apparently unself-conscious participation in the fantasy logic of American commercial imperialism. It presents the Miles-Becky couple's white, middle-class, heterosexual normalcy as that which is both what everyone naturally wants and what America makes freely available to everyone who wants it. The pod people's nightmare vision of a world at peace with itself because all difference and desire have been eliminated from it is the inverted image of an imaginary world at peace with itself because everyone is free to become a normal American.

Space Is the Place obviously sets out from a radically different premise and perspective—the premise that America systematically denies full-fledged humanity to a great many people, particularly to black Americans, and the perspective afforded by that exclusion. Unlike *Invasion of the Body Snatchers*, *Space Is the Place* does not elaborate the contradictions of hegemonic American ideology but rather explores the contradictions and the internal struggle of the black community. There is nothing imaginary in this film about being colonized, subjugated, and alienated. The dilemma acted out in the contest the film stages between Sun Ra (played by himself) and the Overseer (Ray Johnson) concerns whether to accept the degraded status and limited possibilities offered by the dominant culture, or to reject them, and this boils down in good measure to the question of whether such a choice is even available. Thus this film about race and the nation puts the notion of destiny very much at stake. However, the struggle over it is located not in the old context of territorial expansion, but rather at the margins of mass culture. Given the overpowering influence of the dominant culture, is the formation of a viable, autonomous counter-public possible? Or in the political terms contemporary to the film, what version or semblance of a nation can black nationalism aspire to?

The plot and themes of *Space Is the Place* map easily and clearly onto the contest between Sun Ra and the Overseer for the souls of the black community. It is a Manichean setup. Sun Ra stands for an apocalyptic break with the past, and the Overseer for business as usual. To embark upon the "alter destiny" Sun Ra envisions means to exit history as heretofore written, to plunge into the abyss opened up by embracing myth in favor of what passes for reality on "planet Earth" (aka America). This is why the first words we hear in the film, being chanted by June Tyson and the Arkestra, are, "It's after the end of the world. Don't you know that yet?" and why Sun Ra announces in the next sequence, during his rumination on founding a colony for black people in outer space, that "equation-wise, the first thing to do is consider time as officially ended." The Overseer, in contrast, tries in a telling scene to convince the two young blacks Bubbles (John Bailey) and Bernard (Clarence Brewer), who have just been quite impressed by Ra's speech at the local youth center, that Ra does not represent any alternative to the status quo but is only interested in "cold hard cash"—or, in Bubbles's ebullient phrasing, that he has "betrayed his brethren to the exploitative racially and culturally co-opted Caucasian power structure."

The mediating figure between Ra and the Overseer is the sycophantic Jimmy Fey (Christopher Brooks), the spokesperson for the local black radio station, and also the host in the 1943 Chicago nightclub where the contest begins and the emcee at the Sun Ra concert where it ends. The crisis point of the plot might well be identified as the handshake between Sun Ra and Jimmy by which Ra agrees to go into business with the radio station after being assured by Jimmy, "Look, Ra, I got my finger on the impulse of the entire communications network of this country.... We can set it up so you have a nice percentage coming off the top, I'll have a nice percentage coming off the top, everybody will have everything going for them." This is followed by an extraordinary radio interview Jimmy conducts with Ra as they drive around Oakland in a convertible limo. While Ra expounds upon racial hierarchies, the power of music, and the way to a better future, the camera dwells extensively on the lower-class black urban community in the streets. When Jimmy follows up the interview with a commercial for Ra's latest recording, Bernard and Bubbles, listening in, debate whether Ra has confirmed the Overseer's earlier accusation. In all of this the film poses the question of what kind of bargain it is possible to strike with the entertainment industry. To what extent can Ra avail himself of the visibility and distributional power the industry affords without coming under the control of its power brokers?[6] Or, perhaps more to the point, to what extent can Jimmy Fey and Channel Five serve the interests of their black audience as well as that of their owners? The magical ending, when Ra splits Jimmy Fey into his black self, whom he takes with him on his music-powered spaceship, and his white self, who stays behind to suffer the death sentence passed on planet Earth, certainly does not settle the issue. Instead the narrative strategy of the film reaches its limits here. Its Manichean allegory cannot yield any more supple closure to the questions the film raises about assimilation and resistance.

The film's real power does not lie in its narrative, however, but rather in the Arkestra's music, Sun Ra's poetry, and the generic complexity they introduce into its texture. Director John Coney has said that the film's "cheesy" visual effects were meant as both parody and homage to low-budget SF films of the '50s and '60s. But whatever subcultural, campy appeal Coney achieved is itself estranged and repositioned by the genuinely avant-garde and militantly noncommercial musical soundtrack, which, as Nabeel Zuberi has observed, is the film's primary special effect. Ra's poetry —and nearly every line he speaks, all of it written by him, can be taken as poetry—resonates with the mélange of verbal styles and dialects surrounding it, including Bubbles's marvelous riffs on black nationalist ideology, the Overseer's misogynistic, cynical rhetoric of command, Jimmy Fey's jive-ass shtick, the black dialect of the teenagers in the Oakland youth center, and the dominant discourse of white power when a radio news broadcaster announces that Sun Ra's invasion represents a threat "to undermine both the economy and the social structure of the strongest nation on earth." Similarly the rather undefined space of the band's performances, filmed mostly on a visually bare sound stage, when set in contrast to the documentary-style footage on the streets of Oakland, embodies the thematic opposition announced and emphatically reiterated in the poetry between "myth" and "reality," or between the possibility of a free black community and the given condition, especially since both of these visual threads disrupt, stand apart from, and comment upon the narrative.

Thus, in contrast to the fantasy of universality, openness, and freedom of choice at the heart of *Invasion of the Body Snatchers*, *Space Is the Place* takes its point of departure from the exclusions and constrictions America imposes upon its internal subaltern communities. In *Body Snatchers* the antagonism between the invaders and the invaded dissolves upon analysis into ideological homogeneity. *Space Is the Place*, in contrast, derives its energy and distinction from pushing the self-evident contradictions of American society to their breaking point. Where one film paints its nightmare of vampiric absorption within the frame of a boundlessly optimistic fantasy, the other tries to salvage a glimmer of hope from the nightmare of history. And that hope is embodied in the formation of a counter-public galvanized in opposition not simply to the dominant white society but, even more insistently, to the despair and cynicism the history of race relations in the United States bequeaths to its heirs. The film accomplishes this defiance by appropriating and recoding the optimistic ideologies of progress associated with SF's boundless frontier of outer space, seizing upon them for the service of the intellectually elite, economically autonomous position of Sun Ra's avant-garde jazz.

Helen Haig-Brown's *The Cave* seizes upon "science fiction" in an entirely different fashion. In a December 2009 publicity release concerning the film's being showcased at the Toronto International Film Festival as one of the top-ten short films of 2009, Haig-Brown says, "The Cave is the first ever indigenous science fiction film shot in Tsilhqot'in, my native language. This recognition means a lot to me and my community" (Rugged Media). Haig-Brown's emphasis on her use of the Tsilhqot'in language and her appreciation of the recognition conferred upon her and her community by TIFF's selection are important but unsurprising. What is most likely to raise an eyebrow here is the claim that *The Cave*, an adaptation of an oral tale told by Henry Solomon, Haig-Brown's great-uncle, using Solomon's original audio recording of the story as its basis, is "Indigenous science fiction." What does it mean to classify the film adaptation of this Tsilhqot'in traditional narrative as science fiction?

I want to bracket the question of the director's conscious motives here and emphasize instead the effect of calling the film "science fiction" within the context of the mass cultural genre system. Haig-Brown's decision to make a science fiction film was in any event a response to exterior pressures and suggestions. The film was produced as part of a group of six films by Indigenous artists, the Embargo Collective, part of whose creative process involved having certain restrictions imposed by the collective upon individual filmmakers in order to force them into taking "a completely new creative direction" (Wassenberg). Given the directive to make a piece of science fiction, Haig-Brown "knew right away I didn't want to do space and aliens" ("Tsilhqot'in Helen Haig-Brown Splashes at Sundance"). The idea of adapting her great-uncle's story came at the suggestion of a cousin. Nonetheless her choice of using an Indigenous personal narrative to respond to the collective's imposed constraint does create an interesting tension between her refusal to satisfy the expectation that an SF film will involve space and aliens and the way the story and the film very definitely do involve space and aliens. What I propose to explore here is not the director's motives for setting up this tension but rather the effects, deliberate or not, of placing the film within the protocols of interpretation entailed by its genre designation as SF.

Let me give a fairly detailed description of the film, which is not widely distributed or easily available. It begins with Solomon's narration, in Tsilhqot'in with English subtitles, over a black screen, telling us that he is going to tell a story told to him by Sam Bulyan. The story concerns a cowboy (Edmond Lulua) from Gwetsilh in Western Canada, Chilcotin Territory, 1961, who goes bear hunting "because that is what they mainly ate around there." As the film switches into lush, full-color cinematography alternating with the black-and-white credits, we see the cowboy riding his horse through a beautiful landscape, in slow-motion shots that luxuriate in the horse's power and beauty. The credits ended, the cowboy follows the traces left by a bear—a destroyed beehive and claw marks on a tree—to the entrance of a cave. After tying the horse to a nearby tree, the cowboy enters the cave with an improvised torch. As he crawls fully into the cave, he is blinded by an intense white-blue light, and he begins to bleed from his nose. Still bleeding, he emerges from the cave, but not from where he entered. He walks down a grassy hillside to the side of a stream where he sees a woman through some trees and calls to her. But when she turns to him, he sees she is naked, and he stumbles away in confusion, muttering to himself, "How embarrassing." He looks back up to see an entire group of Native people working on the banks of the stream, clothed only in loincloths. They all turn and look at him. The voice of a woman, whose lips do not move, strikes him with physical force, knocking him backward. She says, "This place is not for you. You're not ready yet. Wherever you have crawled from, crawl back." The cowboy flees back through the cave. When he returns to the tree where he had tied his horse, he finds the horse's dried-out skeleton.

The fantastic element that leaps out from this plot as possibly science fictional is the cowboy's journey into another world. However, his passage through the cave into the world on the other side, combined with the time lapse upon his return through the cave, would first suggest to a mass cultural audience the devices of a wonder tale, putting the cowboy into a class of characters including the Japanese Urashima or Washington Irving's Rip Van Winkle. Alternatively, the journey through the cave might be interpreted as a typical convention of portal fantasy, aligning the story with classics like Lewis Carroll's *Alice in Wonderland* or C. S. Lewis's *The Lion, the Witch, and the Wardrobe*. Reading his journey as science fiction, in contrast, means putting it in the context of "space and aliens," that is, within the traditions and conventions of science fiction invasion narratives. The story's distortions of space and time now have to be read as elaborating the structure of a political and historical contact zone between radically alien or alienated groups. As science fiction, the story is all about territories and boundaries and the economy of maintaining them. Furthermore it is not just about encountering aliens but about becoming alien oneself by virtue of the encounter. Part of the effect of calling this adaptation of an Indigenous personal narrative—a story that is not, in its Tsilhqot'in context, "fiction" at all—a piece of science fiction, then, is to suggest, first, that the Tsilhqot'in narrative has already been generically alienated and reconfigured by colonial contact, and second, that adapting the oral narrative to cinematic form itself involves another generic metamorphosis within another reiteration of the colonial contact zone.[7]

Seen from this angle, the opening sequence strikingly juxtaposes three semiotic codes: the Tsilhqot'in language and the oral references to Sam Bulyan and the diet of the people who live around Gwetsilh; the English language in the subtitles, including the place reference to Chilcotin Territory in the settler colonial nation-state of Canada; and the cinematic apparatus of the slow-motion cinematography and non-diegetic music. Any thoughtful viewing should notice the complexity forming around the questions of whom the film is addressing, and how. Several versions of the film's "public" overlap and intersect, including Tsilhqot'in speakers and English speakers, tribal and national identities, and the diverse addressees of oral storytelling and cinematic representation. Calling the film science fiction additionally brings into the foreground the association of these oppositions—oral versus cinematic codes, tribal versus national identities, and Tsilhqot'in versus English—with the hierarchical association of the colonial state with technological modernity and the colonized Indigenous nation with premodern technology, such as horse riding and bear hunting. Calling *The Cave* a piece of science fiction implicitly challenges this hierarchy by revaluing the oral tale, shifting it from its position within a traditional genre system where contemporary oral storytelling is conventionally afforded a subordinate status to literary forms, and instead claiming for it a place within the mass cultural genre system associated with often hyperbolic representations of technological and political modernity. The identification of the *science* in science fiction with industrial technology and the forms of capitalist and scientific rationality associated with it is therefore called into question, opening onto a conversation that is likely to involve what Grace L. Dillon (Anishinaabe) has called "Indigenous scientific literacies," Indigenous modes of knowing and doing that value sustainability, codependence, and integration with natural processes rather than dominance and control over them (7–8).

Issues of territoriality and boundaries—therefore of race, nation, and destiny—arise repeatedly in the hunter's penetration of the cave, his fantastic transportation into the other world beyond the blinding light, and his climactic encounter with the Native people by the stream. The exact nature of the other world is not revealed. Its temporal alterity from the cowboy's home world, as well as the cost of his transportation into and out of the other world, are marked by the dead horse at the conclusion of the story. Yet, although the credits refer to the people by the stream as spirits, and some print accounts of the film contend that the hunter enters into the world of the afterlife, all that one can be sure of is that the cowboy does not understand where he has come to. His first reaction to seeing a bare-breasted woman by the stream, embarrassment at having invaded her privacy, turns out to be wholly inappropriate. Perhaps his embarrassment and his hiding himself are themselves the signs that he has come to a place where he does not belong, but we are not told enough to be sure of that. What we can be sure of is that the Native woman's words carry a power that marks her condition as radically different from his. The interpretive protocols of SF would lead one to regard this as a political and historical difference, the representation of an elsewhere distinguished from the cowboy's world and from the nation-state of Canada by precisely the power and autonomy of the Native group on the stream bank—which is to say, also by their ability to command an unwanted visitor to go away. But the reticence of the narrative is crucial. Haig-Brown comments in the December 2009 publicity release that "it was a challenge to follow protocol as much as possible in order to properly honour my community's traditions of oral story-telling." The film's reticence about the other world is one of the formal effects of the difference between its publics, a strategy that might in its turn evoke questions about the meaning of terms like "nation" and "recognition."[8] Who gets to define what counts as a nation, and to decide what legal and political effects that status of nationhood commands? Who gets to bestow "recognition" upon others, and to determine what conditions of power and self-determination predicate that status? These are questions that the association of science-fictional space and aliens with the story's handling of invasion and misrecognition insists upon raising.

Recoding the Frontier in Andrea Hairston's *Mindscape*

One of the more remarkable SF invasion narratives of recent years is Andrea Hairston's premier novel, *Mindscape* (2006). *Mindscape* is set in a world that is decisively separated from its past by the invasion of a mysterious extraterrestrial entity called the Barrier. The Barrier, "a blood red cloud of unknown material overwhelming Earth," erupts "out of nothing, out of nowhere ... breaking apart land and sea, night and day, yesterday and every other tomorrow" (4). It divides the earth into three "inhabited Zones" that have severely limited contact with one another—acting like a "prison wall," according to some, but like "a blessing for the chosen and a curse for the damned," according to others (4). The question Hairston's narrative premise sets up, then, is whether the world is to be "consumed, rearranged, and forgotten in the pattern of some other being" or whether "this phenomenon will defy humanity to create a new language, a new syntax of life" (5). In short, Hairston's Barrier invasion constitutes the imposition of a *frontier* dividing what was from what is and can be, and forcing those in its "zone" to redefine themselves in relation both to one another and to their lost pasts and possible futures.

The frontier, as theme and setting, is as important to American SF, and as central to the genre's entanglement with the history, discourses, and ideologies of colonialism, as the plot of invasion.[9] Much pulp-era and mid-twentieth-century American SF reconstructs the nation's mythic pioneering past as a science-fictional future, transferring both the symbolic and ideological values of the American frontier and the tropes of the American western to outer space. In elaborating in fictional form what Richard Slotkin calls America's frontier myth, according to which "the conquest of the wilderness and the subjugation or displacement of the Native Americans who originally inhabited it have been the means to our achievement of a national identity, a democratic polity, an ever-expanding economy, and a phenomenally dynamic and 'progressive' civilization" (10), these SF versions of the frontier often participated in the ideology of American exceptionalism, the representation of American political, military, and economic power as free from the corrupting burdens of history that turn it into domination and oppression elsewhere.

The rise to commercial prominence of cinematic SF in the 1970s corresponds with a reconfiguration of the historiography of the American frontier and, in consequence, the ideological force of the American western. In the late nineteenth century, when both the American western and American SF were just beginning to take shape in popular culture, the frontier myth developed along two extremely influential paths, a "populist" version whose greatest exponent was the historian Frederick Jackson Turner, and a "progressive" one whose most influential spokesman was Theodore Roosevelt. Roosevelt's version was social Darwinian and imperialist; Turner's was agrarian, decentralizing, more focused on the cumulative behavior of ordinary pioneering husbandmen than on the heroic deeds of explorers, hunters, and soldiers. But both versions firmly identified the frontier itself as the linchpin for an account of American history that identified the rigors of the frontier as the catalyst of America's capacity for continual renewal and reinvention of itself. Not surprisingly, this highly charged figure held together ambivalent, even contradictory values, simultaneously celebrating progress and bathed in nostalgia, firmly ensconced within an evolutionary notion of historical stages of development based on an opposition of savagery and civilization and at the same time invoking a cyclical logic of redemptive return to the cleansing innocence of the wilderness (Katerberg 18–23; Slotkin 22–24).

This account of the American frontier exerted enormous influence on American popular culture, not least of all or least profitably in cinematic depictions of heroic white pioneers battling red savages in the American western. Its influence faded, however, as the frontier thesis of Turner yielded to the new western historiography that recast the American frontier experience not as what distinguishes and privileges America, but as a typical instance of territorial expansion in capitalist settler colonies. Patricia Limerick, the primary spokesperson for this school of thought, sees the American West as a scene of invasion, conquest, and expansion of the world market, typical of global imperialism (see Limerick's *The Legacy of Conquest*). Although American exceptionalism is far from dead, this change in the dominant historiography can certainly be registered in the difference separating the Wild West of Tom Mix or of John Ford's *Stagecoach* (1939) from that of Clint Eastwood's *Unforgiven* (1992). But the resultant gap in the supply of ideologically comforting, nostalgic fantasies of American righteousness was filled in large part by neo-pulp SF, led by *Star Wars* (1977), and neo-imperial adventure fantasy like Steven Spielberg's *Raiders of the Lost Ark* (1981). The astounding commercial success of *Star Wars* testifies to the mass cultural audience's undiminished appetite for identifying with white heroes battling "the dark side" of things, while fantasies of indigenizing the settler, from *Dances with Wolves* (1990) to *Avatar* (2009), proved to stand in well for the old-fashioned glorification of the genocidal Indian wars. All of this has made the theme and setting of the frontier a more or less inevitable target of the recoding of SF conventions in Afrofuturism and Indigenous futurism.[10]

Hairston's recoding of the frontier is a demystifying, anti-mythic resurrection of the histories buried by the frontier myth, a resurrection that ultimately takes the form of a massive rising of the dead on the site of the great Indian massacre at Wounded Knee. The entire project of naming and identifying Afrofuturism and Indigenous futurism—and Hairston's novel quite clearly falls into both categories—has to do with claiming a place in the cultural present for groups whose history has been systematically distorted or erased and whose future has been scripted predominantly in terms of the disappearance of their specific cultural identity into that of the dominant, white society. During one of the interviews conducted by Mark Dery that established Afrofuturism as a critical term, Samuel R. Delany argues that Afro-Americans have been

> impoverished in terms of future images . . . because, until fairly recently, as a people we were systematically forbidden any images of our past. I have no idea where, in Africa, my black ancestors came from because, when they reached the markets of New Orleans, records of such things were systematically destroyed. If they spoke their own languages, they were beaten or killed. . . . Every effort conceivable was made to destroy all vestiges of what might endure as African social consciousness. When, indeed, we say that this country was founded on slavery, we must remember that we mean, specifically, that it was founded on the systematic, conscientious, and massive destruction of African cultural remnants. (Dery 747)

If Afrofuturism and Indigenous futurism operate, as Sun Ra proclaims, within a postapocalyptic present, it is because of the process of obliteration described by Delany. Bringing a postapocalyptic humanity back from the dead, while simultaneously obliterating its past and imposing upon it a radically new identity, is the plot of Octavia Butler's great *Xenogenesis* trilogy (1987–1989; renamed *Lilith's Brood* in 2000), which remains unmatched for the scope and complexity with which it explores the inextricable intertwining of assimilation, miscegenation, and cultural genocide at the frontier of alien contact. Hairston's *Mindscape* explores the same topics with similar ambition.

If Hairston's recoding of the frontier derives first of all from her antimythic or "new western" identification of it with invasion and historical trauma, the power with which she carries through on this premise has much to do with her success at situating her narrative at the conjuncture of the traumatic Afro-American and Native American histories of colonial encounter with Europe. The three zones in *Mindscape* correspond roughly to the three points of the triangular slave-trade route between Europe, Africa, and the Americas. In each case Hairston invests that historical location with a significance based upon its contemporary relationship to the traumatic past. Paradigma is the neo-European zone that is identified, in the words of its prime minister, with the codependence and practical equivalency of "civilization, democracy, free market, science" (190). New Ougadougou is a neo-African zone inhabited by a society that calls itself Healers, promoting social welfare and spiritual traditions in opposition to the corporate profit motives and militaristic state policies of Paradigma. The third and most bizarre zone is Los Santos, a neo-Hollywood in which the entertainment industry has become a form of organized crime.

Los Santos, located in what was formerly the American West, is also the home of a group of "born-again Sioux" who call themselves Ghost Dancers and follow a prophet named after Wovoka, the Native American leader of the historical Ghost Dances of the late nineteenth century. The novel hints throughout at an alliance forming in the hinterland of Los Santos between the Ghost Dancers and the "Extras," the exploited class of Los Santos workers whose members were routinely raped and murdered in the making of snuff pornography up until the signing of an Interzonal Treaty five years before the main events of the story take place. Most of the story has to do with the protagonists' battling against a conspiracy among leaders of all three zones to undermine the treaty—a conspiracy that Paradigma's leaders see as a way to take over the world for capitalism and democracy, Los Santos's leaders as a way to get back to business as usual, and New Ougadougou's as a way to isolate themselves from the moral and social contamination they see spreading from the "warrior Zones" to their own. Climaxing and overwhelming this interzonal conflict at the end is the vigil of the rebel Extras and Ghost Dancers at Wounded Knee, where the dead rise out of the Barrier to offer the living "an invitation to the future" (430).

This is only a bare skeleton of *Mindscape*'s intricate plot, without any attempt at describing how the convoluted narration interweaves the experiences of its six focal characters. At the heart of this daunting and dazzling complexity, however, lies the issue of cultural power over the narratives that lay the basis for national, ethnic, and personal identities in the ability to connect the past to the future. A speech laying out the rationale for the New Ougadougouian isolationist opposition to the Interzonal Treaty sets the stakes: "To bring an alien culture to its knees, you steal the natives' stories and fill them with lies. You desecrate sacred symbols and replace ancestral wisdom with your story of the world. You obsess the benighted natives with being like you, until finally they forget themselves and become like you. Why waste bullets when a cultural bomb will do? Stealing the future is an old story, a universal cliché" (213). Even though this character's fear of cultural contamination ultimately turns out to be misguided, and she herself becomes the principal actor in using the Barrier as a means of unifying rather than separating the zones and their inhabitants, her analysis of the power of culture to orient desire is right on the mark.

This power accounts for the seemingly odd move of making the neo-American sector of Hairston's global allegory into a version of Hollywood. This future Hollywood is given over, in addition to its penchant for snuff pornography, to commercial fantasy production of a nostalgic past: "Ray Valero [one of the six principals, a star "in a direct line from Cary Grant and Denzel Washington" (7)] rode a Mustang scooter, guzzled Jolt, and saved the world. He promised a taste of before-the-whole-world-was-like-the-Third-World, when humanity ruled the Earth" (364). To the character watching this film clip, the towers of Paradigma's science center look like Emerald City (364). A thread of references to other Hollywood fantasy settings includes "an alpine castle modeled on mad King Ludwig's fairytale palace, Neuschwanstein" (238), the model for the famous Disney Corporation logo; a gangster's mansion modeled to look like Tara, the mansion in *Gone with the Wind*, which one character associates with "nostalgia for knights and ladies or masters and slaves" (337); and, crucially, the Badlands, where "umbrella rocks balanced on spindly columns" (381) recall many an American western cinematic landscape. This last is also the location of Wounded Knee, a site invested with real rather than cinematic history, where the climactic resurrection of the dead takes place.

The rising of the dead is depicted most vividly from the perspective of a filmmaker, Aaron Dunkelbrot: "A face he'd almost forgotten ghosted in front of him on the Barrier screen—Stella Jackson, naked and grinning. She leaned across the ridge right into him" (429). Once Dunkelbrot's memory becomes flesh on the "screen" it closes the gap between presence and representation, merging "right into him" with an impact that delivers what the Hollywood film can only promise, an intimate reconnection to his past. The key to this scene's power is that Stella Jackson and Aaron Dunkelbrot are one and the same. Dunkelbrot is the product of transgender and transracial genetic engineering. In his former life as Stella Jackson he was an Extra raped and left for dead on a Los Santos production site. As Aaron Dunkelbrot he has become a highly successful director who is engaged in making an epic about the Interzonal Treaty, a film whose events dovetail with those of the novel. Aaron's integration of his abandoned past with his present identity is one of several remarkable instances of Hairston's literalizing and playing out W. E. B. Du Bois's figure of African American "double consciousness," a condition Du Bois describes in *The Souls of Black Folk* this way: "One ever feels his two-ness,—an American, a Negro, two souls, two thoughts, two unreconciled strivings; two warring ideals in one dark body, whose dogged strength alone keeps it from being torn asunder" (8).[11] Aaron Dunkelbrot's encounter with Stella Jackson is a moment of healing this wounded condition: "They were close enough to touch. Wounds from torture and rape on her face, neck, breasts, and belly had healed to angry brown scars. This was not his body anymore, but still painful to see. Aaron enveloped Stella in his burnoose. Her rough hand on his cheek was forgiveness for throwing her away before she could find herself. Her lips on his forehead was that awful strain in the back of the throat, behind her eyes, before tears. He had lost so much abandoning her. Stella's heart thudded against his and then she was gone" (429). Like a Hollywood film or a piece of fiction, the Barrier here externalizes and makes palpable an alternative, possible relation to the past. As film or fiction can only aspire to do, it makes the political entirely, irrefutably personal.

A bit later Dunkelbrot describes the rising of the dead in more general terms as an opening up of the Barrier "corridors," transforming it into a mode of access to a whole new set of worlds: "Right before the new corridors opened, all these people . . . people we carry around in our heads, showed up like a waking dream, ghosting across the Barrier, talking up a storm. Nobody could understand what they were saying, it was like in code. I thought the dead would have big things to tell us. But they just got bigger and bigger 'til you couldn't make them out, scattering off in every direction, and the Barrier broke open. Corridors to everywhere, everyone welcome" (435, ellipsis in text). Thus the Barrier does finally become a familiar type of science-fictional frontier, "corridors to everywhere, everyone welcome." But Hairston's "final frontier" is not an empty space waiting to be conquered; it is instead "an invitation to the future" (430) issued by undoing the repression of the traumatic past. Her rising of the dead is not a Day of Judgment, calling all the past's sinners to account, but rather a release of the past from its pathological concealment, allowing its former ghostliness and incomprehensibility to dissipate into a transparent atmosphere of new possibilities. The portent of revelation—"I thought the dead would have big things to tell us"—gives way to the simple freedom to choose one's path. The entire project of *Mindscape* makes it clear that this is not just a matter of wiping the slate clean. Double consciousness is not overcome or healed by simply drowning out one of its parts, but, quite the opposite, by fully acknowledging and reconciling the claims of both its halves. Thus Hairston's Afro/Indigenous futurist recoding of the frontier, like the work of many of the best SF writers before her, knows that in any borderland or contact zone, there are always two sides to any story, and exploring the radical differences between those two sides is the heart of the adventure.

CONCLUSION

Periodizing SF

According to the historically oriented genre theory that underlies this book, the history of SF is not a story of the persistence of a central formal device (i.e., cognitive estrangement), nor of a coherent artistic tradition, nor of a sequence of great innovations and comprehensive syntheses by major writers. It is, rather, the history of a shifting set of conventions and expectations successively laying their various claims to definition of the genre and exercising their influence over an intersecting but heterogeneous array of practices—comprising not just different ways of telling SF stories, but also of taking roles within its production, distribution, and reception—that draw upon vastly different resources and enact correspondingly divergent motives.[1] It is the story of a rhizomatic proliferation of "variation, expansion, conquest, capture, offshoots" (Deleuze and Guattari 21).

Nonetheless, despite its multiplicity and complexity, this history has a shape. Denying the determining force of a formal or ideological center to the genre does not relegate analysis to a merely pluralistic attentiveness to its many competing practices. On the contrary, the deployment of resources and enactment of motives by practitioners of SF always take place within a field of value-laden possibilities where the quality and quantity of access to economic and cultural resources both comprise the stakes of ongoing political and ideological struggles and prove foundational to the way SF's practitioners are able to position themselves toward and within such struggles. The shape of the history of the genre is given to it first and foremost by systemic transformations of the options that make up this field. Such options are by no means distributed evenly around the globe, so let me repeat once more that the history that follows is limited to Anglophone and mostly American SF. Within that limited scope I would point to three systemic transformations that divide the history of SF into three periods. The three transformative events are the formation of the mass cultural genre system, the consolidation of niche market SF, and the metamorphosis of SF into a highly profitable, capital-intensive mass-market genre. The corresponding periods are, first, the early days up until the mid-1920s; second, the period of the formation and dominance of SF's pulp-based subculture from the mid-1920s to the mid-1970s; and third, the period of what I will call the bifurcation of SF practices over the last four decades.

I take seriously Philip Wegner's observation, prefacing his own recent foray into periodizing the history of SF, that "all periodizations are themselves science fictions, forms of the subgenre of the *alternate history*" (2). Many alternate histories could be made out of the patterns of stylistic and thematic change that extend themselves within and across the three watersheds I have posited. These would include histories of the persistence of the formal devices of cognitive estrangement or of the utopian impulse in SF, of the formation of coherent artistic traditions and the eruption of stylistic and thematic challenges to them within the genre, and, assuredly, of great innovations and major syntheses of the genre's possibilities by its most talented writers. The history of SF that I am sketching here differs from these approaches by deliberately resisting the notion that the goal of a generic history should be to isolate what is unique about the genre. No doubt the individuality of the genre's history has to be part of the story, otherwise what story would there be to tell? But I want to insist that SF's identity—or rather its array of shifting identities—be understood as one cluster of options in an evolving and interconnected system of generic choices, so that the genre develops in tension and dialogue with other proximate genres, and, just as important, that this mass cultural system of genres itself operates in tension with other genre systems based on other venues and modes of publicity. I think that the cultural and ideological power of contemporary narrative can be assessed and appreciated most realistically—both in terms of scholarly accuracy and political effectiveness—when questions about its power are set in this systemic context. The periodization of SF that follows aims to support this claim.

Early SF: the formative period. The six decades stretching from Verne's early work to the appearance of *Weird Tales* and *Amazing Stories* form a kind of gestation period during which examples of SF-like texts become more and more common. Unfortunately, early science fiction is more typically conceived of as this set of SF-like texts than as a period. The two best bibliographies, Everett Bleiler's *Science-Fiction: The Early Years* and Thomas Clareson's *Science Fiction in America, 1870s–1930s*, encourage that conceptualization, not by arguing for it, but simply by performing the essential task of assembling that group of texts whose formal and thematic properties constitute a set of precedents for what eventually comes to be recognized and named as science fiction. This procedure presents us with a bundle of similarities woven out of diverse generic threads, the most important of which are future war fiction, utopian speculation, marvelous voyages, stories of time travel, and lost-race fiction. As Michael McKeon observes about the genealogy of the novel, however, they add up to a coherent generic development only in retrospect. To conceive of early SF as a period, rather than a set of texts, requires advancing some sort of explanation why this bundling and intersecting of diverse genres is taking place at this time.[2]

Obviously the increasing number of SF-like stories published in the UK and the United States during these decades indicates the increasing importance of science and technology in the everyday lives of people living in those countries. But it does not explain the ordering of such stories into a distinctive, new genre rather than our simply seeing this new subject matter introduced into the established ones. The new genre responds not just to changing social conditions but also to the new commercial opportunities being opened up by a new mode of publicity—mass cultural distribution—and the new business model that organizes mass cultural publicity around advertising. The genres that form in this vein of opportunity aim at encouraging and exploiting habitual consumption, not because that is what storytellers suddenly decided to do or because the writers who published in the magazines were all untalented and unimaginative hacks, but because the function of fiction in the mass cultural context is to target specific groups of readers and turn them into habitual consumers of a serial publication. The way the new mass cultural genres define themselves according to content rather than form likewise attests to the basic role that targeting plays in the decisions determining the publication and distribution of one or another kind of story. Surprise and innovation were not valued; the predictable attraction of a certain subject matter for a certain group of readers was. Hence we see coming into view genres that target women and genres that target men, a genre based on interest in the western frontier and one based on interest in crime and police work, another targeting fascination with the supernatural and another targeting fascination with science.

These genres do not come out of nowhere, of course, nor does mass culture relegate previous modes of publicity or traditional practices of reading to the void. The new mass cultural venues seized upon existing tools such as the serialized novel and the gender-specific appeal of feminized sentimental romance or boys' adventure fiction. The instrumentalized aesthetics of mass culture resonated throughout the realm of cultural production, accentuating the value of "art for art's sake" and, arguably, playing a large role in inspiring the cultivation of difficulty and formal experimentation in the high-modernist avant-garde. The most important and widespread tension between mass cultural and traditional practices is located, I would argue, in the schools, and particularly in the practices of higher literary education that set "literature" into opposition with technical discourses as well as with the cultural vernacular. But this tension is less important to the initial formation of SF than to its later development.

The central point is that the story of the emergence of SF during its early period is the story of a systemic change. The piecing together of science fiction out of the materials of the utopia, the future war, the imperial adventure fantasy, and so on, takes place in dialogue with the emergence of the other mass cultural genres out of their own more or less complicated genealogical milieus. As my discussion of *Frankenstein* in chapter 3 tried to demonstrate, the development of the marvelous romance and popular melodrama in the late eighteenth and early nineteenth centuries was a significant episode in providing the materials that later composed the mass cultural genre system, and the Victorian reception of Shelley's novel shows how closely interwoven the emergence of science fiction is with that of detective fiction, Gothic romance, and horror. The exaggerated individuation of these genres in the milieu of the niche market magazines initiates another phase in a long development driven by the demands of seriality and structured by the effects of stratification and the sometimes complementary, sometimes antagonistic formations of mass cultural homogeneity and subcultural heterogeneity.

The Formation and maturation of the SF subculture from the 1920s to the 1970s. The history of American SF from the April 1926 appearance of the first issue of Hugo Gernsback's *Amazing Stories* to the May 1977 release of George Lucas's *Star Wars* is dominated by the formation and maturation of a subculture, composed originally of the fandom spawned in response to the early pulp magazines and growing larger, older, more professional, and more diverse with each passing decade. I wrote in chapter 3 that through the 1930s and '40s one can discern three quite distinct practices of SF: a mass cultural SF present mainly in the comics; a literary SF exemplified by heirs of H. G. Wells such as Olaf Stapledon in the UK and Karel Čapek in Czechoslovakia, as well as by the dystopian fictions of Aldous Huxley and George Orwell; and the subcultural SF of the niche magazines, with John W. Campbell and the writers he nurtured at *Astounding* the most influential members. By the end of the 1950s, partly as a result of the increased global reach of American mass culture in the aftermath of World War II, subcultural SF had clearly become the most widespread and widely recognized of these three, the sector of SF practice that set the agenda for literary interlopers and increasingly crept from its origins in cheap print publication (by this time paperbacks had taken over from the pulp magazines as the main vehicle) into the more capital-intensive venues of film and eventually television. It was subcultural SF that established the dominant tropes and conventions of the genre, the megatext with all its peculiar and wonderful "beauties" that Istvan Csicsery-Ronay has so thoroughly anatomized, as it grew out of the pulps and made its presence felt in larger markets and more reputable venues.

Any history of SF focused on stylistic and thematic changes would likely take the mid-'60s as a watershed because of the impact of the New Wave movement led by Michael Moorcock's editorship of *New Worlds* in the UK and its echoes in the United States, well exemplified in Harlan Ellison's *Dangerous Visions* anthologies (1967 and 1972; for a concise summary of the New Wave and the controversies over its significance see Latham).

The version of SF history I am sketching here would see these as episodes playing out the tensions that structured the SF subculture rather than as transformative changes in the genre's field of production, distribution, and reception. On the one hand there is a very significant intergenerational struggle that during the course of the '50s had already largely undermined the dominance of Campbell and *Astounding*. The ideological stakes in this struggle were certainly raised, and its animosities exacerbated, by its intersection with the 1960s youth counterculture and the antiwar movement. On the other hand there is that odd homology I have mentioned several times between the cultishness and exclusivity or elitism of niche subcultures and the intellectual avant-garde. In this connection one might see the New Wave—and particularly the careers of J. G. Ballard in the UK and Samuel R. Delany in the United States, both of whom are at least as strong candidates for literary canonization as Philip Dick—as a rapprochement of literary and subcultural SF that does not so much transform the field as follow one course of opportunities and affinities inherent in its terrain.

Alongside these struggles within the genre, a steadily wider dissemination of SF into the cultural vernacular took place throughout the '50s and '60s. The UFO legends of the 1950s and after, or the startling SF elements in the writings of Elijah Muhammad and their proliferation in what Yusuf Nuruddin calls "black urban mythology," represent one side of a development matched on the other by the futuristic visions of consumerist utopia in advertising displays such as the Motoramas and the Frigidaire Kitchens of Tomorrow of the 1950s (Woodham 375–79). Thus there is not just that steadily wider distribution and reception of SF evident in its penetrating into the film and television industries and in the best-seller status achieved by Robert A. Heinlein's *Stranger in a Strange Land* (1961) or Frank Herbert's *Dune* (1965), but, more importantly, a diversification of its audiences. I would point to these trends in SF's reception to help explain what I would argue was the single most important development within the genre in terms of reshaping its potential and repositioning its resources in the '60s and '70s: the increasing participation and importance of women in every aspect of SF.

The Bifurcation of Mass Cultural and Subcultural SF after Star Wars. The commercial success of *Star Wars* could be considered the culmination of the SF subculture's penetration into the film industry and its dissemination into the mass cultural vernacular. A major problem with this view is that, as anyone reading this book knows, *Star Wars* does not at all represent the state of subcultural SF in the mid-1970s. As I argued in chapter 6, Lucas's film instead reverted to something more like a 1930s *Flash Gordon* serial in state-of-the-art, high-tech special-effects drag, bathing its audiences in the nostalgic fantasies that could no longer be invested in the American western. Thus, rather than bringing the SF subculture into the sphere of blockbuster finances, it initiated a new and drastic bifurcation into the practices and definitions of SF—yielding, on the one hand, the franchise fictions and endless serializations of the *Star Wars* and *Star Trek* universes; and, on the other, leaving the mature SF subculture relatively untouched, or unscathed. A telling comparison is that between *Star Wars* and Stanley Kubrick's *2001: A Space Odyssey* (1968), a film that well and truly melded the resources of Hollywood film with subcultural SF. Kubrick's film may have helped legitimate SF as a major film genre, but it did not change the relationship of print SF to film or change the position held by SF within the mass cultural genre system. *Star Wars* did. It catapulted SF into the very heart of one of the most capital-intensive sectors of the entertainment industry, where studio practitioners of the genre have made a lot of money and occasionally a pretty good film (e.g., Ridley Scott's *Blade Runner* or Michel Gondry's *Eternal Sunshine of the Spotless Mind* [2004]), while formulaic series fiction seems to some observers to have so swamped the marketplace that the pre–*Star Wars* version of the genre has now attained a status akin to poetry, "ignored by most readers but still a vibrant tradition to the minority that values it" (Westfahl, "Marketplace," 91).

I like Westfahl's comparison of contemporary small-press, niche market SF to poetry (even though I disagree with most of the rest of what he has to say about the history and definition of the genre) because one of the more noteworthy and beneficial effects of the bifurcation of SF practices in the last forty years has been to narrow, although certainly not erase, the gap between literary and subcultural SF that was so prominent a feature of the cultural landscape when Suvin was formulating his poetics of the genre. This has been accompanied by the parallel and to some extent interdependent growth of the field of science fiction studies in the academy, a topic I brushed against in my reading of the mock-academic essays by Calder and Carter in the Tiptree anthologies in chapter 5, but which easily could have been the subject of a whole chapter. What I chose to emphasize a bit more in chapters 5 and 6 is the changing demographics of the SF subculture, which as I have said was well under way by the time Hollywood discovered the moneymaking potential of its own brand of SF. Thus SF in the era of bifurcated practices has been significantly feminist in ways that are utterly unlike the dominant tone of the genre before the '70s (in spite of the excellence of a writer like Catherine L. Moore or the importance of Judith Merril's editorial work), and it has become an increasingly important vehicle for nonwhite writers (not just in the United States; see Eric Smith's argument that SF has supplanted magical realism as the dominant genre of postcolonial literature). My argument is not that the success of *Star Wars* caused this to happen, but rather that the rise of blockbuster SF changed the ideological power of recoding SF tropes, raising the stakes by elevating them to the status of normative, hegemonic fantasy vehicles.

A development that has often been noted and commented upon in the period of bifurcated SF practices is the evaporation, as Gary K. Wolfe calls it, of genre boundaries between the varieties of fantastic, nonrealist fiction. The new demographics arguably have much to do with this. The argument would be that, in retrospect, the defense of SF against the incursions of fantasy or romance had everything to do with its bias toward male gender ideology (cf. Larbalestier). Without contesting that argument, which I think is strong and accurate, I would add that the hybridization of SF with neighboring genres in phenomena like the New Weird or slipstream also has a lot to do with its repositioning within the mass cultural genre system. Contemporary SF no longer shares early fandom's heavy investment in the technical discourses of science. The center of energy, or the fund of cultural capital, for the genre now depends much more heavily on its central position within the entertainment industry. Rather than foreshortening SF's "cognitive" dimension, this repositioning in my estimation accentuates SF's powers as a tool of social criticism by highlighting its abilities to imagine alternatives to the dire realities of the neoliberal capitalist regime that, coincidentally or not, coincides pretty closely with the bifurcation of SF. It is this repositioning of SF's cultural role and the complementary or corollary loosening of genre boundaries that opens up (or that is the result of the work of those who opened up) the genre to feminist interventions like those in the Tiptree anthologies and to the serious interrogation of what counts for the science in science fiction characteristic of Afrofuturism and Indigenous futurism.

A new feature of cultural production in the current period is the emergence of digital technology and the new venues of publication and avenues of distribution that it opens up. I have had little to say about this topic for the simple reason, first of all, that it is beyond my expertise. Perhaps it is still too soon to grasp digital technology's historical significance. The work of Henry Jenkins, for example, seems to me more of an activist intervention than the kind of historical rumination offered in this book. I can only hope that my efforts here prove useful to those who, now or later, take on this project. But my sense of things is that the basic contours of the mass cultural genre system have not changed as the result of the new technological vehicles for narrative distribution and reception. The underlying corporate-capitalist structures that place advertising at the center of the system, with their concomitant effects of seriality, stratification, and subculturation, persist undiminished. The advent of widespread electronic broadcasting in the mid-twentieth century did not disrupt these features, and at present it does not seem to me that digital technology is doing so either. Transforming the structure of contemporary capitalist publicity would involve changing the political economic order itself.

Let me finish with a final word on what Fredric Jameson calls the ideology of form. For Jameson the genres that coexist in tension with one another in a given text constitute a quasi-geological or archaeological pattern of strata that carries within it the long history of cultural change and social struggle underlying the narrative choices available at any given time and place. Jameson argues that this sort of pattern comes properly into view when generic form is correlated with changes in the mode of production (*Political Unconscious*, 88–102). For modes of production I would substitute modes of publicity, a substitution that crucially involves taking into account the way that the transformation of genre systems can disrupt and revalue the meaning of any particular generic identity. To deny that genres have any formal essence, as I do, is not to reject the notion of an ideology of form, then, but rather to contend that the relation of formal strategies to ideologies is a constantly moving target, and that the ideological power of a genre at any point in its history has less to do with its formal precedents than with the positions occupied by its practitioners within the set of resources and opportunities currently available. The history of SF I have tried to sketch out here has been an attempt to realize, or at least to point in the direction of realizing, this conception of the ideology of form.

NOTES

Introduction

1. I use the abbreviation "SF" here and throughout this book as an umbrella term that deliberately avoids choosing among contemporary variations on "science fiction" such as "speculative fiction" and "sci-fi," and at the same time includes earlier genre terms such as scientifiction and scientific romance.

2. For a trenchant critique of how the sacralization of literary genres forged in the early modern period persists in modern critical practices, see Beaujour.

3. In *Metamorphoses of Science Fiction* Suvin makes an extended attempt to demonstrate that the literature of cognitive estrangement bears an ancient lineage, including ancestors such as Lucian, Rabelais, and Swift. On the shortcomings of that attempt see Westfahl, *Mechanics of Wonder*, chapter 1.

4. "Cognition effect" is Carl Freedman's term, aligning the literary effect of cognition that Suvin considers crucial to the definition of SF with the "reality effect" of realism as analyzed by Roland Barthes. See *Critical Theory and Science Fiction*, 18, and cf. Rhys Williams's comments, 621.

1. On Defining Science Fiction, or Not

1. Good examples of this kind of discussion: Roberts 1–20; Freedman, *Critical Theory and Science Fiction*, 13–23; Luckhurst, *Science Fiction*, 6–10; Rieder, *Colonialism and the Emergence of Science Fiction*, 15–21.

2. Cf. the discussion of Todorov's distinction between theoretical and historical genres in the introduction of this book.

3. One of the most notable linguistic arguments is that of Tzvetan Todorov, who, in the opening section of his 1978 *Genres in Discourse*, broke with the emphasis he had earlier placed on the category and properties of "literature" (e.g., in *Fantastic*, 6–7) by arguing that there is no clear distinction between literary and nonliterary language. The analysis of literary genres does not have to do with sentences and grammar, he now argued, but rather with discourses composed of "utterances in a given sociocultural context" (9), and therefore genre is a local phenomenon determined by social and cultural practice, not a quasi-grammatical one embedded in the deep structures of language. The same conclusion follows from arguments launched from

the problems of cultural difference that beset translation; see Bacchilega, Naithani, and Owen.

4. Luckhurst makes the same point a different way in *Science Fiction*, 6–10.

5. Suvin and Scholes are quoted in Clute and Nicholls's entry on definitions (310–14).

6. For an example of a reading based on such questions see the section in chapter 6 on Helen Haig-Brown's short film *The Cave*.

7. For identification of Shelley's *Frankenstein* as the grand original of SF see Aldiss and Wingrove 25–52; on the "miraculous birth" of SF in Shelley's *Frankenstein* or Wells's *War of the Worlds* see Jameson, *Archaeologies*, 1 and 57; for Gernsback's role as originator see Westfahl, *Mechanics of Wonder*, 8.

8. For another discussion of the usefulness of Deleuze and Guattari's conception of rhizomes to genre theory see Dimock 74.

9. As already discussed in the introduction, the most drastic example of sorting true SF out from its neighbors is Suvin's (nonetheless informative) bibliography in *Victorian Science Fiction in the UK*, where he lists several hundred texts that fail to qualify as SF (most famously, Stevenson's *Dr. Jekyll and Mr. Hyde*), ignoring, as Luckhurst comments, any "sense that the categories of popular literature and notions of what scientific cognition might be were both undergoing transformation in the nineteenth century, and that SF is itself the very product of this change" (*Science Fiction*, 8). I would say that the more inclusive and broadly based bibliographies of Bleiler and Clareson are to be preferred.

10. On the way that genres construct worlds see Frow, *Genre*, 86–87.

11. What is usually meant by generic hybridity is perhaps simply that the genres being mixed in a text have not conventionally been considered neighbors (like the combination of philosophical speculation with swords and sorcery in Delany's Neverÿon stories), or perhaps that their neighborliness is being foregrounded and exploited in the text rather than allowed a conventionally silent co-presence (as in the explicit use of folkloric material in China Miéville's *King Rat*). That is, the designation of hybridity has more to do with the way a text positions itself within a system of genre values than with the simple and more or less inevitable fact that it uses a multiplicity of genre strategies.

2. The Mass Cultural Genre System

1. On the literary canon as a synchronic construction see Guillory 33–37, and Eliot.

2. See Evans on Verne; Landon 40–50 on the Edisonade; and cf. Csicsery-Ronay's thesis that SF mediates the "ongoing discourse between science as a regulated discipline and a chaotic combinatory popular discourse" (115).

3. On the history of the category of literature see Raymond Williams, *Marxism and Literature*, 45–54; see Blair for an eighteenth-century course of lectures on rhetoric and belles lettres; on the history of higher education see D. J. Palmer, Graff, Court, Eagleton, and Veysey.

4. Guillory traces Macherey and Balibar's critique of the category of "literature" in the French educational system to early Russian formalist attempts at a theoretical elaboration of a literary system. The problem of identifying the "literariness" of literary language strove to ground itself in grammar, but the formalists' investigation always had to do with "different practices of the same language" that would eventually point to the problem of relating dialects, sociolects, and class to different narrative and literary forms (64–71).

5. Ohmann's account is focused entirely on the United States, but Raymond Williams, in "Advertising: The Magic System," makes much the same argument for the UK. According to Williams, the period from 1880 to 1930 saw "the full development of an organized system of commercial information and persuasion, as part of the modern distributive system in conditions of large-scale capitalism" (*Problems*, 179).

6. Cf. Schudson, 209–33, on advertising as a form of "capitalist realism" akin to the socialist realism of Soviet propaganda; and Habermas, 159–235, on the degeneration of the public sphere into "a platform for advertising" (181). On U.S. corporate news as a form of propaganda see Herman and Chomsky, *Manufacturing Consent*.

7. See Gary Wolfe's "Evaporating Genre" on the late appearance of SF in book publishing.

8. The closest anyone has come to compiling a motif index of science fiction is the tremendous "Motif and Theme Index" in Bleiler's *Science Fiction: The Early Years*, 861–924, continued in *The Gernsback Years*, 621–98. Cf. also the "Checklist of Themes" in Clute and Nicholls, xxix–xxx.

9. Cf. Milner: "The binary between Literature and popular fiction is almost entirely an artefact of Literary modernism, designed to valorize form over content, and cannot be applied to SF which, by contrast, is a genre of ideas and therefore privileges content over form" (14).

10. For more on the canonical text as boundary object see my "The Return to the Frontier in the Extraordinary Voyage."

11. On the Futurians see Damon Knight.

12. The UNESCO *Index Translationum* lists Verne as the second-most translated author in the world, behind Agatha Christie. Within a year after the May 1871 publication of "The Battle of Dorking" in *Blackwood's Edinburgh Magazine*, English-language editions appeared in New York, Philadelphia, Toronto, and Melbourne, and translations in Paris, Berlin, Rome, and Rio de Janeiro (Clarke, *Voices Prophesying War*, 227–28).

3. Genealogies of SF

1. A third major candidate is H. G. Wells's *The Time Machine*, which I have discussed in my chapter "Fiction, 1895–1926" in *The Routledge Companion to Science Fiction* in the course of arguing that "what characterizes Wells's great decade on the whole is not the novelty of his invention, but rather the way he breathes vitality into the commonplace plots and devices of an already thriving early sf" (25).

2. P. B. Shelley's review, written in 1817 but not published until 1832, reinforces the impression that political or moral positions, rather than formal elements or the presence or absence of the supernatural, were the dominant factors in the milieu of the contemporary reviews. In Shelley's crystal-clear response to the conservative accusations that the novel lacks a moral, we can see how entirely predictable the conservative reaction was: "In this the direct moral of the book consists; and it is perhaps the most important, and of the most universal application, of any moral that can be enforced by example. Treat a person ill, and he will become wicked. Requite affection with scorn;—let one being be selected, for whatever cause, as the refuse of his kind—divide him, a social being, from society, and you impose upon him the irresistible obligations—malevolence and selfishness" (730).

3. Paul Alkon's excellent discussion of *Frankenstein*'s originality in the opening pages of *Science Fiction before 1900* likewise takes its point of departure from Percy Shelley's preface and compares *Frankenstein* to *Gulliver's Travels*.

4. Scott's emphasis on psychological plausibility may also be echoing Horace Walpole's preface to the second edition of *The Castle of Otranto*, where Walpole declares that "desirous of leaving the powers of fancy at liberty to expatiate through the boundless realms of invention, and thence of creating more interesting situations, [the author of the following pages] wished to conduct the mortal agents in his drama according to the rules of probability, in short, to make them speak, and act, as it might be supposed mere men and women would do in extraordinary positions" (9–10).

5. On the contemporary use of "romance" rather than Gothic see for example Clery, "The Genesis of 'Gothic' Fiction," 22, and Botting, *Gothic*, 24.

6. Miles puts together a chart of the frequency of publication of "Gothic" novels using a set of well-defined criteria (use of Gothic marketing cues and association by reviewers with Gothic writers); it shows a sharp increase in 1788 and again in 1794, peaking in 1800 ("1790s," 41–43).

7. On the construction of "literature" in relation to the public sphere see Keen.

8. For texts of all the adaptations mentioned in this paragraph see Forry.

9. The creature's exaggerated susceptibility to music is one aspect of the stock "wild man" figure; cf. Wierzbicki. For a more extended treatment of the thematic consequences of the creature's muteness and of other consistent changes to the plot of the novel in the stage adaptations see Rieder, "Patriarchal Fantasy."

10. Jeffrey Cox points to a turn away from the supernatural toward "the dangers of scientific experimentation" when, in Peake's *Presumption*, Frankenstein refers to his creature as "a huge automaton in human form" (act 1, scene 3). But Cox continues: "This turn might be read as a rejection of Gothic displacements and an encounter with the actual technological monstrosities that were being created through the factory system; but it is also the case that this turn from the supernatural is a retreat from the Gothic's radical questioning of traditional religion.... Peake's monster might (though I doubt it) raise questions about technology run mad; but the ghosts and ghouls of the earlier Gothic drama raised questions about Providence itself" (67). In Milner's *Frankenstein*, the creature is brought to life in a laboratory with chemical apparatus, but Frankenstein's assistant, Strutt, describes his master's work as alchemy and demonism.

11. An example of magazine fiction with a direct debt to *Frankenstein* is E. E. Kellett's "The New Frankenstein" (*Pearson's*, May 1899); explorations of the plot motifs with little or no direct reference to Shelley include W. C. Morrow, "The Surgeon's Experiment" (*Argonaut*, October 1887), Dick Donovan, "Some Experiments with a Head" (*Cornhill Magazine*, 1889), and Harle Oren Cummings, "The Man Who Made a Man" (*McClure's*, December 1901). All four are reprinted in *The Frankenstein Omnibus* edited by Peter Haining.

12. The point here is not to argue that horror, detective fiction, and science fiction are all expressions of the same Gothic impulse, but rather to suggest that the term "Gothic," having outlived its polemical functions in the early nineteenth century, lives on precisely as that which names the continuity of a certain set of figures and strategies with the marvelous romance of that era. The Gothic names the enduring effects on the articulation of popular fictional genres of that anticlassical, hybridizing episode.

13. For a standard version of the thesis that the creature is Victor Frankenstein's double see Harold Bloom's afterword to the Signet Classic *Frankenstein*; on the shortcomings of the thesis see Rieder, "Patriarchal Fantasy." For a study of the construction of monstrosity that lines up *Frankenstein*, *The Strange Case of Dr. Jekyll and Mr. Hyde*, and *The Picture of Dorian Gray* see Halberstam, *Skin Shows*.

14. Rhodes's and Milne's tales of super-scientific extortion may participate in a peculiarly American nineteenth-century fascination with superweapons, on which see Franklin. However, the plot persists most famously in the adventures of James Bond.

15. For a complete list of the table of contents of *Amazing Stories* see Bleiler, *Science-Fiction: The Gernsback Years*, 551–61.

16. Gernsback coined the portmanteau term "scientifiction" to name the genre in *Amazing Stories* but switched to "science fiction" after driving *Amazing* into bankruptcy, losing control of it and almost immediately using financial resources that perhaps could have played a part in repaying the debts he walked away from at *Amaz-*

ing, starting up *Science Wonder Stories*, *Air Wonder Stories*, and *Radio-Craft*. It is often said that "science fiction" replaced "scientifiction" because the latter term is so awkward, but "scientifiction" remained in use among fans well into the thirties, and Gernsback's switch to "science fiction" probably has more to do with establishing a new term in exclusive association with his new magazines than with any sense of its intrinsic superiority to "scientifiction."

17. Jess Nevins claims in his contribution to *The Oxford Handbook of Science Fiction* that more science fiction appeared in American periodicals outside the pulp magazines before the Second World War than in them. It is difficult to assess this claim without more detailed evidence regarding which stories Nevins is counting as science fiction. However, if, as he claims, there was a significant community practicing science fiction outside the pulps during these years, this would be both of great interest to historians of the genre and entirely consonant with the argument being made here.

18. See also Luckhurst's concise summary of the variety of genres Wells worked in during the 1890s and his many generic predecessors, in *Science Fiction*, 30–31; and cf. note 1 above.

19. The astronomical and imperial perspectives come rather bizarrely together in J. Holt Schooling's "The Lion's Share," the article immediately following the installment of *The War of the Worlds* in the June 1897 issue of *Pearson's*. It begins:

> In looking at facts about the British Empire, as regards its size and its importance as a piece of the Earth, one is quite clearly impressed by a result which soon becomes evident—that we as an Empire now have the Lion's Share of this planet.
>
> We all know, probably, that the area of the British Empire, with its colonies and dependencies, is, in round numbers, eleven millions of square miles. That is, nearly three times as large as Europe, almost as big as Africa, and more than one-fifth part of the land-surface of the earth. Our population is not far short of 400 millions, or, more precisely, one person in every four who crawl, walk, or ride on the surface of this planet is under the rule of Victoria, the greatest monarch in ancient or modern history. (611)

Accompanying the article is a drawing depicting the Earth as a globe on the left of a black background with some stars, the moon on the right, and in between them a sphere somewhat larger than the moon with Victoria's profile on it (man-in-the-moon style) and the caption: "Discovery of the Planet Victoria. The British Empire secedes from the World and takes a place between the reduced Earth and the Moon" (618).

20. The *Buck Rogers* comic was initially based on a short story by Philip Francis

Nowlan, "Armageddon in 2419 A.D.," first published in Gernsback's *Amazing Stories* in August 1928.

21. *Electrical Experimenter* was retitled *Science and Invention* in September 1920, but the numbering of the issues is continuous with the earlier title. According to Bleiler, six pieces of early SF appeared in *Modern Electrics* from 1911 to 1913, twenty-seven in *Electrical Experimenter* from 1915 to 1920, and sixty-eight more in *Science and Invention* from 1920 to 1926 (*Science-Fiction: The Early Years*, 931–34).

22. For instance, a typical *Weird Tales* editorial blurb, in the October 1926 issue, lists among the upcoming fiction "Drome," by John Martin Landry, "a thrilling weird-scientific story"; "The Head," by Bassett Morgan, "a weird and terrible tale of surgery and horror in the jungle wilderness"; "The Metal Giants," by Edmond Hamilton, "a powerful weird-scientific thrill-tale by the author of 'Across Space'"; and "The Last Horror," by Eli Colter, "a tale of weird surgery."

23. For a fuller account of SF and the Edisonade see Landon 40–50.

24. But compare Wells, whose methods as opposed to Verne's form the basis for golden age SF as opposed to Gernsback's project: "For the writer of fantastic stories to help the reader to play the game properly, he must help him in every possible unobtrusive way to *domesticate* the impossible hypothesis" (Wells, *Scientific Romances*, viii).

4. Philip K. Dick's Mass Cultural Epistemology

1. Beginning with his last agent, Richard Galen, who said, "To my mind, his mainstream stuff wasn't one-tenth as good as his science fiction" (Sutin 280).

2. I give dates of first book publication for Dick's novels, except for *We Can Build You*, where the date of composition is necessary for clarity's sake.

3. I am inclined to view Dick's visions themselves and his subsequent, obsessive elaboration and interpretation of them not as signs of the onset of mental illness but rather as what Freud called the delusional system of Dr. Schreber, an attempt at a cure. And in Dick's case the cure was successful in both emotional and artistic terms.

4. Dick's reception in France was also an important factor; see Bozzetto.

5. Cf. Kim Stanley Robinson's judgment that Dick's peculiar virtue as an SF writer was his ability "to stretch generic conventions to the breaking point" (37).

6. A similar example is the "rhetorizor" in *Penultimate Truth* chapter 1, where there is also a kind of reverse image of the Great Books animator in the canonical status enjoyed by twentieth-century TV commercials.

7. In addition to my debts to Jameson, Hayles, C. Palmer, and Rossi, this account of the Dickian sublime is consonant with and partly inspired by Peter Fitting's reading of Dick in "Reality as Ideological Construct."

8. *A Scanner Darkly* is also a notable reworking of the Oedipus story understood as detective fiction—that is, the story in which the detective discovers himself to be the criminal.

9. I offer this as a supplement to my fuller reading of the novel's generic complexity and the hexagram of "Inner Truth" in "The Metafictive World of *The Man in the High Castle*."

10. Dick connects the group hallucination plots of *Eye in the Sky*, *Time out of Joint*, *Palmer Eldritch*, *Ubik*, and *Maze of Death* to one another in a passage in the *Exegesis*, quoted in Sutin 95–96.

11. Dick himself certainly took the option throughout the *Exegesis* of reading backward from the oracular experience of 2-3-74 into the earlier fiction. But one need not follow his example. The "long-range very tight information-rich beam of energy focused on Fat's [i.e., Dick's] head" in *VALIS* is patently another example of an SF broadcasting event, even if Dick's accounts of the experience are accurate autobiography (*VALIS*, 190). Horselover Fat's reception of the beam, in this account, is preceded by pathological aural hallucinations: "The first thing that went wrong, according to Fat, had to do with the radio . . . he heard the radio saying hideous words, sentences which it could not be saying" (207). It is clearly plausible to read the 2–3-74 event as taking its shape from Dick's prior, extensive intellectual investment in the power exercised by mass cultural broadcasting. See Enns's argument that Dick's concern with media establishes a strong continuity between the earlier and late phases of his career; and cf. note 3 above.

5. Communities of Interpretation (1)

1. The box office estimates of this and the three *Matrix* films are the ones given on *The Numbers* (www.the-numbers.com).

2. For an excellent exploration of the ideological ramifications of *The Matrix*'s generic complexity see David Higgins, "Coded Transmissions: Gender and Genre Reception in *The Matrix*."

3. This approximation of time travel to game playing shows signs of becoming a standard Hollywood trope as it is reworked in the 2014 Tom Cruise vehicle *Edge of Tomorrow* (dir. Doug Liman).

4. This echoes, though it is probably not derived from, a similar moment in *The Truman Show*, when a bartender announces to his customers that he is willing to offer two-to-one odds that Truman will not be able to escape the director's machinations.

5. By SF's "realism" Wegner means the period during which the genre is consolidated by a community of readers sharing a common ground. In the terms laid out in this study we might instead speak of the establishment of a predictable megatext

or SF "world" the conventions of which can then be played with and strategically violated by a "modernist" like Dick.

6. An earlier Tiptree Award anthology was published in 1998: *Flying Cups and Saucers: Gender Explorations in Science Fiction and Fantasy*, edited by Debbie Notkin and the Secret Feminist Cabal. This volume's compilation of some of the Tiptree Award winners and short-listed texts from 1992 to 1995, while coherent with the later volumes in the ideological and generic qualities of the fiction, is chiefly distinguished from them by its comparatively minimal editorial apparatus.

7. Judith Butler's *Gender Trouble: Feminism and the Subversion of Identity* appeared in 1990; the first Tiptree Awards were given in 1991.

8. *The Left Hand of Darkness* begins: "I'll make my report as if I told a story, for I was taught as a child on my homeworld that Truth is a matter of the imagination."

9. The impact of the mutagen on British youth culture is compared to "that of 1977, when punk found a short-lived apotheosis in the conjunction of the Sex Pistols and the Queen's Silver Jubilee" [1:107]).

6. Communities of Interpretation (2)

1. Cf. Mark Dery's puzzlement, in the important 1994 essay-interview "Black to the Future" that did much to establish Afrofuturism as a viable critical category, about the relative absence of Afro-American writers within SF given the fact that "the sublegitimate status of science fiction as a pulp genre in Western literature mirrors the subaltern position to which blacks have been relegated throughout American history" (736).

2. It is important to keep in mind that these two categories are academic constructions that collect together a quite diverse set of artists; cf. Kilgore, "Afrofuturism," 566.

3. For example, *Star Trek*'s challenging of the color boundaries of broadcast TV by introducing a black woman onto the bridge of the starship *Enterprise* is well known, but the crucial point here is that the series depicts a postracial future where the ethnicities of Lieutenants Uhura, Sulu, and Chekhov are made either diegetically irrelevant or, in the case of Chekhov, played for laughs. Racial differences are also, of course, coded as alien in the series, a strategy as old as SF. For the argument that *Star Trek: Deep Space Nine* performs a more complex resistance to the overall whiteness of the franchise see Kilgore, "'The Best Is Yet to Come.'"

4. On the history of race as a category see Hannaford. The term "indigenous," likewise, designates a political relationship within the context of colonial domination and expropriation. Before the colonizers arrive, "indigenous" people are just people; only in relation to the colonizers do they become "indigenous." Cf. Patrick Wolfe's

comparison of the contradictory modes of deployment of race in the United States in relation to slavery and the seizure of Indian land (387–88). Wolfe concludes, "We cannot simply say that settler colonialism or genocide have been targeted at particular races, since a race cannot be taken as given. It is made in the targeting" (388).

5. For a more detailed reading of U.S. imperialism and mass culture in the 1890s see Rieder, "John Henry Palmer's *The Invasion of New York, or How Hawaii Was Annexed*: Political Discourse and Emergent Mass Culture in 1897."

6. This question to a large extent determines the shape of Sun Ra's entire career; see Rieder, "Sun Ra's Otherworldliness."

7. Helen Haig-Brown has stated that she wanted to "take the fiction out of science fiction" in this film. Thanks to Grace Dillon for communicating this to me (e-mail, March 28, 2016).

8. For a recent take on the political negotiation of nation and recognition between Canada and the First Nations see Coulthard.

9. For a broader survey of the frontier in American SF see Rieder, "American Frontiers," which I have drawn upon selectively in what follows.

10. For example, Native American writers find it useful to repeatedly resuscitate and recode a frontier myth figure like General George Armstrong Custer: as a corrupt government agent in Gerald Vizenor's (Anishinaabe) "Custer on the Slipstream" (1978); as an evil, shape-shifting trickster in Stephen Graham Jones's (Piegan Blackfeet) *The Fast Red Road* (2000); and as the egomaniacal, incompetent victim of a rebellion of the horses at Custer's Last Stand in Archer Pechawis's (Cree) short film / performance piece *Horse* (2001). William Sanders's lighthearted adventure novel *Journey to Fusang* (1988), set in an alternative history where Europe was devastated by the medieval plagues, the New Orleans slave markets traffic in Englishmen and are run by Islamic traders, and Native Americans have never suffered the genocidal effects of European colonialism, could be read as an elaborate device to set up a sentence such as this, spoken by the novel's hero: "For there is no doubt about it, if those savages hadn't arrived in the nick of time, those cavalrymen would have killed us" (246).

11. Hairston makes the allusion to double consciousness most explicit in section 31, "Miracles," in recounting the history of Celestina Xa Irawo, the author of the treaty. I would argue that it applies in different ways and with different intensities to all the principal characters.

Conclusion

1. If this is true within the limited range of English-language SF, it is all the more true of SF as a global practice. There is no common formal device or coherent artistic tradition shared by texts as different as the Russian Alexander Bogdanov's commu-

nist utopia *Red Star* (1905), the Italian Filippo Tommaso Marinetti's proto-fascist *Mafarka the Futurist* (1909), and the German serial *Perry Rhodan* (beginning in 1961).

2. Thinking about early SF as nothing but a (fuzzy) set of texts that share certain similarities opens up the option of searching back as far as one can for such texts—as far as More's *Utopia* in Bleiler's case, but others have extended the category back into ancient times (e.g., Suvin, *Metamorphoses*, 87–88; Gunn, *Road to Science Fiction: From Gilgamesh to Wells*; Roberts, *History of Science Fiction*, 21–31). The further back one extends the category, the more puzzling becomes the question of why the genre should have taken so long to be recognized.

WORKS CITED

Adorno, Theodor W. *The Culture Industry: Selected Essays on Mass Culture*. Edited and with an introduction by J. M. Bernstein. New York: Routledge, 1991.

Aldiss, Brian, with David Wingrove. *Trillion Year Spree: The History of Science Fiction*. London: Gollancz, 1986.

Alkon, Paul. *Science Fiction before 1900: Imagination Discovers Technology*. New York: Routledge, 2002.

All-Story Magazine. 110 vols. New York: Frank Munsey, 1905–1920.

Althusser, Louis. "Ideology and Ideological State Apparatuses: Notes towards an Investigation." In *Lenin and Philosophy and Other Essays*, 127–86. New York: Monthly Review Press, 1970.

Altman, Rick. *Film/Genre*. London: British Film Institute, 1999.

———. "A Semantic/Syntactic Approach to Film Genre." *Cinema Journal* 23, no. 3 (1984): 6–18.

Amazing Stories. Edited by Hugo Gernsback. New York: Experimenter Publishing, 1926–1929.

Anderson, Benedict. *Imagined Communities: Reflections on the Origin and Spread of Nationalism*. Rev. ed. London: Verso, 2006.

Anonymous. Review of *Frankenstein; or, The Modern Prometheus*. *La Belle Assemblée*, 2nd Series, vol. 17 (March 1818): 139–42.

Attebery, Brian. *Decoding Gender in Science Fiction*. New York: Routledge, 2002.

———. "Science Fiction, Parables, and Parabolas." *Foundation: The International Review of Science Fiction* 34 (Autumn 2005): 7–22.

———. *Strategies of Fantasy*. Bloomington: Indiana University Press, 1992.

Attebery, Brian, and Veronica Hollinger, eds. *Parabolas of Science Fiction*. Middletown, Conn.: Wesleyan University Press, 2013.

Bacchilega, Cristina. *Legendary Hawai'i and the Politics of Place: Tradition, Translation, and Tourism*. Philadelphia: University of Pennsylvania Press, 2007.

Baldick, Chris. *In Frankenstein's Shadow: Myth, Monstrosity, and Nineteenth-Century Writing*. Oxford: Clarendon, 1987.

Banerjee, Anindita. *We Modern People: Science Fiction and the Making of Russian Modernity*. Middletown, Conn.: Wesleyan University Press, 2012.

Barthes, Roland. *S/Z*. Translated by Richard Howard. New York: Farrar, Straus and Giroux, 1974. First published Paris: Éditions du Seuil, 1970.

Beaujour, Michel. "Genus Universum." *Glyph* 7 (1980): 15–31.
Bennett, Tony. *Outside Literature*. London: Routledge, 1990.
Berger, John. *Ways of Seeing: A Book Made by John Berger [and others]*. London: British Broadcasting, 1972.
Blair, Hugh. *Lectures on Rhetoric and Belles Lettres*. Reprint of London: W. Strahan and T. Caddell, 1783 edition. Edited by Harold F. Harding. 2 vols. Carbondale: Southern Illinois University Press, 1965.
Bleiler, Everett F., with the assistance of Richard J. Bleiler. *Science-Fiction: The Early Years*. Kent, Ohio: Kent State University Press, 1990.
———. *Science-Fiction: The Gernsback Years*. Kent, Ohio: Kent State University Press, 1998.
Bloch, Ernst. "A Philosophical View of the Detective Novel." In *The Utopian Function of Art and Literature: Selected Essays*, translated by Jack Zipes and Frank Mecklenburg, 245–64. Cambridge, Mass.: MIT Press, 1988.
Botting, Fred. *Gothic*. London: Routledge, 1996.
———. "In Gothic Darkly: Heterotopia, History, Culture." In *A Companion to the Gothic*, edited by David Punter, 3–14. Oxford: Blackwell, 2000.
Bould, Mark. "The Dreadful Credibility of Absurd Things." *Historical Materialism* 10, no. 4 (2002): 51–88.
———. "The Ships Landed Long Ago: Afrofuturism and Black SF." *Science Fiction Studies* 34, no. 2 (2007): 177–86.
Bould, Mark, and Sherryl Vint. "There Is No Such Thing as Science Fiction." In *Reading Science Fiction*, edited by James Gunn, Marleen Barr, and Matthew Candelaria, 43–51. New York: Palgrave Macmillan, 2009.
Bourdieu, Pierre. "The Field of Cultural Production, or: The Economic World Reversed." *Poetics* 12 (1983): 311–55.
Bowker, Geoffrey C., and Susan Leigh Starr. *Sorting Things Out: Classification and Its Consequences*. Cambridge, Mass.: MIT Press, 1999.
Bozzetto, Roger. "Dick in France: A Love Story." 1988. Reprinted in *On Philip K. Dick*, edited by Mullen et al., 153–60.
Broderick, Damien. *Reading by Starlight: Postmodern Science Fiction*. London: Routledge, 1995.
The Cabin in the Woods. 2012. Directed by Drew Goddard. Lionsgate.
Campbell, John W., Jr. "Concerning Science Fiction." In *The Best of Science Fiction*, edited by Groff Conklin, v–xi. New York: Crown, 1946.
Cawelti, John. *Adventure, Mystery, and Romance: Formula Stories as Art and Popular Culture*. Chicago: University of Chicago Press, 1976.
Cheng, John. *Astounding Wonder: Imagining Science and Science Fiction in Interwar America*. Philadelphia: University of Pennsylvania Press, 2012.

Clareson, Thomas. *Science Fiction in America, 1870s–1930s: An Annotated Bibliography of Primary Sources*. Westport, Conn.: Greenwood, 1984.

Clarke, I. F. *Voices Prophesying War: Future Wars, 1763–1984*. New York: Oxford University Press, 1966.

Clery, E. J. "The Genesis of 'Gothic' Fiction." In *The Cambridge Companion to Gothic Fiction*, edited by Jerrold E. Hogle, 21–39. Cambridge: Cambridge University Press, 2002.

———. *The Rise of Supernatural Fiction, 1762–1800*. Cambridge: Cambridge University Press, 1995.

Clute, John, and Peter Nicholls, eds. *The Encyclopedia of Science Fiction*. London: Orbit, 1999.

Cohen, Ralph. "Genre Theory, Literary History, and Historical Change." In *Theoretical Issues in Literary History*, edited by David Perkins, 85–113. Harvard English Studies 16. Cambridge, Mass.: Harvard University Press, 1991.

Coulthard, Glen Sean. *Red Skins, White Masks: Rejecting the Colonial Politics of Recognition*. Minneapolis: University of Minnesota Press, 2014.

Court, Franklin. *Institutionalizing English Literature: The Culture and Politics of Literary Study, 1750–1900*. Stanford, Calif.: Stanford University Press, 1992.

Cox, Jeffrey N., ed. *Seven Gothic Dramas, 1789–1825*. Athens: Ohio University Press, 1992.

Croker, John Wilson. Review of *Frankenstein, or the Modern Prometheus*. *Quarterly Review* 36 (January 1818): 379–85.

Csicsery-Ronay, Istvan, Jr. *The Seven Beauties of Science Fiction*. Middletown, Conn.: Wesleyan University Press, 2008.

Curran, Stuart. *Poetic Form and British Romanticism*. New York: Oxford University Press, 1986.

Delany, Samuel R. "About 5,750 Words." In *The Jewel-Hinged Jaw: Notes on the Language of Science Fiction*, 21–37. New York: Berkley, 1978.

———. "Science Fiction and 'Literature'—or, the Conscience of the King." In *Speculations on Speculation: Theories of Science Fiction*, edited by James Gunn and Matthew Candelaria, 95–117. Lanham, Md.: Scarecrow Press, 2005. First published in 1979.

Deleuze, Gilles, and Felix Guattari. *A Thousand Plateaus: Capitalism and Schizophrenia*. Translated and foreword by Brian Massumi. Minneapolis: University of Minnesota Press, 1987.

Denning, Michael. "The End of Mass Culture." In *Modernity and Mass Culture*, edited by James Naremore and Patrick Brantlinger, 253–68. Bloomington: Indiana University Press, 1991.

Dery, Mark. "Black to the Future: Interviews with Samuel R. Delany, Greg Tate, and Tricia Rose." *South Atlantic Quarterly* 92, no. 4 (1993): 735–78.

Dick, Philip K. *Clans of the Alphane Moon.* 1964. New York: Mariner, 2013.

———. *Eye in the Sky.* 1957. New York: Mariner, 2012.

———. *Five Novels of the 1960s and 1970s: "Martian Time-Slip," "Dr. Bloodmoney," "Now Wait for Last Year," "Flow My Tears, the Policeman Said," "A Scanner Darkly."* Edited by Jonathan Lethem. New York: Library of America, 2008.

———. *Four Novels of the 1960s: "The Man in the High Castle," "The Three Stigmata of Palmer Eldritch," "Do Androids Dream of Electric Sheep?," "Ubik."* Edited by Jonathan Lethem. New York: Library of America, 2007.

———. *The Penultimate Truth.* 1964. New York: Mariner, 2011.

———. *The Shifting Realities of Philip K. Dick: Selected Literary and Philosophical Writings.* Edited with an introduction by Lawrence Sutin. New York: Vintage, 1995.

———. *The Simulacra.* 1964. New York: Mariner, 2011.

———. *Solar Lottery.* 1955. New York: Mariner, 2012.

———. *Time out of Joint.* 1959. New York: Vintage, 2002.

———. *VALIS and Later Novels: "A Maze of Death," "VALIS," "The Divine Invasion," "The Transmigration of Timothy Archer."* Edited by Jonathan Lethem. New York: Library of America, 2009.

———. *The World Jones Made.* 1956. New York: Mariner, 2012.

———. *The Zap Gun.* 1965. New York: Mariner, 2012.

Dillon, Grace L. "Imagining Indigenous Futurisms." In *Walking the Clouds: An Anthology of Indigenous Science Fiction*, edited by Grace L. Dillon, 1–12. Tucson: University of Arizona Press, 2012.

Dimock, Wai Chee. *Through Other Continents: American Literature across Deep Time.* Princeton, N.J.: Princeton University Press, 2006.

Du Bois, W. E. B. *The Souls of Black Folk.* Edited with an introduction by Brent Hayes Edwards. Oxford: Oxford University Press, 2007.

Eagleton, Terry. *Literary Theory: An Introduction.* Minneapolis: University of Minnesota Press, 1983.

Electrical Experimenter. Edited by Hugo Gernsback. New York: Experimenter Publishing, 1913–1920.

Eliot, T. S. "Tradition and the Individual Talent." In *Selected Essays, 1917–1932*, 3–11. New York: Harcourt Brace, 1932.

Enns, Anthony. "Media, Drugs, and Schizophrenia in the Works of Philip K. Dick." *Science Fiction Studies* 33, no. 1 (March 2006): 68–88.

Evans, Arthur B. *Jules Verne Rediscovered: Didacticism and the Scientific Novel.* New York: Greenwood, 1988.

Fitting, Peter. "Reality as Ideological Construct: A Reading of Five Novels by Philip K. Dick." 1983. Reprinted in *On Philip K. Dick*, edited by Mullen et al., 92–110.

Forry, Steven Earl. *Hideous Progenies: Dramatizations of "Frankenstein" from Mary Shelley to the Present*. Philadelphia: University of Pennsylvania Press, 1990.

Foucault, Michel. "Nietzsche, Genealogy, History." In *Language, Counter-Memory, Practice: Selected Essays and Interviews*, edited with an introduction by Donald F. Bouchard, translated by Donald F. Bouchard and Sherry Simon, 139–64. Ithaca, N.Y.: Cornell University Press, 1980. First published in 1977.

Fowler, Alistair. *Kinds of Literature: An Introduction to the Theory of Genres and Modes*. Cambridge, Mass.: Harvard University Press, 1982.

Fowler, Karen Joy, Pat Murphy, Debbie Notkin, and Jeffrey D. Smith, eds. *The James Tiptree Award Anthology*. 3 vols. San Francisco: Tachyon, 2005–7.

Franklin, H. Bruce. *War Stars: The Superweapon and the American Imagination*. New York: Oxford University Press, 1988.

Freedman, Carl. *Critical Theory and Science Fiction*. Middletown, Conn.: Wesleyan University Press, 2000.

———. "Editorial Introduction: Dick and Criticism." 1988. Reprinted in *On Philip K. Dick*, edited by Mullen et al., 145–52.

———. "Towards a Theory of Paranoia: The Science Fiction of Philip K. Dick." 1984. Reprinted in *On Philip K. Dick*, edited by Mullen et al., 111–18.

Frow, John. *Genre*. London: Routledge, 2006.

———. "'Reproducibles, Rubrics, and Everything You Need': Genre Theory Today." *PMLA* 122, no. 5 (October 2007): 1626–34.

Glut, Donald F. *The Frankenstein Legend: A Tribute to Mary Shelley and Boris Karloff*. Metuchen, N.J.: Scarecrow Press, 1973.

Gopnik, Adam. "Blows against the Empire: The Return of Philip K. Dick." *New Yorker*, August 20, 2007.

Graff, Gerald. *Professing Literature: An Institutional History*. Chicago: University of Chicago Press, 1987.

Gramsci, Antonio. *Prison Notebooks*. Edited by Joseph A. Buttigieg. Translated by Joseph A. Buttigieg and Antonio Callari. New York: Columbia University Press, 1992.

Guillory, John. *Cultural Capital: The Problem of Literary Canon Formation*. Chicago: University of Chicago Press, 1993.

Gunn, James. *Alternate Worlds: The Illustrated History of Science Fiction*. Englewood Cliffs, N.J.: Prentice-Hall, 1975.

———. *The Road to Science Fiction*. Vol. 1, *From Gilgamesh to Wells*. New York: New American Library, 1977.

Habermas, Jürgen. *The Structural Transformation of the Public Sphere: An Inquiry into a Category of Bourgeois Society.* Translated by Thomas Burger. Cambridge, Mass.: MIT Press, 1991. First published in 1965.

Haggerty, George E. *Queer Gothic.* Urbana: University of Illinois Press, 2006.

Haining, Peter, ed. *The Frankenstein Omnibus.* London: Orion, 1994.

Hairston, Andrea. *Mindscape.* Seattle: Aqueduct, 2006.

Halberstam, Judith. *Skin Shows: Gothic Horror and the Technology of Monsters.* Durham, N.C.: Duke University Press, 1995.

Hall, Stuart. "Encoding, Decoding." In *Culture, Media, Language,* edited by Stuart Hall, Dorothy Hobson, Andrew Love, and Paul Willis, 128–38. London: Hutchinson, 1980.

Hannaford, Ivan. *Race: The History of an Idea in the West.* Baltimore: Johns Hopkins University Press, 1996.

Hayles, N. Katherine. *How We Became Posthuman: Virtual Bodies in Cybernetics, Literature, and Informatics.* Chicago: University of Chicago Press, 1999.

Haywood Ferreira, Rachel. *The Emergence of Latin American Science Fiction.* Middletown, Conn.: Wesleyan University Press, 2011.

Heinlein, Robert A. "Science Fiction: Its Nature, Faults and Virtues." In *Turning Points: Essays on the Art of Science Fiction,* edited by Damon Knight, 3–28. New York: Harper & Row, 1977. First published in 1959.

Herman, Edward S., and Noam Chomsky. *Manufacturing Consent: The Political Economy of the Mass Media.* New York: Pantheon, 2002.

Higgins, David M. "Coded Transmissions: Gender and Genre Reception in *The Matrix.*" In *Parabolas of Science Fiction,* edited by Brian Attebery and Veronica Hollinger, 143–160. Middletown, Conn.: Wesleyan University Press, 2013.

Hogle, Jerrold E. "Introduction: The Gothic in Western Culture." In *The Cambridge Companion to Gothic Fiction,* edited by Jerrold E. Hogle, 1–20. Cambridge: Cambridge University Press, 2002.

Invasion of the Body Snatchers. Directed by Don Siegel. Walter Wanger Productions, 1956.

Jakobson, Roman. "The Dominant." In *Readings in Russian Poetics: Formalist and Structuralist Views,* edited by Ladislav Matejka and Krystyna Pomorska, 82–87. Ann Arbor: Michigan Slavic Publications, 1978.

James, Louis. "Frankenstein's Monster in Two Traditions." In *Frankenstein, Creation and Monstrosity,* edited by Stephen Bann, 77–94. London: Reaktion Books, 1994.

Jameson, Fredric. "After Armageddon: Character Systems in *Dr. Bloodmoney.*" 1975. Reprinted in *On Philip K. Dick,* edited by Mullen et al., 26–36.

———. *Archaeologies of the Future: The Desire Called Utopia and Other Essays*. London: Verso, 2005.

———. "Futurist Visions That Tell Us about Right Now." *In These Times* 6, no. 23 (May 5–11, 1982): 17.

———. *The Political Unconscious: Narrative as a Socially Symbolic Act*. Ithaca, N.Y.: Cornell University Press, 1981.

———. "Reification and Utopia in Mass Culture." *Social Text* 1 (Winter 1979): 130–48.

Jauss, Hans-Robert. *Toward an Aesthetic of Reception*. Translated by Timothy Bahti. Minneapolis: University of Minnesota Press, 1982.

Jenkins, Henry, with Ravi Purushotma, Margaret Weigel, Katie Clinton, and Alice J. Robison. *Confronting the Challenges of Participatory Culture: Media Education for the 21st Century*. Cambridge, Mass.: MIT Press, 2009.

Katerberg, William H. *Future West: Utopia and Apocalypse in Frontier Science Fiction*. Lawrence: University Press of Kansas, 2008.

Keen, Paul. *The Crisis of Literature in the 1790s*. Cambridge: Cambridge University Press, 1999.

Kilgore, De Witt Douglas. "Afrofuturism." In *The Oxford Handbook of Science Fiction*, edited by Rob Latham, 561–72. Oxford: Oxford University Press, 2014.

———. "'The Best Is Yet to Come'; or, Saving the Future: *Star Trek: Deep Space Nine* as Reform Astrofuturism." In *Black and Brown Planets: The Politics of Race in Science Fiction*, edited by Isiah Lavender III, 31–47. Jackson: University Press of Mississippi, 2014.

Kilgour, Maggie. *The Rise of the Gothic Novel*. New York: Routledge, 1995.

Kincaid, Paul. "On the Origins of Genre." *Extrapolation* 44 (Winter 2003): 409–19.

Knight, Damon. *The Futurians: The Story of the Science Fiction "Family" of the 30's That Produced Today's Top SF Writers and Editors*. New York: John Day, 1977.

———. "Science Fiction Adventures." *Science Fiction Adventures* 1 (1952): 122.

Landon, Brooks. *Science Fiction after 1900: From the Steam Man to the Stars*. New York: Twayne, 1997.

Larbalestier, Justine. *The Battle of the Sexes in Science Fiction*. Middletown, Conn.: Wesleyan University Press, 2002.

Latham, Rob. "The New Wave." In *A Companion to Science Fiction*, edited by David Seed, 202–16. Oxford: Blackwell, 2005.

Lavalley, Albert J. "The Stage and Film Children of *Frankenstein*: A Survey." In *The Endurance of "Frankenstein": Essays on Mary Shelley's Novel*, edited by

George Levine and U. C. Knoepflmacher, 243–89. Berkeley: University of California Press, 1979.

Lavender, Isiah, III. *Race in American Science Fiction*. Bloomington: Indiana University Press, 2011.

Le Guin, Ursula. *The Left Hand of Darkness*. New York: Walker, 1969.

Lem, Stanisław. "Philip K. Dick: A Visionary among the Charlatans." 1975. Reprinted in *On Philip K. Dick*, edited by Mullen et al., 49–62.

———. "Science Fiction: A Hopeless Case—with Exceptions." 1975. Reprinted in *Philip K. Dick: Electric Shepherd*, edited by Bruce Gillespie, 69–94. Melbourne: Norstrilia, 1975.

Lévi-Strauss, Claude. "The Structural Study of Myth." *Journal of American Folklore* 68, no. 270 (October–December 1955): 428–44.

Lewis, Matthew G. *The Monk*. London: J. Saunders, 1796.

Limerick, Patricia Nelson. *The Legacy of Conquest: The Unbroken Past of the American West*. New York: W. W. Norton, 1987.

Luckhurst, Roger. "The Many Deaths of Science Fiction: A Polemic." *Science Fiction Studies* 21, no. 1 (March 1994): 35–50.

———. *Science Fiction*. Cambridge: Polity, 2005.

Macherey, Pierre, and Étienne Balibar. "Literature as an Ideological Form: Some Marxist Propositions." Translated by James Kavanagh. *Praxis* 5 (1981): 43–58.

Malzberg, Barry. "Some Notes toward the True and the Terrible." In *Speculations on Speculation: Theories of Science Fiction*, edited by James Gunn and Matthew Candelaria, 239–42. Lanham, Md.: Scarecrow Press, 2005. First published in 1982.

The Matrix. Directed by the Wachowski brothers. Warner Bros., 1999.

McKeon, Michael. *The Origins of the English Novel, 1600–1740*. Baltimore: Johns Hopkins University Press, 1987.

Miéville, China. "Cognition as Ideology." In *Red Planets: Marxism and Science Fiction*, edited by China Miéville and Mark Bould, 231–48. Middletown, Conn.: Wesleyan University Press, 2009.

Miles, Robert. *Gothic Writing, 1750–1820: A Genealogy*. 2nd ed. Manchester: Manchester University Press, 2002.

———. "The 1790s: The Effulgence of Gothic." In *The Cambridge Companion to Gothic Fiction*, edited by Jerrold E. Hogle, 41–62. Cambridge: Cambridge University Press, 2002.

Miller, Carolyn R. "Genre as Social Action." *Quarterly Journal of Speech* 70 (1984): 151–67.

Milne, Robert Duncan. "A Question of Reciprocity." In *Into the Sun and Other Stories*, edited by Sam Moskowitz, , 217–53. *Science Fiction in Old San Francisco*, vol. 2. West Kingston, R.I.: Donald Grant, 1980. First published in 1891.

Milner, Andrew. *Locating Science Fiction*. Liverpool: Liverpool University Press, 2012.

Mittel, Jason. *Genre and Television: From Cop Shows to Cartoons in American Culture*. London: Routledge, 2004.

Mullen, R. D., Istvan Csicsery-Ronay Jr., Arthur B. Evans, and Veronica Hollinger, eds. *On Philip K. Dick: 40 Articles from Science-Fiction Studies*. Terre Haute and Greencastle, Ind.: SF-TH Inc., 1992.

Naithani, Sadhana. *The Story-Time of the British Empire: Colonial and Postcolonial Folkloristics*. Jackson: University Press of Mississippi, 2010.

Nevins, Jess. "Pulp Science Fiction." In *The Oxford Handbook of Science Fiction*, edited by Rob Latham, 93–103. Oxford: Oxford University Press, 2014.

Nuruddin, Yusuf. "Ancient Black Astronauts and Extraterrestrial Jihads: Islamic Science Fiction as Urban Mythology." *Socialism and Democracy* 20, no. 3 (November 2006): 127–65.

Ohmann, Richard. *Selling Culture: Magazines, Markets, and Class at the Turn of the Century*. London: Verso, 1996.

Owen, Stephen. "Genres in Motion." *PMLA* 122, no. 5 (October 2007): 1389–93.

Pagetti, Carlo. "Dick and Meta-SF." 1975. Reprinted in *On Philip K. Dick*, edited by Mullen et al., 18–25.

Palmer, Christopher. *Philip K. Dick: Exhilaration and Terror of the Postmodern*. Liverpool: Liverpool University Press, 2003.

Palmer, D. J. *The Rise of English Studies*. London: Oxford University Press, 1965.

Pearson's Magazine. 88 vols. London: C. A. Pearson, 1896–1939.

Pope, Alexander. *The Poems of Alexander Pope*. Edited by John Butt. New Haven, Conn.: Yale University Press, 1961.

Propp, Vladimir. *Morphology of the Folk Tale*. First Edition translated by Laurence Scott with an introduction by Svatava Pirkova-Jakobson; second edition revised and edited with a preface by Louis A. Wagner and new introduction by Alan Dundes. Austin: University of Texas Press, 1968.

?E?ANX (The Cave). Directed by Helen Haig-Brown. Canada, 2009.

Radcliffe, Ann. *The Mysteries of Udolpho: A Romance Interspersed with Some Pieces of Poetry*. London: G. G. and J. Robinson, 1794.

Rhodes, William Henry. "The Case of Summerfeld." In *Caxton's Book*. San Francisco: A. L. Bancroft, 1876. First published in 1871.

Rieder, John. "American Frontiers." In *The Cambridge Companion to American Science Fiction*, edited by Eric Carl Link and Gerry Canavan, 167–78. New York: Cambridge University Press, 2015.

———. *Colonialism and the Emergence of Science Fiction*. Middletown, Conn.: Wesleyan University Press, 2008.

———. "Fiction, 1895–1926." In *The Routledge Companion to Science Fiction*, edited by Mark Bould, Andrew M. Butler, Adam Roberts, and Sherryl Vint, 23–31. London: Routledge, 2009.

———. "John Henry Palmer's *The Invasion of New York, or How Hawaii Was Annexed*: Political Discourse and Emergent Mass Culture in 1897." In *Future Wars: The Anticipations and the Fears*, edited by David Seed, 85–102. Liverpool: Liverpool University Press, 2012.

———. "The Mad Scientist, the Failed Experiment, and the Queer Family of Man: *Sirius*, *Frankenstein*, and the SF Stockroom." In *Parabolas of Science Fiction*, edited by Brian Attebery and Veronica Hollinger, 161–79. Middletown, Conn.: Wesleyan University Press, 2013.

———. "The Metafictive World of *The Man in the High Castle*: Hermeneutics, Ethics, and Political Ideology." 1988. Reprinted in *On Philip K. Dick*, edited by Mullen et al., 223–31.

———. "Patriarchal Fantasy and the Fecal Child in Mary Shelley's *Frankenstein* and Its Adaptations." In *Romantic Circles Praxis Series: Frankenstein's Dream*, edited by Jerrold E. Hogle. February 2003. http://www.rc.umd.edu/praxis/frankenstein/rieder/rieder.html.

———. "The Return to the Frontier in the Extraordinary Voyage: Verne's *The Mysterious Island* and Kubrick's *2001*." *Extrapolation* 51, no. 2 (Summer 2010): 201–15.

———. "Sun Ra's Otherworldliness." In *Africa SF*, edited by Mark Bould. *Paradoxa* 25, (2013): 235–52.

Roberts, Adam. *The History of Science Fiction*. London: Palgrave Macmillan, 2005.

Robinson, Kim Stanley. *The Novels of Philip K. Dick*. Ann Arbor, Mich.: UMI Research Press, 1984.

Rossi, Umberto. *The Twisted Worlds of Philip K. Dick: A Reading of Twenty Ontologically Uncertain Novels*. Jefferson, N.C.: McFarland, 2011.

Rugged Media. "The Cave: Tsilhqot'in Language Sci-Fi Short Film in TIFF's Top Ten Selection." *Vancouver Media Co-op*, December 9, 2009. http://vancouver.mediacoop.ca/newsrelease/2235.

Russ, Joanna. "Somebody's Trying to Kill Me and I Think It's My Husband: The Modern Gothic." In *The Female Gothic*, edited by Juliann E. Fleenor, 31–56. Montreal: Eden, 1982.

Sanders, William. *Journey to Fusang*. New York: Warner, 1988.

Scholes, Robert. *Structural Fabulation: An Essay on Fiction of the Future*. Notre Dame, Ind.: Notre Dame University Press, 1975.

Schudson, Michael. *Advertising, the Uneasy Persuasion: Its Dubious Impact on American Society*. New York: Basic Books, 1984.

Science and Invention. Edited by Hugo Gernsback. New York: Experimenter Publishing, 1920–1931.

Scott, Walter. "Remarks on *Frankenstein, or the Modern Prometheus; A Novel.*" *Blackwood's Edinburgh Magazine* 2, no. 12 (March 1818): 611–20.

Shelley, Mary. *Frankenstein.* London: Colburn and Bentley, 1831.

———. *Frankenstein; or, The Modern Prometheus.* London: Lackington, Hughes, Harding, Mayor, and Jones, 1818. Published anonymously.

———. *Frankenstein, or The Modern Prometheus.* With an afterword by Harold Bloom. New York: Signet Classics, 1983.

Shelley, Percy Bysshe. "On Frankenstein." *Atheneum* 263 (November 10, 1832): 730.

Slotkin, Richard. *Gunfighter Nation: The Myth of the Frontier in Twentieth-Century America.* Norman: University of Oklahoma Press, 1998.

Smith, Eric D. *Globalization, Utopia, and Postcolonial Science Fiction: New Maps of Hope.* London: Palgrave Macmillan, 2012.

Smith, Erin A. "How the Other Half Read: Advertising, Working-Class Readers, and Pulp Magazines." *Book History* 3 (2000): 204–30.

Source Code. Directed by Duncan Jones. Vendome Pictures, 2011.

Space Is the Place. Directed by John Coney. North American Star System, 1974.

Spencer, Kathleen. "'The Red Sun Is High, the Blue Low': Towards a Stylistic Description of Science Fiction." *Science Fiction Studies* 10, no. 1 (March 1983): 35–49.

Spinuzzi, Clay. "Describing Assemblages: Genre Sets, Systems, Repertoires, and Ecologies." Computer Writing and Research Lab White Paper Series, No. 040505-2, University of Texas at Austin, May 5, 2004.

Stableford, Brian. *Scientific Romance in Britain, 1890–1950.* New York: St. Martin's, 1985.

St. Clair, William. "The Impact of *Frankenstein.*" In *Mary Shelley in Her Times*, edited by Betty T. Bennett and Stuart Curran, 38–63. Baltimore: Johns Hopkins University Press, 2000.

Stevenson, Robert Louis. *The Strange Case of Dr. Jekyll and Mr. Hyde.* London: Longman, Green, 1886.

Stoker, Bram. *Dracula.* London: Archibald Constable, 1897.

Strand Magazine: An Illustrated Monthly. 118 vols. London: George Newnes, 1891–1950.

Sutin, Lawrence. *Divine Invasions: A Life of Philip K. Dick.* New York: Carrol & Graf, 2005.

Suvin, Darko. "Goodbye and Hello: Differentiating within the Later P. K. Dick." *Extrapolation* 43, no. 4 (Winter 2002): 368–97.

———. *Metamorphoses of Science Fiction: On the Poetics and History of a Literary Genre.* New Haven, Conn.: Yale University Press, 1979.

———. "On the Poetics of the Science Fiction Genre." *College English* 34, no. 3 (December 1972): 372–82.

———. *Victorian Science Fiction in the UK: The Discourses of Knowledge and of Power*. Boston: G. K. Hall, 1983.

Thrill Book. 3 vols. New York: Street and Smith, March–October 1919.

Todorov, Tzvetan. *The Fantastic*. Translated by Richard Howard. Ithaca, N.Y.: Cornell University Press, 1975.

———. *Genres in Discourse*. Translated by Catherine Porter. Cambridge: Cambridge University Press, 1990. First published Paris: Éditions du Seuil, 1978.

Trujillo Muñoz, Gabriel. *Biografías del futuro: La ciencia ficción mexicana y sus autores*. Mexicali: Universidad Autónoma de Baja California, 2000.

The Truman Show. Directed by Peter Weir. Paramount, 1998.

"Tsilhqot'in Helen Haig-Brown Splashes at Sundance." *Indian Country Today Media Network*. January 31, 2011. http://indiancountrytodaymedianetwork.com/2011/01/31/tsilhqotin-helen-haig-brown-splashes-sundance-14833.

UNESCO. *Index Translationum: World Bibliography of Translation*. http://www.unesco.org/xtrans/.

Veysey, Laurence. *The Emergence of the American University*. Chicago: University of Chicago Press, 1965.

Wassenberg, Anya. "Film News—ImagineNATIVE Embargo Collective at the Berlin Film Fest." *Art & Culture Maven*, February 9, 2010. http://www.artandculturemaven.com/2010/02/film-news-imaginenative-embargo.html.

Wegner, Philip E. *Shockwaves of Possibility: Essays on Science Fiction, Globalization, and Utopia*. Oxford: Peter Lang, 2014.

Weird Tales. Edited by Edmond Baird (March 1923–October 1924) and Farnsworth Wright (November 1924–March 1940). 279 issues, 1923–1954.

Wellbery, David E. Foreword to *Discourse Networks, 1800/1900*, by Friedrich A. Kittler, vii–xxxiii. Translated by Michael Metteer and Chris Cullens. Stanford, Calif.: Stanford University Press, 1990.

Wellek, René, and Austin Warren. *Theory of Literature*. 3rd ed. New York: Harcourt Brace Jovanovich, 1977.

Wells, H. G. *The Invisible Man: A Grotesque Romance*. London: Pearson's, 1897.

———. *The Island of Dr. Moreau: A Possibility*. London: Heineman, 1896.

———. *The Scientific Romances of H. G. Wells*. London: Gollancz, 1933.

Westfahl, Gary. "The Marketplace." In *The Oxford Handbook of Science Fiction*, edited by Rob Latham, 81–92. Oxford: Oxford University Press, 2014.

———. *The Mechanics of Wonder: The Creation of the Idea of Science Fiction*. Liverpool: Liverpool University Press, 1998.

Whedon, Joss, and Drew Goddard. *The Cabin in the Woods: The Official Visual Companion*. London: Titan, 2012.

Wierzbicki, James. "How Frankenstein's Monster Became a Music Lover." *Journal of the Fantastic in the Arts* 24 (2013): 246–63.

Williams, Raymond. *Marxism and Literature*. New York: Oxford University Press, 1977.

———. *Problems in Materialism and Culture*. London: Verso, 1997. First published in 1980.

Williams, Rhys. "Recognizing Cognition: On Suvin, Miéville, and the Utopian Impulse in the Contemporary Fantastic." *Science Fiction Studies* 41, no. 3 (November 2014): 617–33.

Wittenberg, David. *Time Travel: The Popular Philosophy of Narrative*. New York: Fordham University Press, 2013.

Wittgenstein, Ludwig. *Philosophical Investigations*. Translated by G. E. M. Anscombe. Oxford: Basil Blackwell, 1978.

Wolf, Mark J. P. *Building Imaginary Worlds: The Theory and History of Subcreation*. New York: Routledge, 2012.

Wolfe, Gary K. "Evaporating Genre: Strategies of Dissolution in the Postmodern Fantastic." In *Edging into the Future: Science Fiction and Contemporary Cultural Transformation*, edited by Veronica Hollinger and Joan Gordon, 11–29. Philadelphia: University of Pennsylvania Press, 2002.

Wolfe, Patrick. "Settler Colonialism and the Elimination of the Native." *Journal of Genocide Research* 8 (2006): 387–409.

Woodham, Jonathan M. "Advertising and Design." In *The Oxford Handbook of Science Fiction*, edited by Rob Latham, 364–82. Oxford: Oxford University Press, 2014.

Zuberi, Nabeel. "The Transmolecularization of [Black] Folk: *Space Is the Place*, Sun Ra and Afrofuturism." In *Off the Planet: Music, Sound, and Science Fiction Cinema*, edited by Phillip Hayward, 77–95. Eastleigh, UK: John Libbey, 2004.

INDEX

academic genre system, 1, 8–9, 39–44, 69, 164. *See also* genre systems; literature
Adorno, Theodor, 42, 46
Adventures in Time and Space, 127
advertising: in Philip K. Dick's fiction, 102–3, 107–10; in the mass cultural genre system, 35, 44–50, 52–53
Afrofuturism, 127, 140, 145–48, 155, 168–69
Aldiss, Brian, 66, 79
Alkon, Paul, 66
Allison, Dorothy, 132
"All of Us Can Almost . . ." (Carol Emshwiller), 132
All-Story Magazine, 85, 87–88
Althusser, Louis, 40
Altman, Rick, 8, 13, 14, 33, 50, 54
Always Coming Home (Ursula Le Guin), 133
Amazing Stories, 52–53, 66, 81, 85, 163
Andersen, Hans Christian: "The Snow Queen," 131
Anderson, Benedict, 61, 141
"Another Story or A Fisherman of the Inland Sea" (Ursula Le Guin), 133
Astounding, 90–91, 165–66
Astounding Science Fiction Anthology, The, 127
Attebery, Brian, 18, 30–31, 56–57

Ballard, J. G., 166
Baudrillard, Jean, 135

Belle Assemblée, La, 68
Bennett, Tony, 23
Best of Science Fiction, The, 127
Big Book of Science Fiction, The, 127
"Birth Days" (Geoff Ryman), 131
Blade Runner, 97, 167
Blair, Hugh: *Lectures on Rhetoric and Belles Lettres*, 69
Bleiler, Everett, 21, 163, 172n9, 173n8
"Bluebeard," 131
Botting, Fred, 70
Bould, Mark, 14, 27, 141
boundary objects, 29–30, 39–40, 61
Bourdieu, Pierre, 7, 23, 51, 58–59
Bowker, Geoffrey, 29–30, 34
"Boys" (Carol Emshwiller), 131–32
"Brains of Female Hyena Twins, The" (Gwyneth Jones), 132–33
Brandon Society, Carl, 129, 140
broadcasting: in *Invasion of the Body Snatchers*, 144; and national community, 62; in Philip K. Dick's fiction, 106–12; telepathic, 107–10, 143
Broderick, Damien, 56
Buck Rogers in the 25th Century, 85, 90
Burroughs, Edgar Rice, 87
Butler, Octavia: *Xenogenesis*, 155

Cabin in the Woods, The, 117–19, 122–26
Calder, Richard: "The Catgirl Manifesto," 134–35
Camouflage (Joe Haldeman), 131

Campbell, John W., 90–91, 127, 165–66; "Who Goes There?," 143
canon: in the academy, 40, 43–44; as boundary object, 61, 94. *See also* Dick, Philip K.; *Frankenstein*
Čapek, Karel, 81, 165
capitalism, 45, 62
Carr, Terry, 75
Carter, Raphael: "Congenital Agenesis of Gender Ideation by K. N. Sirsi and Sandra Botkin," 134–35
"Case of Summerfield, The" (William Rhodes), 79
"Catgirl Manifesto, The" (Richard Calder), 134–35
Cave, The (?E?ANX), 140, 148–52
Cawelti, John, 8–9
Charnas, Suzy McKee: "Judging the Tiptree," 128–29
Cheng, John, 82
Chesney, George: "The Battle of Dorking," 63
Chiang, Ted: "Liking What You See," 135
Clans of the Alphane Moon (Philip K. Dick), 96, 97–98, 104, 106
Clareson, Thomas, 163, 172n9
class, 40–43, 51–53, 58
Clery, E. J., 70
Clute, John, and Peter Nicholls: *Encyclopedia of Science Fiction*, 18, 85
Cohen, Ralph, 13
Coleridge, Samuel Taylor, 73
communities of practice, 11, 27–31, 113–14. *See also* mass culture; science fiction
Conan Doyle, Arthur, 53, 77, 84–85
"Congenital Agenesis of Gender Ideation by K. N. Sirsi and Sandra Botkin" (Raphael Carter), 134–35
Conklin, Groff, 127
Cooper, James Fenimore, 53
Croker, John Wilson, 68
Csicsery-Ronay, Istvan, Jr., 91, 165
culture industry, 41–43
Curran, Stuart, 69
"Custer on the Slipstream" (Gerald Vizenor), 180n10

Dalkey, Carol: "The Lady of the Ice Garden," 131
Dangerous Visions, 127, 165
Dark Matters, 127
Dear, Nick: *Frankenstein*, 80
Delany, Samuel R., 22, 91–92, 132, 155, 166, 172n11
Deleuze, Gilles, 20
Denning, Michael, 43
detective fiction, 3–4, 38, 53, 74, 76–77, 115, 178n8
Dick, Philip K.: advertising in, 102–3, 107–10; broadcasting in, 106–12; canonical status of, 93–95, 112, 166; career of, 95–97; *Clans of the Alphane Moon*, 96, 97–98, 104, 106; comic vignettes in, 98–99; critique of mass culture, 102–12; *Do Androids Dream of Electric Sheep?*, 96, 97, 98, 105–6; *Dr. Bloodmoney*, 106; "Drugs, Hallucination, and the Quest for Reality," 100–101; *The Exegesis*, 96; *Flow My Tears, the Policeman Said*, 97, 108; "How to Build a Universe That Doesn't Fall Apart Two Days Later," 101–2, 105; *The Man in the High Castle*, 96, 100, 101, 107; *Martian Time-Slip*, 96, 103–4, 107; *A Maze of Death*, 108–9; *Now Wait For Last Year*, 96, 110; *The Penultimate Truth*, 96, 104; *A Scanner Darkly*, 96, 105,

INDEX

178n8; *The Simulacra*, 96, 104–5, 108; *Solar Lottery*, 96, 103, 106; sublime in, 99–102; *The Three Stigmata of Palmer Eldritch*, 96, 98–99, 100, 105–6, 110–12; *Time out of Joint*, 96, 100, 103, 106–7, 108, 110, 116; *The Transmigration of Timothy Archer*, 96; 2-3-74 experience, 96, 177n3, 178n11; *Ubik*, 96, 98, 100, 109–10; *The Unteleported Man*, 104; *VALIS*, 96, 106, 178n11; *We Can Build You*, 96; *The World Jones Made*, 106; *The Zap Gun*, 96, 104, 107

Dillon, Grace W., 127, 151

distribution: 3, 10, 16, 38, 50, 54, 166; and genre attribution, 25–26; and nationalism, 61–62

Do Androids Dream of Electric Sheep? (Philip K. Dick), 96, 97, 98, 105–6

Dracula (Bram Stoker), 75, 76–77

Dr. Bloodmoney (Philip K. Dick), 106

"Drugs, Hallucination, and the Quest for Reality" (Philip K. Dick), 100–101

Dryden, John, 70

Du Bois, W. E. B.: *The Souls of Black Folk*, 158

Duchamp, L. Timmel, 128; "The Gift," 131

du Maurier, Daphne: *Rebecca*, 75

Dunciad, The (Alexander Pope), 70

Dune (Frank Herbert), 166

Earthsea trilogy (Ursula Le Guin), 132

Edisonade, 38, 88

Electrical Experimenter, 86

Ellison, Harlan, 127, 165

Emshwiller, Carol: "All of Us Can Almost…", 132; "Boys," 131–32

Encyclopedia of Science Fiction (John Clute and Peter Nicholls), 18, 85

Enns, Anthony, 105–6

Eternal Sunshine of the Spotless Mind, 167

ethnography, 133–34

exceptionalism, American, 142, 153–54

Exegesis, The (Philip K. Dick), 96

fairy tale, 56, 130–32

fan fiction, 62

fantasy (genre), 6, 22, 60–61, 130, 132, 150, 168

Fast Red Road, The (Stephen Graham Jones), 180n10

Feeling Very Strange: The Slipstream Anthology, 127

Fielding, Henry: *Tom Jones*, 2

field of production, 7, 23, 50–51, 58–59, 168

First Men in the Moon (H. G. Wells), 84

"Five Fucks" (Jonathan Lethem), 131–32, 135

Flash Gordon, 85, 167

Flow My Tears, the Policeman Said (Philip K. Dick), 97, 108

folk narrative, 133, 148, 150–51

Foucault, Michel, 66, 135

Fowler, Alistair, 18, 24–25

Fowler, Karen Joy, 128–29; "What I Didn't See," 17, 131

Frankenstein (Mary Shelley), 25, 66, 164; adaptations of, 71–74, 77–81; canonical status of 67, 79–81; contemporary reviews of, 68; doubling in, 74–79; gender ideology in, 75–77, 80; and the Gothic revival, 69–72; intertextuality of, 80–81; and late-Victorian Gothic, 74–77; as marvelous romance, 68–72; and profession-

Frankenstein (Mary Shelley) (*cont.*) alism, 74–77; science and scientists in, 67, 73–79, 175n10; Walter Scott on, 68–69
Frankenstein (Nick Dear), 80
Freedman, Carl, 66, 93, 102–3, 171n4
frontier: American ideology of, 141, 153–54
Frow, John, 7–8, 21–23, 56
Frye, Northrop, 35–36

gender: and the SF audience, 62, 113, 127, 139
gender ideology: in *Frankenstein*, 75–77, 80; in Gothic romance, 74–76; in horror cinema, 123; in *Invasion of the Body Snatchers*, 145; in Philip K. Dick's fiction, 112; in post-70s SF, 168–69; and the Tiptree Award, 128–38
genre systems: formalist, 35–36; and hierarchies of value, 23–25, 70–72, 93; mass cultural versus academic, 1, 3–4, 8–9, 33, 35, 42–44, 60–61; rhetorical approach to, 33–35; transformation of, 3, 26, 35–36, 69–72. *See also* academic genre system; mass cultural genre system
genre theory: assemblages in, 20–21, 66–67, 161–62; boundary objects in, 29–30; communities of practice in, 27–31; family resemblance in, 14–15, 17–20; fuzzy sets in, 18–19; hierarchies of value in, 23–24; historical approach to, 16–27, 161; hybridity in, 22, 168, 172n11; and the ideology of form, 169–70; and institutional venues, 33, 42–43; labeling in, 25–26, 148–52; origins in, 19–21, 28, 65; paradigm shift in, 13, 16; problems of definition in, 3–6, 13–15, 17–19, 28, 31; protocols of interpretation in, 21–22; rhetorical approach to, 7–8, 25–26, 33–35; textual dominant in, 18–19; theoretical versus historical genres in, 5–7. *See also* academic genre system; genre systems; mass cultural genre system
Gernsback, Hugo, 28, 52, 81–82, 85–88, 175n16. *See also Amazing Stories*
"Gift, The" (L. Timmel Duchamp), 131
"Girl Who Was Plugged In, The" (James Tiptree), 135
"Glass Bottle Trick, The" (Nalo Hopkinson), 131
Godwin, William, 68–70
Gopnik, Adam, 93
Gothic, the: continuity of, 175n12; and doubling, 74–77, 80–81; revival, 69–74; late-Victorian, 74–77
Gothic romance, 74–76
Gramsci, Antonio, 9, 35, 42–43
Guattari, Felix, 20
Guillory, John, 39–40, 43
Gulliver's Travels (Jonathan Swift), 68, 174n3
Gunn, Eileen, and Leslie What: "Nirvana High," 131, 136
Gunn, James, 81

Habermas, Jürgen, 71
Haig-Brown, Helen, 140, 148–49, 152
Hairston, Andrea: *Mindscape*, 140–41, 152–53, 155–59
Haldeman, Joe: *Camouflage*, 131
Hall, Stuart, 54–55
Hayles, N. Katherine, 99
Haywood Ferreira, Rachel, 63
Healy, Raymond, 127

"Heat Death of the Universe, The" (Pamela Zoline), 17
Hebdige, Dick, 135
Heinlein, Robert A., 92, 112; *Stranger in a Strange Land*, 166
Herbert, Frank: *Dune*, 166
Hetzel, Pierre-Jules, 87
History of English Poetry (Thomas Warton), 69
Hogle, Jerrold, 71
Hollinger, Veronica, 56–57
Hollywood, 50–51, 115–26, 154, 156–58, 166–67
Hopkinson, Nalo: "The Glass Bottle Trick," 131; "Looking for Clues," 132
horror (genre), 74, 76, 79, 118, 122–25
Horse (Archer Pechawis), 180n10
"How to Build a Universe That Doesn't Fall Apart Two Days Later" (Philip K. Dick), 101–2, 105

Indigenous Futurism, 140, 148–52, 155, 168–69, 180n10
intellectuals, 9, 44
Invasion of the Body Snatchers, 120, 140, 143–45, 147–48
Invisible Man, The (H. G. Wells), 67, 75, 77–79
Island of Dr. Moreau, The (H. G. Wells), 67, 75, 77

Jakobson, Roman, 18–19
Jameson, Fredric: 41–42, 95, 100, 169
James Tiptree Award, 128–30
James Tiptree Award Anthology, The: academic form in, 132–35; editorial apparatus, 128–30; fiction in, 130–38; generic hybridity in, 130–32

Jauss, Hans-Robert, 20, 24, 36–37
Jenkins, Henry, 43–44, 169
Jones, Gwyneth: "The Brains of Female Hyena Twins," 132–33
Jones, Stephen Graham: *The Fast Red Road*, 180n10
Journey to Fusang (William Sanders), 180n10
"Judging the Tiptree" (Suzy McKee Charnas), 128–29

Kafka, Franz, 98
Kelly, James Patrick, 127
Kessel, John, 127
Kilgour, Maggie, 70–71
Kincaid, Paul, 14, 17, 20, 27
"Kissing Frogs" (Jaye Lawrence), 131
Knight, Damon, 14, 27
Kornbluth, Cyril, and Frederik Pohl: *The Space Merchants*, 103

"Lady of the Ice Garden, The" (Carol Dalkey), 131
Lanagan, Margo: "Wooden Bride," 132, 135
Larbalestier, Justine, 30
Lavender, Isiah, III, 141
law, 124
Lawrence, Jaye: "Kissing Frogs," 131
Lectures on Rhetoric and Belles Lettres (Hugh Blair), 69
Left Hand of Darkness, The (Ursula Le Guin), 133
Le Guin, Ursula: *Always Coming Home*, 133; "Another Story or A Fisherman of the Inland Sea," 133; Earthsea trilogy, 132; *The Left Hand of Darkness*, 133; "Mountain Ways," 131, 133
Lem, Stanislaw, 95

Lethem, Jonathan: "Five Fucks," 131–32, 135
Lévi-Strauss, Claude, 55
Lewis, Matthew G., 72–73, 75
"Liking What You See" (Ted Chiang), 135
Limerick, Patricia, 154
Link, Kelly: "Travels with the Snow Queen," 131
literary history: 161–62; genre definitions in, 31; individual innovation versus systemic change in, 2–3, 26
literature: as academic boundary object, 39–40; and diglossia, 40, 44; and national vernacular, 39, 69; as the nongeneric genre, 24, 55–56
"Little Faces" (Vonda McIntyre), 131, 136–38
"Looking for Clues" (Nalo Hopkinson), 132
"Looking through Lace" (Ruth Nestvold), 131, 134
Luckhurst, Roger, 23–24, 37–38, 83, 88–89, 172n

Malzberg, Barry, 27–28
Man in the High Castle, The (Philip K. Dick), 96, 100, 101, 107
Martian Time-Slip (Philip K. Dick), 96, 103–4, 107
mass cultural genre system: advertising in, 35, 44–50, 52–53, 117; authorial signature in, 56; and digital media, 169; emergence of, 37–41, 45, 85, 163–65; and escapism, 48, 51, 56, 118–19, 122, 125–26; genre specialization in, 51, 85, 163–64; in Gernsback's editorials, 89–90; and the Gothic revival, 73, 80; hybridity in, 50, 116, 128, 130–31; narrative in 35; news in, 35, 49; niche market magazines in, 51–54, 85; and propaganda, 35, 47; serial fiction in, 49, 51–54; seriality in, 54–57, 114–15; stratification in, 54–55, 57–61; and subcultures, 54–55, 61–64; and technical discourses, 38–44, 56–57, 73–74; venues of production in, 50–51, 53, 125–26
mass culture: defined, 45; emergence of, 45–46; as instrument of US international hegemony, 63–64, 141; versus modernism, 40–44, 58; and national homogeneity, 61–63, 140; in Philip K. Dick's fiction, 102–12; prediction as cognition in, 106–7, 115, 117–26; and race, 140; seriality in, 62, 84, 114–15, 121–22; subcultural formations in, 62–63, 90–91, 113–14, 126, 140
Matrix, The, 108, 116–17, 119
McComas, Frank, 127
McIntyre, Vonda: "Little Faces," 131, 136–38
McKeon, Michael, 2, 28, 163
Memoirs of Victor Frankenstein, The (Theodore Roszak), 80
Merritt, A., 87
Miéville, China, 6–7, 172n11
Miles, Robert, 71, 80
Miller, Carolyn, 25–26
Milne, Robert Duncan: "A Question of Reciprocity," 79
Milner, Andrew, 10–11, 60, 93
Milton, John: *Paradise* Lost, 73, 77
Mindscape (Andrea Hairston), 140–41, 152–53, 155–59
Mirrorshades: The Cyberpunk Anthology, 127
Mittel, Jason, 8, 15, 33, 65
Modern Electrics, 86

INDEX

modernism, 40–44, 58
Moorcock, Michael, 165
"Mountain Ways" (Ursula Le Guin), 131, 133
Munsey, Frank, 85
Murphy, Pat, 128

Nestvold, Ruth: "Looking through Lace," 131, 134
New Weird, The, 127
Nicholls, Peter, and John Clute: *Encyclopedia of Science Fiction*, 18, 85
Night of the Living Dead, The, 135
Nineteen Eighty-Four (George Orwell), 92, 103
"Nirvana High" (Eileen Gunn and Leslie What), 131, 136
Noles, Pam: "Shame," 132
Notkin, Debbie, 128
Now Wait for Last Year (Philip K. Dick), 96, 110

Oedipus the King, 3–4
Ohmann, Richard, 40–41, 45, 47, 51, 61–62
Orwell, George: *Nineteen Eighty-Four*, 92, 103

Pagetti, Carlo, 97
Palmer, Christopher, 99
Paradise Lost (John Milton), 73, 77
Paul, Frank R., 86
Pearson's Magazine, 83–84
Pechawis, Archer: *Horse*, 180n10
Penultimate Truth, The (Philip K. Dick), 96, 104
Percy, Thomas: *Reliques of Ancient English Poetry*, 69
Philosophical Investigations (Ludwig Wittgenstein), 14, 17–20

Picture of Dorian Gray, The (Oscar Wilde), 75
Pocket Book of Science Fiction, 127
Poe, Edgar Allan, 52, 53, 77, 88
Pohl, Frederik, and Cyril Kornbluth: *The Space Merchants*, 103
Pope, Alexander: *The Dunciad*, 70
postmodernism, 43
Propp, Vladimir, 55
publicity, 1–2, 59
publics, 59, 140–41, 145, 150–52

?E?ANX. See *Cave, The*
"Question of Reciprocity, A" (Robert Duncan Milne), 79

race: in American imperialist ideology, 141–42; in mass culture, 140; in science fiction, 141, 145–48, 179n3. See also Afrofuturism; Indigenous Futurism
Radcliffe, Ann, 72–73, 75
Rebecca (Daphne du Maurier), 75
reception: and genre attribution, 25–26, 53–54
Reliques of Ancient English Poetry (Thomas Percy), 69
Rhodes, William: "The Case of Summerfield," 79
romance (mass cultural genre), 38, 56, 121, 130–31, 133, 135, 168. See also Gothic romance
Roosevelt, Theodore, 153
Rossi, Umberto, 100
Roszak, Theodore: *The Memoirs of Victor Frankenstein*, 80
Ruoff, Matt: *Set This House in Order*, 130
Russ, Joanna, 75, 128
Ryman, Geoff: "Birth Days," 131

Sanders, William: *Journey to Fusang*, 180n10
Sargent, Pamela, 127
Scanner Darkly, A (Philip K. Dick), 96, 105, 178n8
Science and Invention, 86–87
science fiction: and the academy, 1, 7, 130–35, 167–68; anthologies, 126–27; and book industry, 54, 113, 126–27; canon formation in, 60–61; definitions of, 14–15; different practices of, 58–59, 82, 89–92, 113–14, 139, 165–66; emergence of: 2–3, 21, 25, 28, 37–38, 82, 162–65; fandom, 62, 90–91, 132; and late-Victorian Gothic, 74–77; Latin American, 63; as literature of cognitive estrangement, 4–7, 16–17, 130–31; in Hollywood, 97, 113–14, 166–67; invasion narratives in, 140, 143, 150; mass cultural, 85, 113–14, 139, 166–68; neologism in, 91; nonwhite participants in, 132, 139; organic to mass culture, 9–10, 89; periodization of, 127, 162–69, 178n5; and pulp milieu, 27–28, 82–83, 85–92, 165, 176n17; race in, 141, 145–48, 179n3; and scientific romance, 82; and scientifiction, 175n16; as selective tradition, 10–11, 127; and seriality, 55–57, 94; as subculture, 27–31, 51–52, 82, 91–92, 113–14, 139, 165–66, 168; white male domination of, 62, 128, 139; women participants in, 113, 126–30, 139, 166
Science Fiction Hall of Fame, Volume One, 1929–64, The, 127
Science Wonder Stories, 81, 85
Scott, Walter, 68–69
"Screwfly Solution, The" (Racoona Sheldon), 134–35

Set This House in Order (Matt Ruoff), 130
"Shame" (Pam Noles), 132
Sheldon, Alice, 128–29, 134–35
Sheldon, Racoona: "The Screwfly Solution," 134–35
Shelley, Mary, 3. See also *Frankenstein*
Shelley, Percy Bysshe, 68, 174n2, 174n3
Simulacra, The (Philip K. Dick), 96, 104–5, 108
slipstream, 132
Slotkin, Richard, 153
Smith, Erin, 52
Smith, Jeffrey D., 128–29
"Snow Queen, The" (Hans Christian Andersen), 131
Solar Lottery (Philip K. Dick), 96, 103, 106
Souls of Black Folk, The (W. E. B. Du Bois), 158
Source Code, 114, 117–22, 125–26
Space Is the Place, 140, 145–48
Space Merchants, The (Frederik Pohl and Cyril Kornbluth), 103
space opera, 136–38
Spencer, Kathleen, 91–92
Spinuzzi, Clay, 34–35, 41
Stableford, Brian, 82, 92
Stapledon, Olaf, 81, 92, 165
"Star, The" (H. G. Wells), 86–87
Starr, Susan Leigh, 29–30, 34
Star Trek, 167, 179n3
Star Wars, 97, 113–14, 154, 166–68
Stevenson, Robert Louis: *The Strange Case of Dr. Jekyll and Mr. Hyde*, 67, 75, 76, 172n9
Stoker, Bram: *Dracula*, 75, 76–77
Strand, The, 83–85
Strange Case of Dr. Jekyll and Mr. Hyde,

The (Robert Louis Stevenson), 67, 75, 76, 172n9
Stranger in a Strange Land (Robert A. Heinlein), 166
Sun Ra, 140, 145–48, 155
Suvin, Darko, 4–7, 16–17, 18–19, 36, 60, 130–31, 172n
Swift, Jonathan: *Gulliver's Travels*, 68, 174n3

Thomas, Sheree, 127
Three Stigmata of Palmer Eldritch, The (Philip K. Dick), 96, 98–99, 100, 105–6, 110–12
Thrill Book, The, 88
Thrilling magazine chain, 85
Time Machine, The (H. G. Wells), 81, 174n1
Time out of Joint (Philip K. Dick), 96, 100, 103, 106–7, 108, 110, 116
time travel, 120, 133
Tiptree, James, 128–29; "The Girl Who Was Plugged In," 135
Tiptree Award. *See* James Tiptree Award
Tiptree Award Anthology. *See James Tiptree Award Anthology*
Todorov, Tzvetan, 5, 7, 171–72n3
Tom Jones (Henry Fielding), 2
tragedy, 3–4
Transmigration of Timothy Archer, The (Philip K. Dick), 96
"Travels with the Snow Queen" (Kelly Link), 131
Treasury of Science Fiction, A, 127
Truman Show, The, 108, 116, 119
Turner, Frederick Jackson, 153
2001: A Space Odyssey, 167

Ubik (Philip K. Dick), 96, 98, 100, 109–10

Unteleported Man, The (Philip K. Dick), 104
Urashima, 133, 150

VALIS (Philip K. Dick), 96, 106, 178n11
Vandermeer, Ann, 127
Vandermeer, Jeff, 127
Verne, Jules, 3, 38, 53, 63, 79, 84, 87, 89, 162
Vint, Sherryl, 14, 27
Vizenor, Gerald: "Custer on the Slipstream," 180n10

Walking the Clouds: An Anthology of Indigenous Science Fiction, 127
Walpole, Horace, 71–72, 174n4
War of the Worlds, The (H. G. Wells), 79, 83–84
Warren, Austin, 16
Warton, Thomas: *History of English Poetry*, 69
We Can Build You (Philip K. Dick), 96
Wegner, Philip, E., 5, 127, 130, 162
Weird Tales, 88, 163
Wellek, René, 16
Wells, H. G., 3, 53, 177n24; *First Men in the Moon*, 84; *The Invisible Man*, 67, 75, 77–79; *The Island of Dr. Moreau*, 67, 75, 77; "The Star," 86–87; *The Time Machine* 81, 174n1; *The War of the Worlds*, 79, 83–84
Wertenbaker, G. Peyton, 86
western (genre), 38, 53, 141, 153–54
Westfahl, Gary, 28, 82, 92, 167
What, Leslie, and Eileen Gunn: "Nirvana High,"131, 136
"What I Didn't See" (Karen Joy Fowler), 17, 131
"Who Goes There?" (John W. Campbell), 143

Wilde, Oscar: *The Picture of Dorian Gray*, 75
Williams, Raymond, 10, 47–48
Williams, Rhys, 4–5, 130
WisCon, 126, 129–31
Wister, Owen, 53
Wittenberg, David, 120
Wittgenstein, Ludwig: *Philosophical Investigations*, 14, 17–20
Wolfe, Gary K., 116–17
Wollheim, Donald A., 127
Women of Wonder, 127

"Wooden Bride" (Margo Lanagan), 132, 135
World Jones Made, The (Philip K. Dick), 106

Xenogenesis (Octavia Butler), 155

Zap Gun, The (Philip K. Dick), 96, 104, 107
Zoline, Pamela: "The Heat Death of the Universe," 17

JOHN RIEDER is a professor of English at the University of Hawai'i at Mānoa, where he has taught since coming there from graduate school at Yale University in 1980. After publishing a book on William Wordsworth and essays on English Romanticism, particularly the poetry of Percy Shelley, on horror cinema, on Mary Shelley's *Frankenstein* and its dramatic and film adaptations, and on problems of periodization, the professionalization of literary studies, and the canon, he has focused his research agenda on science fiction for the last fifteen years, contributing essays to *Extrapolation, Science Fiction Studies, Science Fiction Film and Television, Paradoxa,* and other venues. His book on early science fiction, *Colonialism and the Emergence of Science Fiction,* was published by Wesleyan University Press in 2008. He was awarded the SFRA's Pioneer Award in 2011 for his 2010 essay "On Defining SF, or Not," which appears in revised form as the first chapter of *Science Fiction and the Mass Cultural Genre System.* He currently serves as a coeditor of *Extrapolation.*